SECOND EDITION

Homeland Security and Private Sector Business

Corporations' Role in Critical Infrastructure Protection

SECOND EDITION

Homeland Security and Private Sector Business

Corporations' Role in Critical Infrastructure Protection

ELSA LEE

CRC Press
Taylor & Francis Group
Boca Raton London New York

CRC Press is an imprint of the
Taylor & Francis Group, an **informa** business

CRC Press
Taylor & Francis Group
6000 Broken Sound Parkway NW, Suite 300
Boca Raton, FL 33487-2742

First issued in paperback 2020

© 2015 by Taylor & Francis Group, LLC
CRC Press is an imprint of Taylor & Francis Group, an Informa business

No claim to original U.S. Government works

ISBN-13: 978-1-4822-4858-6 (hbk)

ISBN-13: 978-0-367-77911-5 (pbk)

Library of Congress Cataloging-in-Publication Data

Lee, Elsa.
    Homeland security and private sector business : corporations' role in critical infrastructure protection elsa lee. -- Second edition.
        pages cm
    Includes bibliographical references and index.
    ISBN 978-1-4822-4858-6 (hardcover : alk. paper) 1. Infrastructure (Economics)--Security measures--United States--Planning. 2. Corporations--Security measures--United States--Planning. 3. Business enterprises--Security measures--United States--Planning. 4. Industries--Security measures--United States--Planning. 5. Preparedness--United States. 6. Terrorism--Prevention. 7. United States. Department of Homeland Security. National infrastructure protection plan. I. Title.

HC110.C3L44 2015
363.325'936360973--dc23   2014043746

Visit the Taylor & Francis Web site at
http://www.taylorandfrancis.com

and the CRC Press Web site at
http://www.crcpress.com

CONTENTS

PREFACE

The main difference between this book and the first edition is that it has been updated with current case studies and current relevant information about terrorism and homeland security. It aims to serve global readers. I started out with a vision of decoding terrorism for the private sector and providing a template for preparedness to owners and operators of our nation's 16 critical infrastructure sectors. This template would be derived from my 20 years of successful counterintelligence practices securing and protecting national security assets from terrorism, espionage, sabotage, and other foreign and domestic threats.

To achieve what I set out to do was not practical, as it would have required starting with an overview of our Homeland Security laws. They are not the best laws in the world, but they suffice. We are a young nation, and our existing laws are the best we have to work with for now. So far, we have been able to introduce laws that allow us to maintain a delicate balance between being a "free society" and not a "police state" nation. We do need laws, and I am sure our friends in the legal system will continue to draft laws that preserve our civil liberties but hopefully with enough enforceability to protect us from future 9/11s. I quickly realized that taking this approach would have taken up all the chapters of the book.

Instead, I decided to focus on my ultimate goal—to educate the private sector on terrorism preparedness by framing problems and solutions in a way that everyone can understand so that mind-sets can evolve quickly to improve our security posture as a nation. My vision is to infuse current leaders, future leaders, and the 300 million or so people in America with knowledge that bends the minds, teases the brain, and stumps emotional intelligence—through rhetorical questions, lighthearted humor, anecdotal material, and tactical and strategic perspectives—to help put terrorism back where it belongs: in the Dark Ages.

Through "critical, scholarly, and intellectual thinking," we can accelerate our security evolution, our security awakening—maybe even put ourselves in "turbo mode" and bolt into action right now. We can start by securing exploitable vulnerabilities.

Terrorist groups who conspire to carry out attacks in this country or elsewhere already know the limits of our laws and use them to their advantage. They know our laws prevent us from investigating them without solid information. We cannot investigate someone simply on the basis of a notion "in their head." This is largely due to intelligence oversight changes introduced after the Watergate events of the 1970s. Thus, terrorists are free to live among us, conduct meetings, raise funds, send funds to other plotters abroad, and engage in surveillance of U.S. facilities that they would like to target—right under our noses.

I was 39 when I retired from the U.S. Army and I could have easily stayed retired and taken up gardening, but I could not take my eyes off "the prize"—making our nation a safer place to live and preserving our way of life.

Really, how could someone like myself—who at the age of 22 served on an international terrorism task force that captured terrorists and who could've, would've, should've died in three different terrorist attacks in three different countries on three random days of my life—simply roll over and go away, all while watching events like 9/11 unfold?

I cannot change what is. I cannot undo the political decisions or historical events that got us here, but I must do something. You must do something too. For years, I saw the threat of terrorism and "tenacity" building up, but not in a way that I alone could stop. Together, we can do something about it today. Those of us who have served in this field do it because we care. We do it because we have skills that are suited for this kind of work—it's not that we're brave or crazy—well, maybe a little. But we are just a few, and we 10 percent of the population can no longer carry the workload of the other 90 percent—rhetorically speaking, of course.

The prize is worth fighting for, worth dying for—the prize being "a safer America." I love this country more than the blood that runs through my veins, which is why I served for 20 years in the U.S. Army—a noble and fine profession. I believe I have earned the right to grab a megaphone and communicate my message loudly and freely. Get out there and secure your vulnerabilities! Train your people! Hurry up and harden your facilities!

We don't want suicide bombers approaching our parking lots. We don't even want to put ourselves "out there" and see how we would react to subway attacks. Help secure tomorrow today. Don't let our government try to carry the full load. The U.S. government needs our help regardless of our political affiliation. Government, if you need our help, please be more specific about what you need. Business owners, when there is a lull in terrorist activity, that is the time to hurry up and put defenses in place. Use the time wisely—look inward and revamp or restructure the security architecture that protects your assets. Doing so positions you to deter and effectively mitigate risk. It can also solidify market shares, strengthen your brands, lower insurance premiums, and endear customers and stakeholders to you because of the confidence you will instill in them through your security actions.

There are more than 1 million action items that you could probably come up with in the race to secure your assets before catastrophe strikes again, but the fastest and most prudent way to go about this is through the National Infrastructure Protection Plan (NIPP)—which the Department of Homeland Security (DHS) published in June 2006. Of all the plans, strategies, programs, and best practices observed over my 28 years in the business of preventing and deterring terrorism and managing security risks—this is the closest thing to an "oracle."

Our government is working hard to make the nation safer. The DHS, Federal Bureau of Investigation (FBI), Central Intelligence Agency (CIA), and other state and local agencies are reaching out to private industry for assistance in technology development and advice on how to protect our critical resources—they are trying to wade through the bureaucracy and put as much effort as possible into sharing information, making informational resources available, and drafting legislation that protects us from terrorists while still maintaining a delicate balance to protect our civil liberties. But they can't do the job alone, and even within government there are influences at work that hamper efforts—political agendas, the inability to self-reform, and the inability to overcome or adapt organizational cultures overnight.

This book is not the answer to all your problems—though I wish it were. It is not meant to give technical advice in one specific area or on which security technology to select. You should not readily defer a selection like that to someone communicating to you through a book. This book is meant to open your mind, and entice you to embrace other ideas and approaches so that you can solve problems with solutions that you never thought of before. Please find three things that you can change, improve, or secure, and calculate how much you saved by catching what would be an exploitable problem—early on. I want to do something measureable that will help you. Please allow me that privilege.

ACKNOWLEDGMENTS

This book is the result of my 34 years of experience in counterintelligence and security. It would not have been possible to write it without the events that shaped me, serving as a counterintelligence agent in the U.S. Army from the age of 19 to 39—personal and professional experiences in 19 countries—living to tell about three countries in which I did not die in terrorist attacks—and being touched by those who died horrific deaths in terrorist attacks. I thank God that I am here today with the capacity, experience, and credentials to share proven methods for preparedness, risk management, and response strategies to effectively deal with terrorism, homeland security programs, and disaster management.

I am grateful to Mark Listnewik for spotting me in the crowd almost a decade ago and building a path to this publishing milestone—to Stephanie Morkert, Jennifer Abbott, and Linda Leggio for their hard work on this book project—to all my friends, family, quiet warriors, and colleagues still serving who supported, assisted, and collaborated with me to make this book possible—and to all the quiet warriors who still serve and cannot be named. Another important acknowledgment goes to the publisher, Taylor & Francis Group, who provided me the opportunity to achieve my vision of transferring important knowledge to academic, professional, corporate, first responder, and government communities so that together—we can secure tomorrow, today.

For helping to make the second edition of my book possible, I wish to thank:

> Elisa Gutierrez, my mother, life coach, and biggest champion. She wears many hats and provides limitless support to help me achieve my life goals—from serving as my little four dogs' nanny, to making sure I eat three home cooked meals, and assisting in any task at hand. I owe her a big "thank you" for lending a helping hand with her administrative assistance for this edition. I was proud to give her the opportunity to feel good about serving her country even at this stage of her life—as a wise elder of this nation.
> Cynthia Ziegenhirt, who wears many hats in support of my company and homeland and national security vision from employee, to editor, to researcher, to sage advisor. I can always count on her government experience, sharp wit, and her honest and practical

points of view. I owe her much gratitude for a major portion of the research and editing. I'm fortunate to have her as a lifelong friend.

I want to thank my book contributors who are featured in various chapters. Although they all took time out of their busy schedules to provide contributions to various chapters of this book, I especially wish to thank former DHS Secretary and the Honorable Michael Chertoff for his chapter contribution and for generously sharing his words of wisdom with me, and you, the reader.

I am deeply indebted to everyone who made the first edition of the book possible.

- Jessica Farias, my lovely daughter, for working under a tight deadline and providing me with her valuable time, expertise, and creative talent to design and create all the graphics and tables needed for this book.
- My best friend, Traci Britton, for her sacrifices, for providing non-military civilian insight on security, conducting research, and giving me the encouragement to write this book, but mostly for taking on a greater workload at Advantage SCI so that I could dedicate the time needed to write this book.
- My friend Gary Berntsen, author of *Jawbreaker* and a former CIA officer with extensive experience in Iraq and Afghanistan, who provided me with the encouragement to write this book.
- My parents for teaching me the basics of survival and going the distance in everything I pursue; and my siblings Gracie, Javier, and Rene for supporting me throughout my career.

To those who are currently fighting in Iraq, Afghanistan, and other places across the globe, I salute and support you 100 percent. Another group I wish to recognize are former U.S. military personnel who continue to serve as civilian and government employees sharing their security and intelligence expertise in protecting our nation. May God bless all of you.

And, most of all to my husband and partner, Pete Lee. Pete works hard every day in support of national security and gives selflessly to our company, Advantage SCI, as the Vice President of Operations. He knows this business better than I. With his 24 years in the U.S. Army Special Forces, he is the best partner to help my mission to keep America safe and secure. Without his leadership and support, and contributions to Chapters 5, 8, and 9, this book would still be in my head and Advantage SCI would not exist today. Thank you to my loving partner and husband—Pete Lee!

ABOUT THE AUTHOR

Elsa Lee is a lecturer and the CEO and founder of Advantage SCI, LLC, a professional services firm with offices in Washington, DC, Texas, and California providing corporate, homeland, and national security services to government and private industry. Lee has been quoted extensively in national and international newspapers and professional journals and has appeared on Univision, Telemundo, CNN, Fox News, CBS News, Voice of America, and Canada Business Channel. These days, Lee works with key member representatives of the critical national infrastructures, the academic community, and the U.S. government.

Lee served as a U.S. Army Counterintelligence Officer and Special Agent for 20 years in the fight against terrorism and espionage in the United States, Europe, Central America, and Asia. During her career, she worked closely with the Federal Bureau of Investigation (FBI), the Central Intelligence Agency (CIA), the U.S. Secret Service, the National Security Agency (NSA), Great Britain's Security Service (MI-5), and Germany's Special Operations and Counterterrorist Forces (Grenzschutzgruppe—GSG-9). She is one of the few experts in this nation trained in U.S., British, and Israeli counterintelligence and counterterrorism methods and operations. Her intelligence contributions included presenting high-level training to U.S. and foreign national audiences, including U.S. presidential staff; White House executives; diplomats and German, Russian, Central American, and U.S. military leaders; and international law enforcement and intelligence audiences worldwide.

Lee's most recent professional accomplishment is assisting with and promoting the establishment of the Homeland Security and Emergency Management Certificate at the University of California, Los Angeles (UCLA) Extension. She serves as a member of the program's Advisory Board and is also an instructor.

Through her firm, Advantage SCI, Lee has helped global clients effectively manage risk and improve security programs. Over the years, she has taught homeland security, leadership, global cultural relations, resource management, and business communications courses as an adjunct professor in Los Angeles. She speaks Spanish and German. Her education includes a master's degree in organizational leadership and a graduate certificate in human resources, both from Chapman University (Orange, California), and a bachelor's degree in behavioral science from the University of Maryland. Recent accomplishments include providing support to national counterintelligence programs, delivering antiterrorism training overseas for the U.S. Department of State, and conducting first-time studies on railway, port, and critical infrastructure vulnerability to terrorism in partnership with the University of Southern California (USC) homeland security center "The Center for Risk and Economic Analysis of Terror Events" (CREATE), RAND Corporation, and the Los Angeles County Economic Development Corporation (LAEDC).

While in the military, Lee served in the Defense Intelligence Agency, the U.S. Army Intelligence and Security Command (INSCOM), U.S. Army Europe, the Pentagon, the U.S. Army Intelligence Center and School, and the Defense Nuclear Agency (DNA). At DNA, her liaison efforts with local, state, federal, and international law enforcement facilitated threat and vulnerability assessments, incident response, and contingency planning for terrorist attacks against nuclear facilities, including weapons of mass destruction (WMD) attacks.

In 1995, she served as the Chief Intelligence Officer of a joint task force in Central America directing intelligence operations for peacekeeping operations of the U.S. Army. Her diplomacy skills with U.S. Embassy diplomats, senior military executives, and Central American officials facilitated timely and safe conduct of the many peacetime operations, ensuring Force Protection of U.S. forces and zero incidents and fatalities on her watch.

From 1980 to 1986, at the height of terrorist attacks against Americans in Europe, Lee served on an international terrorism task force responsible for the capture of two terrorists and survived three terrorist attacks. She presented terrorism awareness, methodology, and ways to protect against terrorism to U.S. Armed Forces in Europe. Her intelligence contributions influenced U.S. Presidential policy decisions. During her 20-year career as a Counterintelligence Special Agent with the U.S. Army, Lee received numerous recognition awards and military honors, including the highest military peacetime award possible, the Legion of Merit.

1

Introduction
Homeland Security Vision

The will of God prevails. In great contests each party claims to act in accordance with the will of God. Both may be, and one must be, wrong. God cannot be for and against the same thing at the same time. In the present civil war it is quite possible that God's purpose is something different from the purpose of either party—and yet the human instrumentalities, working just as they do, are of the best adaptation to affect His purpose.

Abraham Lincoln

THE DESIRED STATE OF HOMELAND SECURITY

In the ideal world of security, society, businesses, and government work together in synchronicity as true partners. Concepts, ideas, and insights from the soft and hard sciences merge to enable remarkable capabilities in prevention, detection, and response to terrorism and disasters. Whether in Washington, DC, Texas, or California, the response is coordinated and orchestrated like a well-oiled machine—it is decisive and automatic. No one shudders at the sound of *terrorist attack* or *disaster* because everyone has been trained. They understand their roles. Everyone is accountable and owns a share of preparedness. There are documented procedures that have been tested, validated, and rehearsed across all environments and industries.

1

In personal and professional settings, people got past the shock, fear, and denial stages of terrorism; reached a level of acceptance; and bought into it emotionally and intellectually to do something about it. Everyone went through the "forming, storming, norming, and performing"* stages of team dynamics to collectively establish effective security and preparedness measures to ensure all operations would run smoothly. This was just one of the many great models learned over time and adopted as an effective training tool. Terrorism is managed and controlled smartly in this perfect world, so that even my grandmother knows what to do if she were to stumble upon something that smelled remotely terroristic. Members of all communities were trained to recognize and report suspicious behaviors in a timely manner to the right office—from recognizing a person who is seeking employment in an organization for the purposes of collecting information needed to plan an attack, to an ill-intentioned culprit studying a facility's security practices to identify and exploit vulnerabilities for personal gain. Suspicious reports are received, managed, properly tagged, tracked, and acted on. They do not disappear into an abyss of backlog in an obscure basement, nor are they relegated to binary data trapped in some virtual bin.

On the off chance that a disaster occurs, people are sensitized to go into action and not slip into psychological paralysis. This is where the soft sciences were best utilized. Psychologists and behavioral scientists introduced training and exercises that helped everyone understand how the body responds under stress. People learned that the release of chemicals in the body causes people to freeze or kick into autoresponse mode. The brain's hidden potential is unleashed when survival depends on it. Everyone quickly learned that immobility, shock, and a lack of confidence cause situations to quickly go from manageable to fatal. On the terrorism front, there are no soft targets. Public and private sector organizations successfully hardened their facilities and reinforced security just like mini "Fort Knoxes" except that they do not look like fortresses. Security designs are pleasing to the eye, safe, and environmentally friendly. Crime prevention through environmental design principles is effectively used. Everywhere the eye can see, adequate technology complements layers of security, and no one broke the bank to achieve it.

People were not always this way, though. One day everyone came together—learned to think differently, learned to change—and merged

---

* Bruce Tuckman's model of team development and behavior, introduced in 1965; in 1970, he added the fifth stage, adjourning.

ideas from different disciplines to become highly evolved and effective at risk mitigation and disaster preparedness. People had to learn three things: prevention, detection, and response. We made the learning process interesting and provided incentives that would entice people to participate. Most people were not interested in the incentives but finally realized the importance of their role. We realized that there were over 300 million in our population and each was viewed as a potential contributor if we could just get them to learn and practice basic security. We found the right methods—one of them was an interactive learning game. Prior to the launching of the game, some felt we had to mandate that everyone register and take the training, but instead we helped most of them understand the importance, and for others we created incentives that enticed them to play. Developing the game was done with the help of psychologists, professional development trainers, and branding and marketing experts who came in after the game designers. The training became a game and a contest. It cost $25 to play. Everyone who played and learned was automatically entered in the contest. We gave everyone 18 months to participate or, rather, play the interactive game. We called it *Play PDR!* It was a simple concept and stood for prevent, detect, and respond. The overall effort was managed on the Internet—through 10 servers that could handle the daily bandwidth of millions of participants online at any given time.

We had calculated that at least 200 million people were of age and had the ability to participate. This was determined through an organized team effort. We brought in the "numbers people," Web site administrators, lawyers, accountants, lottery commissioners, and fund administrators to help launch and manage the game. We were right; 202 million people logged on and played. When people got to the end of *Play PDR!* they were issued a number generated by the interactive game and stamped onto a certificate of graduation. At the end of the 18-month period, half the funds were set aside as a giveaway, and 5,000 people were randomly selected (through the certificate numbers generated) to receive $1,000,000. The winners were televised on local news over a 12-month period. This one-time campaign cost $900,000 (covered from the fees to participate), but it proved to be an explosive success. After the giveaways and the cost of designing, launching, and managing the game was settled, the remaining funds were reinvested into homeland security enhancements. The game signaled a defining moment in our evolution. People changed not just because the game sparked interest and brought everyone together, but also because they had an epiphany and finally understood that society could not tolerate barbaric acts of terrorism that belonged to earlier centuries—not in modern times. Survival and world order depended on society's ability to control the spread of terrorism. Security has one common meaning in this world, and now everyone is on the same page.

But that is in the ideal world. To get there, we still have to chart a map.

THE CURRENT STATE OF HOMELAND SECURITY

As I address homeland security throughout this book, the audience that I am primarily addressing is the private sector, security managers, facility managers, risk managers, emergency management and response resources, and students enrolled in homeland security courses aimed at contributing and implementing effective practices. This book can also help government agencies to understand private sector business needs.

This book aims to provide strategies, techniques, models, case studies, and lessons learned to bridge security knowledge or practice gaps between the DHS and private sector critical infrastructure owners, and strengthen preparedness and response to terrorist attacks, natural disasters, or other catastrophic events. DHS identifies roles and responsibilities for federal departments and agencies but relies heavily on private sector partnerships to strengthen the security and resilience of the nation's critical infrastructure. DHS provides guidance and a wide array of resources but often leaves the private sector wondering what precisely is expected of them in securing their facilities.

It has been a decade since the 9/11 attacks. Although Osama bin Laden no longer lives, Al Qaeda-inspired networks, affiliates, and other terrorist groups still present a terrorist threat to the United States. Terrorism cannot be eliminated but it can be managed. Globalization, technology, and culturally diverse workforces intertwine, collide, and clash creating situations that bring risk into our daily lives. The United States and the core Al Qaeda (post bin Laden) are two civilizations from different centuries fighting with the knowledge of our eras.* The "values" system of today's terrorists is centuries old, and our society has evolved too much to understand this threat. They fight with tools of ancient times and we are trying to fight with tools of modern times.

---

* Excerpts from the Middle East Media Research Institute (MEMRI), "There Is No Clash of Civilizations But a Clash between the Mentality of the Middle Ages and That of the 21st Century," interview with Arab American psychiatrist Wafa Sultan, clip no. 1050, February 21, 2006, http://www.memri.org (accessed February 10, 2008).

Other threats are morphing and surfacing at phenomenal rates, like out-of-control viruses. Today's "homegrown" terrorists, Islamic extremists, cyberattacks, insider threats, and active shooters cannot be managed without a wide-scale community effort. Our society only feels the pain of these threats intermittently when an attack takes us by surprise, but we are rarely compelled to put in place sustaining countermeasures. We need to master the ability to address threats more effectively as quickly as they surface, so that we do not scramble about chaotically when they strike. This requires that we gain an understanding of effective frameworks for managing threats and then apply what we learn accordingly. The United States is one of the world's most advanced nations when it comes to defense and technology, but despite its status as a world power, its citizens still do not fully understand the elements of preparedness and threat management.

Many will argue that much has been done in the name of homeland security. Yes, many solutions are in place as a result of 9/11, and the public now realizes that terrorism is something to worry about. Nevertheless, the progress still consists of elementary steps when considering the desired state described at the beginning of this chapter. To reach the desired state, we need framers to frame the problems in ways we can understand, implementers to introduce plans that work against the threats we face, visionaries to show us how to get to the desired state, creative thinkers to pave the way, leaders and managers who are not afraid to take risks for improvement, and citizens primed for necessary change.

When too much time lapses between terrorist attacks and people do not witness localized terrorist activity, they become complacent and drop their guard. They lose interest in threat awareness, and the momentum created by the last catastrophe quickly fades away. Managers begin to think their risk management measures are sufficient and that no further actions or security improvement expenditures are necessary. Employees begin to find ways to circumvent security measures because they see them as cumbersome and unnecessary. Imagination is no longer used to identify ways that threats might bring down physical or cyber infrastructures.

Just as it was echoed in the 9/11 Commission Report that a "failure of the imagination" made the 9/11 attacks possible, people can't seem to imagine that during times of lull where no attack has been witnessed, "the threat" is training, honing skills, and planning for the next attack.[*] Maybe

---

[*] National Commission on Terrorist Attacks upon the United States (9/11 Commission), 2004, 9/11 Commission Report, http://www.gpoaccess.gov/911/index.html, ch. 11.

attacks have not occurred because security was tight and visible. Maybe there was sufficient observance of "hustle and bustle" in strengthening security. Perhaps such measures created a perception of preparedness. Perhaps it appeared too difficult to strike. Whether there was an elaborate security program in place or not is not so important if the program succeeds at protecting assets and deterring threats. What matters is that even if one did not have the resources to implement the most robust security program, there was a perception that the best security strategy was in place and discouraged "would be" attackers.

To illustrate how true this is we simply have to look at our historical experiences with attacks. After the first World Trade Center attack of 1993, the attacker, Ramzi Ahmed Yousef, explained that he worried he would not get out of the garage before the bomb he had just placed there would explode. Later, as he watched from the Jersey City waterfront, he explained that he was so disappointed that the explosion did not cause the tower that had just been attacked to topple over and knock down the other tower and kill 250,000 people, as he expected.[*] He had carried out this attack in retaliation for U.S. aid to Israel. When asked why he didn't select Israeli targets, Yousef remarked that "they were too difficult therefore, if you cannot attack your enemy, you should attack friend of your enemy." The attack was meant to let Americans know they were "at war." The fact that he said they "were too difficult" (referring to Israeli targets) speaks volumes about what we must do.

It is difficult to buy into the idea that we are walking targets. This mind-set can make us complacent and set us up to be blindsided the next time an attack is carried out or attempted. Terrorists train. They wait. They plan. They plot, and then they carry out the attack.

The core purpose of Al Qaeda is to carry out violent attacks against military and civilian personnel of the United States and other countries regarded as "infidels" who do not govern in a manner consistent with the group's extremist interpretation of Islam. Another reason that the United States is targeted is that it is viewed as providing essential support to other "infidel" governments and institutions, particularly the governments of Saudi Arabia and Egypt, the nation of Israel, and the United Nations organization, all regarded as enemies of Al Qaeda.[†]

---

[*] Stephen Emerson, *American Jihad* (New York: Free Press, 2002).
[†] KLRN Frontline, Inside the Network, http://www.pbs.org/wgbh/pages/frontline/shows/network/alqaeda/indictment.html.

Terrorists have repeatedly given us warnings since the 1993 World Trade Center attack but, as a society, we have difficulty getting that message. How we became targets is immaterial. We cannot erase time, political decisions, or actions that appear to have inspired attacks against Americans, but we must take action and be accountable for our share of homeland security preparedness as citizens, business owners, and critical infrastructure sector owners and operators.

Where will terrorists strike next? Probably in the locations where they have already told us they will attack, as they did repeatedly with the Twin Towers. They like to impress upon us and embarrass us by letting us know what they are targeting and then proving that no matter what we do they can still accomplish their mission. If Osama bin Laden's successors are inspired by what he said, "We are working for a big operation; namely, dragging the United States into a confrontation with the entire Islamic world,"* then we should expect to be confronted with terrorism as a way of life. Terrorists do not care how they are orchestrated.

One step that we could take to improve our terrorist threat analysis is to identify all the blatant warnings that have been stated in the past, and reassess and secure those facilities. We need to discern realistic threats sooner rather than later and not on the day of the attack, as we tried to do on 9/11. On that day, we could not have imagined that humanity could inflict such atrocity and harm to other humans.

Counterterrorism and antiterrorism efforts require collaboration among intelligence, law enforcement, justice department, psychologists, religious leaders, and social scientists to name a few. First and foremost, this ambitious goal requires leaders and managers with superior skills in communications and interpersonal skills to develop and implement results-driven plans.

To do this, we must first come to terms with an understanding of the "words" being used—or "misused"—across sectors and agree to standard terms and definitions. The word *security* has broad meanings to different people depending on what industry they come from. Some think "security" means to invest in or buy stock, while others think it refers exclusively to information technology networks. The multiple uses of this word easily conjure an image in my mind. I am picturing a team of rowers in a boat; each member rows in a different direction and none is unaware that the boat is not going anywhere. Each one is proud of his

---

* Peter L. Bergen, *An Oral History of Al Qaeda's Leader: The Osama bin Laden I Know* (New York: Free Press, 2006).

or her team's contribution, but no one is aware that the boat never moved in any direction.

The use of the words *antiterrorism* and *counterterrorism* is typically intermixed and misused. These words have lost their original meanings. Those who have worked in counterterrorism units for decades would never use the word "antiterrorism" interchangeably with "counterterrorism." Traditionally, "counterterrorism" has been used to describe quick-reaction forces that break down doors and "take out terrorists" so to speak. To this group, "antiterrorism" signifies another type of security professional, one who might focus on preventative measures and perhaps give advice on where to place perimeter barriers at the front gates to protect against terrorism. It would be an insult to counterterrorism forces to refer to them as antiterrorism forces. Conversely, a consultant advising customers on barrier placement who has only book knowledge of terrorism and who has never served in a counterterrorism unit would be receiving undue credit if he or she were referred to as a counterterrorism expert. But the lines of definition have become blurred since 9/11, and now the words are used interchangeably by nearly everyone so that the respect that once belonged to small elite groups of specialized forces who endangered their lives is now lost.

There are pockets of vulnerability or weakness in many areas of homeland security resulting from security gaps and a lack of understanding about the threats and the appropriate role of homeland security officials, intelligence gathering resources, and law enforcement entities. This is further compounded when you add to the equation nonexperts who are out there giving terrorism-related advice. After 9/11, many people surfaced as homeland security experts. Some are considered experts because they are well-read, published, noted cultural experts, or perhaps were chiefs of police, but they have no operational experience in terrorism, unlike the experts who acquired their knowledge operationally where terrorism is a primary focus. Prior to 9/11, police officers and intelligence resources had no way of sharing intelligence information and thus law enforcement had no way of being utilized to be on the lookout for the 9/11 attackers. Law enforcement was strictly in a policing and crime response role, not an intelligence gathering or national security role. With terrorism being a national security concern, counterterrorism investigators and quick reaction forces are constantly in an "intelligence collection and action mode" where one is acting on intelligence information versus a criminal act, which has already taken place.

A security professional, on the other hand, may claim to have expertise gained while with the Federal Bureau of Investigation (FBI), Central

Intelligence Agency (CIA), Secret Service, military, law enforcement, or a security position held prior to 9/11. Do not be fooled by fancy acronyms or military and law enforcement experience. Just because they served in those organizations does not make them an expert in terrorism or countering terrorism. It is important to validate where the expertise originated. It may have been obtained from something other than an active role in counterterrorism units. While it is prudent to reach out to counterterrorism and antiterrorism professionals—American or international—it is most crucial to validate expertise, or else people who lack field or operational experience will unwittingly put many others in harm's way. The number of people who served in operational counterterrorism roles prior to 9/11 was small, and by my calculation many of them will reach retirement age soon if they have not already retired. The public sector consists of government agencies. The private sector consists of corporations, small businesses, and sole proprietors, in essence those who are in business but not a part of a government entity. Private and public sector organizations should do everything possible to reach out to the true experts and solicit their knowledge and expertise before it becomes obsolete and loses utility. Even lessons from the Cold War are applicable in today's global war on terror. At the same time, we must take time to educate the next wave of America's homeland security and national security leaders.

HOMELAND SECURITY ISSUES AND CHALLENGES

Even though DHS and many related legislative and security programs were introduced in the aftermath of 9/11 to protect against attacks in the future, several years later there are still many obstacles that hinder progress. They include the following:

- Lack of reliable early warning methods
- Communication and coordination gaps between public and public sectors
- Confusion and ambiguity about public and private sector homeland security roles
- Lack of trust between the government and private sector on information sharing
- Legal impediments to sharing classified information between public agencies and between government and the private sector
- A global and stateless adversary

Figure 1.1 Our nation's security hierarchy. (Illustration by Jessica Farias. With permission.)

To successfully implement homeland security programs, it is essential to understand security within our nation. There are three major components that comprise our nation's security hierarchy. They are national security, homeland security, and private sector security or corporate security, as illustrated in Figure 1.1.

National security entities are focused on protecting our nation from hostile takeovers, have the most authority in comparison with the other two components, and have jurisdiction in the United States and abroad. At the national security level, workers have a greater amount of responsibility than anyone else in the hierarchy. This group has been focused on threats since the birth of this nation. It is responsible for ensuring that national security is preserved at all times and never compromised. Ever wonder what life would be like if another nation came into our country, overthrew the government, and took over our nation? It is not something we think of often, but ensuring that such a thing never happens is the main reason for national security programs. Our nation's survivability depends on national security being preserved. This is achieved through economic, military, and political power; the use of diplomacy; and the use of the nation's intelligence resources—and this is true of most nations. Agencies with classified missions are the cornerstone to national defenses.

Even though the DHS was officially introduced after 9/11; it previously existed in the form of multiple agencies chartered with various security functions, protecting our country's borders, and responding to natural disasters. The authority and jurisdiction were nationwide. Agencies that comprise DHS have some of the same roles, responsibilities, and authority as national security-level players, but jurisdiction for the most part is inside the United States—with frequent requirements to reach into collaboration with the private sector and other nations on activities related to ports, travelers, and movement of goods into the United States.

Corporate security, of course, has existed since the birth of the private enterprise, and its focus has always been on asset protection and market share protection in order to be profitable. Private sector security is a critical component of our nation's security, and many members of the business community do not yet recognize this. There is no formal requirement mandating the three groups in the hierarchy collaborate. Thus, any partnerships, relationships, or collaboration that takes place among the three is good and can only contribute to preparedness efforts that can then reduce the impact of losses in the subsequent response stages of an event.

Within this hierarchy, there are intangible factors and interdependencies that affect homeland security success. There are security practices within each component that, if shared with the other two, could help solve some of the problems faced in homeland security today. Collaboration among the three would enable them to work in unison toward the same preparedness goals, and sharing methods would minimize duplicative, wasteful, and ineffective measures.

Despite all the work and progress in homeland security, we still do not have a "core foundation" for preparedness across the critical infrastructure sectors. "There is no common core foundation for educational programs in homeland security offered in over 400 colleges and universities," noted Enrique Aragon, during an interview with Elsa Lee. Aragon is the Program Manager for the University of California in Los Angeles (UCLA) Extension's Homeland Security and Emergency Management Certificate launched in 2012.* The program was introduced when educators at UCLA Extension recognized the need to educate businesses about the threat of terrorism in Los Angeles, a city of interest to terrorists. Introducing this program was UCLA Extension's proactive way of educating and creating awareness to improve preparedness and resilience. Partnerships between government and the private sector are the best way to ensure effective communications and establish an understanding about standard and expected practices at the national, homeland, and corporate security levels. Effective communications with everyone in the nation's

---

* Enrique Aragon, Program Manager, UCLA Extension, interview by Elsa Lee, April 2014.

security hierarchy, illustrated in Figure 1.1, would certainly contribute to preparedness and resilience.

A critical component of preventing terrorism is "intelligence capability." Many organizations need to improve their intelligence and information gathering capabilities. Intelligence is necessary in the public sector, within law enforcement, DHS agencies, and within the private sector. This requires knowing a few basics about gathering information, analyzing it, and processing it for action or sharing (connecting the dots).

A major component of this "intelligence" deficiency is the collection of quality data and predictive analysis—analysis that is not just "nice to know stuff" but also predictive and actionable. This includes timely analysis and proper sharing, which would then make it "actionable intelligence." The intelligence community has experienced losses over the years due to the following:

- Budget cuts of recent decades
- Capabilities that diminished after the Nixon Watergate event
- White House administrations forcing budget cuts to intelligence ("Everything is good in moderation ... but look where it put us on 9/11")
- Prevailing mind-set after the Cold War ended that there is no more threat

EVERYONE HAS A ROLE IN HOMELAND SECURITY

When a terrorist attack or disaster strikes, organizations and citizens have a tendency to blame ill-preparedness or failed responses on government, but they often fail to see their own contributions to the perceived failures. They are not even aware that they too had an active role in preparedness, prevention, response, or recovery. To effectively prepare for any homeland security event requires mass participation of the public and private sectors and citizens. If everyone were properly trained, it would enable us as a nation to achieve homeland security objectives and resilience. Our ability to effectively respond to terrorism, natural disasters, insider threats, cyberattacks, or active shooters depends on a unified framework and standard emergency management practices. City, state, and federal emergency management offices typically handle emergencies using the four phases of emergency management: mitigation/prevention, preparedness, response, and recovery. A partnership that includes society's participation and essential training is likely to produce a population that can contribute to preparedness, proper response, and effective recovery. Not only should we as citizens or businesses have preparedness plans, but we should also understand disasters are typically managed using the *National Incident Management System* (NIMS). NIMS is a national systematic approach for government, nongovernmental organizations, and the private sector to work seamlessly in response to catastrophes.

If everyone knew how to apply basic fundamentals of security and emergency management across physical and cyber infrastructure, the target list for terrorist or insider attacks would simply diminish. With preparedness on a national scale, risk would become manageable, and targets would become minimal because every facility would be hardened.

According to the U.S. Census Bureau, the population of the United States in 2013 was 316,128,839.* In this statistic, except of course for toddlers and newborns, nearly everyone has the potential to be a contributor to national security, homeland security, or corporate security. If millions of people had the same level of fundamental knowledge regarding security, it would enable prevention, detection, and response to threats in a way that could minimize damage and a negative economic impact on our nation.

America's citizens—whether at work or at home—could properly respond to terrorism with security fundamentals. Not only could this knowledge be used for terrorist attacks but many of the same procedures would also be applicable to natural disasters. Terrorism and disasters differ in that terrorism is the outcome of a plan concocted and carried out by fellow humans who mean to inflict torturous pain on others in a grand display of blood and carnage. This utter awareness is enough to catapult people into paralyzing shock. This is because people are so far removed from, and no longer live in, barbaric times when such atrocities were an everyday occurrence. In contrast to terrorist attacks, in natural disasters, Mother Nature is not acting out of malice or premeditation, so the shock factor is not the same even though the scale of the disaster may be the same as that generated by a terrorist attack.

Security-conscious citizens could contribute to the protection of homeland threats—not as street-corner posses to hunt terrorists down, but as educated people who would know how to plan for, prevent, respond, or recover from an event. This would simply contribute to security and resilience. It is safe to assume that in a major disaster, most of us would have to be self-reliant because first responders may not be able to get to us right

---

* U.S. Census Bureau, http://quickfacts.census.gov/qfd/states/00000.html.

away. Educating over 300 million people on such topics is not easy but it needs to be a primary goal through any avenue that will work.

HISTORY OF TERRORISM

There are terrorism fundamentals that we should all be aware of. Terrorism is the oldest form of warfare. On the war scale, it is the lowest form of low-intensity conflict, in line with insurgencies.* Originally, terrorism was intended to be an attack tactic that a nation would use against another nation through small unconventional forces to force political changes within the adversary nation. The unconventional force carried no banners and wore no uniform during the attack, thereby allowing the nation that launched the attack the ability to make a plausible denial if accused. Now we should all know that to say "the war on terror" is confusing and redundant because it is like saying "the war on war"—which does not make sense. The context of the original meaning seems to have been lost, like many other things that were lost on 9/11. If we were a society that highly valued preparedness education and emergency management, which comprises preparedness, we would know the essential fundamentals. This education should now be a priority so that we can all contribute to our nation's and our own preparedness.

Terrorist groups of the 1980s relied on state sponsors for support and safe haven. Today, the only countries on the U.S. Department of State sponsors list are Cuba, Iran, North Korea, Sudan, and Syria.† If we do not succeed at fighting terrorism abroad, we face a strong probability of doing it inside our own borders.

---

* U.S. Army, "Military Operations in Low Intensity Conflict," in Field Manual 100-20 (Washington, DC: Government Printing Office, 1990); and U.S. Army, "Operations in Low Intensity Conflict," in Field Manual 7-98 (Washington, DC: Government Printing Office, 1992). "Low-intensity conflict" is defined by the U.S. Joint Chiefs of Staff as a political-military confrontation between contending states or groups below conventional war and above the routine, peaceful competition among states. It frequently involves protracted struggles of competing principles and ideologies. Low-intensity conflict ranges from subversion to the use of armed forces. It is waged by a combination of means, employing political, economic, informational, and military instruments. Low-intensity conflicts are often localized, generally in the Third World, but contain regional and global security implications.

† Countries determined by the Secretary of State to have repeatedly provided support for acts of international terrorism.

In the last 50 years, terrorism has expanded due to instant communication, the Internet, and quicker continental travel methods. Attacks, methods, recruitment, funding, training, and target selection have dramatically changed, and terrorism has spread uncontrollably. No human in any corner of the world is immune from it. Targets historically consisted of airplanes, people, trains, buses, cars, restaurants, shopping centers, and buildings. When they were against American interests, targets were often U.S. government or embassy buildings or military personnel, but again, they usually took place outside U.S. borders. In all the years that we witnessed terrorist threats against American interests, the attack profiles were the same. They took place abroad. This made most Americans feel safe inside the United States because the attacks seemed so far removed from our world of reality. This mind-set made it impossible to imagine that anyone would ever carry out a terrorist attack inside U.S. borders. The attacks of the 1970s and 1980s were politically motivated for the most part and were perpetrated by groups sponsored by Communist or Middle Eastern states. Terrorist attacks carried out today are likely to be motivated by religious ideals (Old World versus New World), and the perpetrators fit no particular profile. Physical traits or ethnic characteristics are not reliable indicators or predictors of people who engage in terrorist activities. Today it can be anyone who has been recruited for the cause. The suicide bomber of today may think nothing of taking her own life and those of others as a martyr.

There are critical infrastructure facilities that provide public services that we have come to rely on for everyday life activities. Now these facilities are on target lists. In 2014, there continues to be prosecutions, arrests, and foiled attacks in the United States, Yemen, India, Italy, Britain, Spain, Azerbaijan, Thailand, Romania, Scotland, Germany, Denmark, and Turkey. In the United States, there will continue to be groups or lone terrorists—homegrown terrorists, Islamic extremists, and Al Qaeda terrorists that plot attacks against the U.S. critical infrastructure, all 16 sectors (see later section titled "What Is at Stake with Today's Terrorist Attacks").

THE DIRECT IMPACT OF MODERN-DAY TERRORISM

Al Qaeda, global Al Qaeda affiliate networks, and homegrown terrorists will continue to present the greatest terrorist threats to America for years to come.

15

Noted author and terrorism expert Peter Bergen states that

> After the Iraq war broke out, many fighters who fought in Afghanistan against the Soviets alongside Osama bin Laden showed up in Iraq to fight against the U.S. and coalition forces and Iraq became one of Al Qaeda's prime training grounds. When the Iraqi war is over, many of these fighters can be expected to focus future attacks against the U.S. in the U.S. We once thought terrorist attacks against America would only take place in foreign soil—not in the United States. That notion proved to be wrong on 9/11. There is no reason to expect that the same won't be true of the Islamic extremists fighting in Iraq today.*

He also believed that

> Several factors could make blowback from the Iraqi war even more dangerous than the fallout from Afghanistan. Foreign fighters started to arrive in Iraq even before Saddam Hussein's regime fell. They have conducted most of the suicide bombings—including some that have delivered strategic successes such as the withdrawal of most international organizations and the United Nations. They are more battle-hardened than the Afghan Arabs, who fought demoralized Soviet Army conscripts. Foreign fighters in Iraq today are testing themselves arguably against the best army in history, acquiring skills in their battles against coalition forces that will be far more useful for future terrorist operations than those their counterparts learned during the 1980s. Mastering how to make improvised explosive devices or how to conduct suicide operations is more relevant to urban terrorism than the conventional guerilla tactics that were used against the Soviet Union in Afghanistan.†

As America gets better at protecting assets and law enforcement interdicts plots to carry out attacks, the core Al Qaeda and its affiliates will continue to look for ways to stay a step ahead and also change their methods. Terrorist cells are very adept at self-funding, self-equipping, and self-training through the Internet—in contrast to 1980s groups like Abu Nidal and the Red Army Faction who relied on making a physical appearance at training camps. Today's terrorists are savvy in marketing and networking, better educated, and more radical than any other group in history. Osama bin Laden began making threats against the United States and other Western nations in the 1990s and delivered on his threats. His successors are in this war (Jihad) for the long run. His impact is already

---

* Bergen, *An Oral History of Al Qaeda's Leader*.
† Ibid.

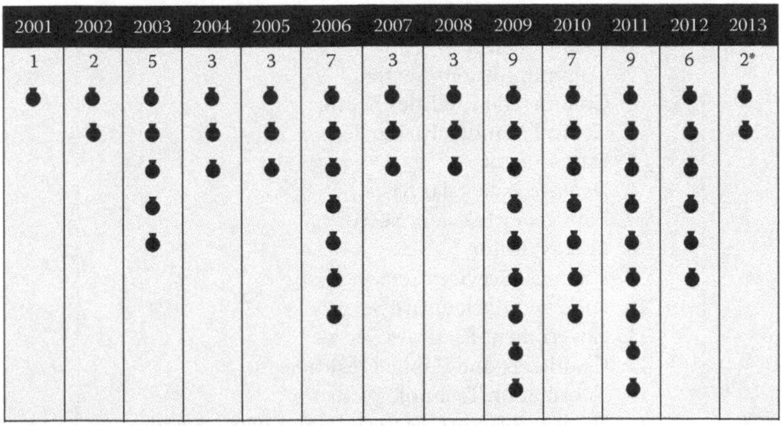

2001	2002	2003	2004	2005	2006	2007	2008	2009	2010	2011	2012	2013
1	2	5	3	3	7	3	3	9	7	9	6	2*

* As of June 24, 2013

Figure 1.2 Number of terrorist plots since 9/11 as of June 24, 2013. (Based on numbers compiled by The Heritage Foundation.)

made. Al Qaeda is no longer just a group but rather a movement that has successfully recruited people worldwide, even converted Americans and other Westerners. According to The Heritage Foundation, there have been at least 60 terrorist plots against the United States, including the Boston Marathon bombing, since 9/11 (see Figure 1.2). An increasing number of Islamist-inspired terrorist attacks are originating within the United States.[*]

WHAT IS AT STAKE WITH TODAY'S TERRORIST ATTACKS

The attacks of September 11, 2001, were pivotal because commercial facilities, defenseless against terrorism, were attacked. Shortly after 9/11, we saw mass transit and other critical infrastructure attacked in Europe. Prior to 9/11, no one really worried about threats against infrastructure except during Y2K or when engineers raised concerns about "infrastructure" reaching capacity levels due to growing populations. Today, we still have to worry about infrastructure but for different reasons. Are we going to

---

[*] Jessica Zuckerman, Steven P. Bucci, and James Jay Carafano, "60 Terrorist Plots Since 9/11: Continued Lessons in Domestic Counterterrorism," The Heritage Foundation, http://www.heritage.org/research/reports/2013/07/60-terrorist-plots-since-911-continued-lessons-in-domestic-counterterrorism (accessed May 29, 2014).

1. Chemical Sector
2. Communications Sector
3. Commercial Facilities Sector
4. Critical Manufacturing Sector
5. Dams Sector
6. Defense Industrial Base
7. Emergency Services Sector
8. Energy Sector
9. Financial Services Sector
10. Food and Agriculture Sector
11. Government Facilities Sector
12. Healthcare and Public Health Sector
13. Information Technology Sector
14. Nuclear Reactors, Materials, and Waste Sector
15. Transportation Security Sector
16. Water and Wastewater Systems Sector

Figure 1.3 The 16 critical infrastructure sectors according to the DHS.

experience attacks to our critical infrastructure like Britain and other European countries?

The greatest devastation from terrorist attacks can result from attacks to critical infrastructure and key resources (CI/KRs), including public venues where masses congregate.

The greatest threat from terrorism in the United States and in most Western countries is to critical infrastructure. Preparedness across infrastructure sectors is the area that needs the most improvement because the public depends on them to sustain everyday life. There are 16 critical infrastructure sectors,* but they do not all have the same level of criticality. They are listed in Figure 1.3.

Of the 16 critical infrastructure sectors, DHS is most worried about some more than others because the economic and psychological impact of some are higher than others. They include nuclear and energy facilities,

---

* "Critical infrastructure" describes systems and assets, whether physical or virtual, so vital to the United States that their incapacity or destruction would have a debilitating impact on national security, national economic security, national public health or safety, or any combination thereof. Key resources are publicly or privately controlled resources essential to minimal operations of the economy or government, including individual targets whose destruction would not endanger vital systems but could create a local disaster or profoundly damage the nation's morale or confidence.

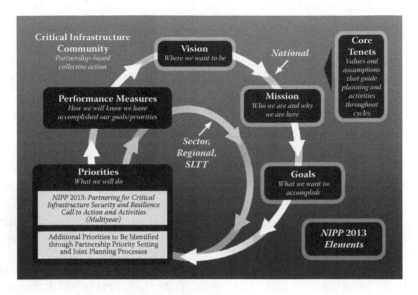

Figure 1.4 Critical infrastructure community.

chemical/petroleum industry, transportation systems, water systems, food industry, and electric power grids.* However, historically, attacks have been carried out against commercial facilities, defense industrial bases, government facilities, and transportation systems. So essentially, there are about 10 we should all really be concerned about.

Government officials estimate that approximately 85 percent of the U.S. infrastructure is owned and operated by the private sector; the critical infrastructure community is illustrated in Figure 1.4.

This puts our country in a vulnerable position because the private sector does not have its own armies, fortresses, or intelligence resources like the federal government. The federal government has an assumption that, given the guidance published by DHS, private sector security professionals know exactly what they need to do to help protect infrastructure. There are many ambiguities and assumptions on both sides that place infrastructure and the private sector in vulnerable positions. For example, in addition to assumptions, what are the compliance requirements, and what are the consequences if the private sector does not meet them? We are a young nation compared to European countries that have been

---

* Robert McCreight, "Soft Targets in Your Backyard: Building Our Own Hometown Readiness," *Homeland Defense Journal* 5, no. 10 (October 2007).

```
Public Sector <> Private Sector

Public Sector <> Public Sector

Private Sector <> Private Sector
```

Figure 1.5 Homeland security and sector communications.

dealing with terrorism for decades. There's much that we can learn from them. Again, caution should be exercised as some of their practices may not be appropriate for our nation, our way of life, or our Constitution. Collectively, we need to quickly grasp the fundamentals of terrorism and master the ability to prevent, detect, and respond so that we can help prevent another 9/11, so that we will not be taken by surprise ever again, so that our infrastructure can be properly secured and protected to sustain everyday life as we know it and expect it to be. Effective communication is not taking place at various levels of response to share threat knowledge and warnings, or properly handle recovery efforts in the face of a disaster. Figure 1.5 depicts the formal and informal relationships that currently exist between and among government and industry. There are various types of relationships that exist among these groups—from formal to informal to nonexistent. An example of a public-to-public relationship would be government-to-government at any level, in any state. Public-to-private would be all critical infrastructure owners and DHS (as well as other government members), and private-to-private would be all critical infrastructure owners and operators communicating with each other and with other private sector community members to share information. Dynamics that affect these relationships are the authority and regulator role of government and the political, technical, and organizational barriers that are ingrained in various organizations. Some of the obstacles that need to be overcome include understanding organizational cultures and rules, removing distrust, and placing aside egos and jealousy.[*]

---

[*] Kumar, Amir. Unabridged version of doctoral dissertation "Developing Homeland Security Partnerships: Comparative Analysis of the Development of Homeland Security Partnerships." *HIS Journal of Homeland Security*, August 2007, http://www.homelandsecurity.org/newjournal/Articles/displayArticle2.asp?article=163 (accessed March 2008).

COUNTERING TERRORISM WITH HELP FROM THE DEPARTMENT OF HOMELAND SECURITY

Many applicable homeland security laws and directives were introduced since 9/11 to help guide preparedness and protective efforts. The key roadmaps for critical infrastructure protection (otherwise referred to as CIP) are Homeland Security Presidential Directive 7 (HSPD-7) and the National Infrastructure Protection Plan (NIPP) prepared by DHS. The NIPP is designed to bring infrastructure protection under one national unified effort. HSPD-7, signed by President George W. Bush in December 2003, established a national policy for federal departments and agencies specific to identification, prioritization, and protection of the CIs and KRs in the United States, and this led to the creation of the NIPP. The NIPP, originally published in June 2006 by DHS and updated in 2013, "provides the coordinated approach to critical infrastructure and key resource protection roles and responsibilities for federal, state, local, tribal, and private sector security partners."

Countering the threat of terrorism requires that all facets of society and communities of teams come together to manage the problem. No nation or government agency alone can fight terrorism. To effectively manage or control terrorism requires a basic understanding of terrorism and how we got to this point: worrying about the security of our infrastructure. The attacks of September 11, 2001, began to unfold in the 1990s, when Islamic extremists began to focus on the United States as a target. Within a matter of years, attacks would cross U.S. borders and 9/11 would come to be marked indelibly in everyone's mind as the worst terrorist attack in history. Would a cruise ship attack in the middle of the ocean have caused the same psychological effect as the Twin Towers and Pentagon attacks? Probably not, because the cruise ship would need to be close enough for media and news cameras to capture and broadcast the attack in order to achieve the desired mass reaction. The cruise ship attack might affect the cruise industry, but it would not have the same effect that the 9/11 targets had on the larger economy. The message to the world on 9/11 was clear: Here is a super world power that was brought to its knees, not in some remote part of the world but here in America. In the mastermind's view, this was a plan conceived and executed by "low-tech" means, not by a high-tech Army of a rival nation. "Wow! It was successfully carried out to fruition, and was not that hard to pull off—imagine that" Osama bin Laden's cohorts might have said as they gave each other the "high five" after the attacks.

What does it take for us—the targets—to heed these messages? Are we smart enough to detect and deter the next attack? Are we taking the time to keep up with terrorist trends at home and abroad? Do we understand the methods that homegrown terrorists might employ compared to sleeper terrorists who still live among us? At our level, can we connect the dots? Do we even know how to connect the dots? Osama bin Laden inspired many followers and asked them to "kill Americans everywhere" and that is not a message that will simply go away just because bin Laden no longer lives.

Public and private sector partnerships are critical to the success of homeland security and managing disasters. It requires building relationships and formal agreements of understanding as well as facilitating information sharing and collaboration. Under the NIPP, this collaboration is absolutely required.* Government officials believe that collaboration between the private sector owners of critical infrastructure and key resources and the government sector councils exist for the most part, but they are not yet efficient or effective with timely sharing of information. The NIPP is a starting point for ensuring that we execute a unified approach to terrorism preparedness, but there are too many obstacles hindering progress between government agencies and the private sector. For example, the private sector is uncertain about the steps that follow risk and vulnerability assessments; see Figure 1.6.

The private sector is afraid to share risk or vulnerability results for fear that information will not be protected by the government and will be leaked to competitors or to the media. This is due in part to past experience, where allegedly the government inadvertently leaked information. The government is not perfect but has its heart in the right place and has

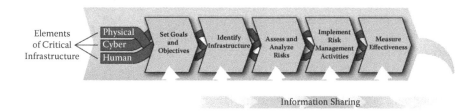

Figure 1.6   Critical Infrastructure Risk Management Framework.

---

* Department of Homeland Security, *National Infrastructure Protection Plan (NIPP)* (Washington, DC: Department of Homeland Security, 2013).

apologized for such leaks. All actions called for in the updated 50-page NIPP (plus supplements) may seem daunting and intimidating, but it is possible to work within the framework by dissecting and working on issues one at a time. This book offers ways the NIPP can be useful to assess and secure critical infrastructure sector vulnerabilities. Throughout my 34-year career I have witnessed or successfully carried out NIPP activities at many agencies, organizations, and private sector companies—effectively and at reasonable costs to secure vulnerabilities and diminish risks.

Addressing terrorism requires educating and updating public and private sector preparedness programs. Both sectors need to work together with a strong spirit of collaboration, but the cultures are so different that often this barrier hinders their endeavors. It is essential to understand the differing natures of government and business in order to capitalize on what they can achieve together to contribute to homeland security.

Businesses exist to provide a product or service in exchange for fees, thus producing profits. Governments also exist to provide services but also to enforce rules, maintain order, and ensure the well-being of the people. Private industry is driven by profitability, and businesses take risks in the hopes that they will be profitable. New and innovative approaches can be tried easier in the private sector than in government organizations. Generally, the worst that will happen in a business is that the effort may not prove to be profitable. When it comes to homeland security, the government must implement preparedness plans and counterterrorism through proven measures—this fits in with government's risk-averse nature. The government expects that businesses will do the same: implement proven methods.

As former DHS Secretary Michael Chertoff makes clear in his contribution to follow, in order to establish true partnerships, government and private industry need to take time to learn about each other's organizational traits as they build relationships. Their differences often result in frustrations and misunderstandings about each other. Every catastrophe in the last few years has shown that these huge differences have a way of impeding response and recovery efforts—as well as prevention measures. Both sectors have to interact, but the methods for coordination and communication are disjointed. Both sectors must get past the misconceptions and frustrations, and simply bolt into action to achieve homeland security objectives.

I have attended hundreds of security conference events over the last 14 years, which has provided me with a unique opportunity to hear the concerns of public and private sector leaders. Private sector workforces

CRITICAL INFRASTRUCTURE OWNERS AND CONTRIBUTING TO HOMELAND SECURITY

Michael Chertoff[*]

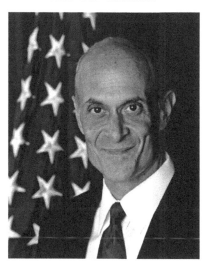

Critical infrastructure owners can contribute to homeland security by developing comprehensive strategies that manage risk without building barriers that interfere with business operations. Critical infrastructure and key resources can be attacked by both physical and cyber means and intrusions, or by the effects of natural or man-made disasters. Efforts to secure the homeland must be driven with

---

[*] Michael Chertoff became the second U.S. Secretary of Homeland Security under President George W. Bush in 2005. Since leaving government service in 2009, Chertoff has worked as a senior of counsel and member of the White Collar Defense and Investigations practice group at Covington & Burling LLP. He is also the cofounder and chairman of The Chertoff Group, a global advisory firm that provides business strategy, risk management, and merger and acquisition (M&A) advisory services. Chertoff graduated magna cum laude from Harvard College and Harvard Law School. As a federal prosecutor, he investigated and prosecuted cases of political corruption, organized crime, corporate fraud and terrorism— including the 9/11 terrorist attacks investigation. He also served as a federal judge on the U.S. Court of Appeals for the Third Circuit.

a sense of urgency because threats to our country are constantly changing and adapting and we too must be nimble and decisive.

The first step in enhancing security and disaster preparedness is to ensure that organizations have security processes that support national preparedness. This can be achieved by first establishing baseline measures to effectively monitor risk environments to prevent, protect against, and respond to terrorist acts or disasters. Then, match possible threats against possible targets, and map the current state of prevention, protection, and response planning with respect to each. Critical infrastructure owners should utilize in-house processes and tools as well as the Department of Homeland Security's resources designed to meet national preparedness goals. Last, strong partnerships, both inside and outside of the organization, can help build the right capabilities in the right places and at the right level to protect the entire infrastructure.

have often declared that they do not know whom to trust or what to do when it comes to homeland security requirements. Many are not even aware that the Homeland Security Advisory System has been replaced by the National Terrorism Advisory System (NTAS). NTAS alerts provide a concise summary of the potential threat including geographic region, mode of transportation, or critical infrastructure potentially affected by the threat, actions being taken to ensure public safety, as well as recommended steps that individuals, communities, business, and governments can take to help prevent, mitigate, or respond to a threat. NTAS alerts are supposed to include a clear statement on the nature of the threat, which is to be defined in one of two ways:[*]

- Elevated Threat—Warns of a credible terrorist threat against the United States
- Imminent Threat—Warns of a credible, specific, and impending terrorist threat against the United States

---

[*] "Secretary Napolitano Announces Implementation of National Terrorism Advisory System," April 20, 2011, http://www.dhs.gov/news/2011/04/20/secretary-napolitano-announces-implementation-national-terrorism-advisory-system.

HELP FROM THE DEPARTMENT OF HOMELAND SECURITY IS NOT ENOUGH

The United Kingdom, Germany, Italy, France, Israel, and Ireland had been dealing with terrorism well before 9/11. Experts in the FBI, the U.S. military, CIA counterintelligence, and U.S. Military Special Operations Forces have been preventing, detecting, and responding to terrorist threats since the 1960s. This nation is missing out on the ability to infuse homeland security programs with their expertise. These experts should be rounded up and debriefed. We would find that counterterrorism forces can tell us how they breached security just before they kicked down the door to neutralize terrorists. We should then take that information and implement appropriate security countermeasures to harden our critical infrastructure facilities. The counterintelligence professionals who have monitored, surveilled, and investigated terrorists could provide information on what are the terrorist behaviors to look for when terrorists are in the plotting stages. We should then take that information and present it to critical workforces in training and education. We need to put their expertise in "offensive tactics" to work to develop "better defensive measures" against terrorism threats. Their job was once to neutralize or capture the threat. Today, everyone's job is to protect America from the same threats.

Terrorism will be around for centuries, but societies must not get to the point where they can tolerate it. In contrast to crime, which we deal with and tolerate, terrorism can affect world order and turn our lives upside down. We may not be able to wipe out terrorism, but we can and we must work to control and manage it. Our history with terrorism shows that in the 1970s and 1980s, U.S. interests were attacked abroad. The attacks of 9/11 changed that trend. Compared to interests abroad, attacks inside the United States threaten not just homeland security but also national security. We can strike at terrorists abroad where U.S. interests are at stake, but, given our laws, in the United States we are limited in what we can do, especially if the only evidence of a planned attack is the "intent" in the mind of a "would-be" terrorist.

2

Essential Threat Factors

The so called religious awakening has turned everything upside down ... the dead have taken control of the living. ... Arab society and culture are regressing in a superstitious and unreasonable manner ... living in a world of the supernatural—not today's world of logic.

Saudi author and reformist Turki Al-Hamad

THE PROBLEM WE FACE WITH THREATS

We live in a world of ever-growing threats that we cannot seem to foresee or stop. Combating terrorism will be a continuous challenge but it does not have to be a burden on everyday life. The last decade has enormously taxed our counterterrorism resources because we have been tactically and strategically fighting terrorism on a global scale. After 9/11, U.S. counterterrorism efforts all got rolled up under one label, the *"global war on terror."* It included an insurgency in Afghanistan, an insurgency in Iraq, disabling Al Qaeda, bringing all Jihadist extremists responsible for heinous crimes to justice, tracking militant Islamists who were plotting to carry out attacks, and controlling homegrown radicalized groups that are planning destruction inside our borders.* Controlling the spread of terrorism is important but we have to find a way to incorporate vigilance, deterrence, and resilience into everyday life or we will remain overwhelmed.

---

* J. Straw, "What's Wrong with the War on Terrorism?" interview with Brian Jenkins, *Security Management*, September 2007, http://www.securitymanagement.com/article/what-s-wrong-war-terrorism?page=0%2C2.

To properly address these concerns requires seeing them in new ways—or facing a world with more 9/11s or a counterterrorism tempo that we will not be able to sustain. Although the threat of terrorism is real and 9/11 proved that we were no match for what hit us that day, it is possible to live in a state of preparedness without fear and panic. The average American has a 1 in 8,000 chance of dying in a car accident, about a 1 in 18,000 chance of being a victim of a homicide, and a less than 1 in 500,000 chance of dying in a terrorist attack based on figures charted from the deaths of 9/11.[*]

Other problems we face are identifying and reporting individuals who perform the acts without stereotyping them. If everyone reporting suspicious activities focused strictly on Middle Eastern men or Muslims, we would open ourselves up to being completely oblivious to valid threats. There is no profile for terrorists that we can rely on today. History has shown that terrorists change tactics as soon as they determine that their methods can be countered. Al Qaeda successfully recruits Westerners, Europeans, blue-eyed men, women, and even professionals like engineers and doctors. In observing terrorists during activities that lead up to an attack, the only attribute that has been reliable at all times is behavior. Behaviors translate into actions, and action is required to carry out attacks. That has not changed throughout history. There are essentially three stages in terrorist attacks: planning, preparation, and execution. The planning and preparation stages are the only points in the attack timeline with a high probability of detection because they require physical access to the target location by the terrorists to confirm information for the attack. If activities are not detected in these stages, it will be nearly impossible on the day of the attack to detect and stop the terrorists. On that day, moreover, different role players than those involved in the earlier stages will appear.

Because of the major impact that a terrorist attack would have on our economy, our infrastructure, and our physical and psychological well-being, everyone (government, private businesses, employees, and citizens) needs to take an active role in helping to prevent them. One way to do this is to look at ways that it has been done in other organizations and countries, and mimic those successful practices that would apply in the United States. Why reinvent the wheel? Using the best practices of others will put us in a position to better respond to threats and meet DHS objectives.

---

[*] J. Straw, "What's Wrong with the War on Terrorism?"

GENERAL THREATS TO SECURITY
HIERARCHY COMPONENTS

Threat can be defined as anything that can cause, or aims to cause, losses, harm, or damage. Threats are viewed, defined, and perceived in various ways across industries. However, we will all feel the impact of the blow if the most deadly of threats—terrorism—strikes one of our critical infrastructure facilities. All components of this nation's security hierarchy face threats but with a few differences in the characteristics of the threats faced by each. Many organizations in the hierarchy have very good methods for addressing them. Let's compare and put into contrast some of the threats faced in the United States. The threats the U.S. government is most concerned about at a national level are as follows:*

1. *Terrorism*—Premeditated, politically motivated violence perpetrated against noncombatant targets by subnational groups or clandestine agents to influence an audience.
2. *Proliferation*—The provision of chemical, biological, radiological, or nuclear weapons and/or technology by states that have controls in place and possess them to states that do not.
3. *Chemical warfare*—The military or terrorist use of toxic substances such that the chemical effects of these substances on exposed personnel result in incapacitation or death.
4. *Biological warfare*—The deliberate use of pathogens or toxins for military or terrorism purposes; more toxic than chemical warfare nerve agents on a weight-for-weight basis, and potentially providing broader coverage per pound of payload than such agents; attacks can be masked as naturally occurring epidemics due to the presence of anthrax in the environment.
5. *Information infrastructure attack*—Political activism on the Internet ranging from using e-mail and Web sites to organize for purposes of attacking the United States, to Web page defacements and denial-of-service attacks or hacking for political activism.
6. *Narcotics trafficking*—A chronic problem created by drug dependence and related activity; it is a chronic problem and a relapsing disorder that exacts an enormous cost on individuals, families, businesses, communities, and nations. Addicted individuals frequently engage in self-destructive and criminal

---

* U.S. Intelligence Community, http://www.intelligence.gov/2-threat.shtml (accessed January 2008).

behavior. Illegal drug trafficking inflicts violence and corruption on our communities.

7. *Foreign intelligence services*—Identifying, understanding, prioritizing, and counteracting the intelligence threats from foreign powers from espionage, sabotage, assassinations, or international terrorism. It involves more than simply the capture of spies (counterespionage); neutralizing all aspects of the intelligence operations of foreign nations. U.S. counterintelligence activities are governed by executive order, and "information gathered" as well as "activities conducted" undergo extensive oversight.

Defense and federal contracting firms have typically been targeted by foreign intelligence services interested in industry's intelligence information, critical technology, and any classified material or research. Companies who hold government contracts are required to report foreign intelligence threats or indicators of potential foreign interest. In a 2013 Defense Security Service (DSS) report, top items of interest to foreign intelligence collectors included information systems, electronics, lasers/optics/sensors, aeronautics, space systems, positioning/navigation/time, and information security. The annual "Targeting U.S. Technologies" is DSS's premier publication on foreign intelligence collection against the Defense Industrial Base (Figure 2.1).*

At the homeland security level, among the 16 critical infrastructure facilities, owners and operators face some of the same threats as the national level but with slight differences. These threats can also apply to businesses and corporations that are not associated with critical infrastructure. Here are some of the most common threats faced by critical infrastructure:

1. *Terrorism*—Activities ranging from undue interest to full-force attacks. Undue interest includes surveillance of facilities for the purposes of identifying security program effectiveness or vulnerabilities that could be exploited at a later time to carry out an attack.
2. *Sabotage*—A deliberate act of perpetrating physical damage to a facility or its assets to inflict losses or damage, or to disrupt operations.
3. *Workplace violence*—Acts originating from employees or others whereby the employer and its employees are threatened; this

---

* "Targeting U.S. Technologies: A Trend Analysis of Cleared Industry Reporting," http://www.dss.mil/isp/count_intell/ci_reports.html (accessed May 30, 2014).

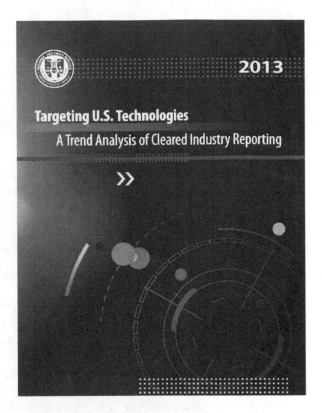

Figure 2.1 The Defense Security Services annual publication "Targeting U.S. Technologies."

includes incidents of abuse, threats, assaults, or an explicit or implicit challenge to their safety, well-being, or health.

4. *Theft*—Involves acts of stealing, larceny, or the taking of property of employees or the facility or employer without authorization or consent.

5. *Espionage*—Involves a human physically stealing or taking information without permission from the holder of the information for uses other than what the owner intended or would consent to.

6. *Bomb threat*—An effective means of disrupting business operations by claiming that a bomb will explode in the facility; the threat may be telephoned or physically brought to the site by any means; used by terrorists, extortionists, and disgruntled employees.

7. *Cyberthreats*—Threats to information systems that could disrupt or bring down operations, including online masquerading; password and identity theft; phishing, spyware, malware, and theft of hardware; criminal use of botnets; cyberterrorism; spying and theft of data by governments, industry, terrorists, other criminals, or insiders; denial-of-service attacks; and organized cyberattacks capable of causing debilitating disruption to the critical infrastructure, economy, or national security.

8. *Active shooters*—Defined by DHS as an individual who is actively engaged in killing or attempting to kill people in a confined and populated area, often using firearms and shooting indiscriminately.

GENERAL THREAT EFFECT ON HOMELAND SECURITY

Despite the differences in the threat characteristics to national security and homeland security components, terrorism is the one threat that can do serious damage to both. We do not have a standardized nationwide method for preparedness or deterrence. Response and recovery guidelines are pretty straightforward through the Federal Emergency Management Agency's (FEMA) Incident Command System. Some states have better preparedness plans than others, and the federal government certainly has tremendous resources it can dedicate to terrorism threats. Terrorist threats have a way of emerging out of nowhere and thus, with this particular threat, we can never let our guard down or become complacent. The critical infrastructure sectors we rely on most are transportation, commercial buildings, defense industrial bases, and government facilities. These sectors have historically been targeted by terrorists and foreign intelligence services for exploitation of classified information.

A terrorist attack to our critical infrastructure would have a detrimental impact on the public and the nation. We all are dependent on the various modes of transportation to get to and from work. Goods we use daily are also delivered through these nodes. We conduct all business using the financial sector. We depend on government and defense to protect the nation. We visit public venues and theme parks with our families. We are totally dependent on critical infrastructure, and even if we do not work at critical infrastructure facilities, we have access to them and use them frequently. That means that we have the potential to witness threats, report them, and deter them—or be present when the full blow of an attack is already in progress.

- At yourself for having been blind to the way threats work
- At the government for being too bureaucratic and slow at times
- At everyone who remained blind to the threat instead of acting proactively
- At the threat for knowing your weaknesses and using them against you
- At all the funds wasted on technology instead of investing in the human factors

Figure 2.2 Emotional anger and blame.

The sooner we remove the aura of fear or strangeness from the word *terrorism*, the sooner we can all contribute to preparedness and deterrence. This would also enable us to think outside the box so that we can face homeland security challenges head on—or save our own lives if caught in the middle of an attack. When a word sounds scary, we resist having anything to do with the subject. But we must get past the shock, fear, and denial stages and reach the acceptance stages of "terrorism" to avoid being passive or pessimistic about this topic.

Ordinary people would not find anything comforting, fun, or exciting about being assigned to an organization where the risk of attack is high or where there has been an actual attack (e.g., the Pentagon or the Navy Yard). They would simply be scared at first. Then, upon witnessing something short of an attack, such as a bomb threat, or an actual attack, the first logical reaction would be shock. If people do not recognize that all the emotions they are likely to feel are part of a logical progression, they might get stuck in the stages of shock or fear and never take the necessary action to assess and secure vulnerabilities or enhance preparedness measures.

When they finally get to acceptance, they realize that they must take action, learn everything possible to avoid ever having that experience again. They would buy into it emotionally and intellectually, but at some point, as addressed in Figure 2.2, they would experience anger and possibly not fully understand how to use it to their advantage.

THREAT MANAGEMENT THROUGH INTELLIGENCE

Properly managing risk in all work environments requires a thorough understanding of the cause and effect of threats. Threat variables must be viewed objectively and subjectively by diverse threat review teams with the objective of highlighting information that would otherwise be missed, then taking steps to apply risk mitigation. Even when the information is right in front of us, sometimes we cannot see it. Critical information we are likely to miss can be brought to our attention through the use of "intelligence" and threat assessment processes used by national security resources.

Our nation's first line of defense against adversarial threats occurs through something called the *intelligence process.** It takes raw collected data and converts it to useful information so that policy makers can make decisions on the diplomatic, economic, and military actions needed to maintain national security. If the intelligence process fails and our first line of defense is compromised or ineffective, we could potentially see a range of surprise attacks, from "low-intensity conflict," to full-scale war abroad or an invasion within our borders. This is why it is critical that the "first line of defense" capability not be compromised. The intelligence process involves five steps that are highly formal and heavily scrutinized by oversight committees.†

1. *Planning and direction*—Management of the entire intelligence cycle, from identifying the need for data to delivering an intelligence product to a consumer.
2. *Collection*—Gathering of raw data from which finished intelligence is produced.
3. *Processing and exploitation*—The synthesis of raw data into a form usable by the intelligence analyst or other consumers.
4. *Analysis and production*—Integration, evaluation, and analysis of all available data, and the preparation of a variety of intelligence products.
5. *Dissemination*—Delivering the products to consumers who request them through categories of finished intelligence available to consumers.

The private sector could develop and model an "early-warning" capability based on similar concepts: the ability to have a program that looks at threats and how they would impact the company and what options exist for dealing with them. To some degree, this already happens in companies through risk management strategies, business intelligence, and competitive intelligence; however, the focus rarely includes the gathering and analysis of terrorism information—groups, methods, tactics, and so on. The focus tends to be on economics: how to protect assets, how to protect market share, and how to protect company secrets and trademarks.

---

* U.S. Intelligence Community, http://www.intelligence.gov/2-business.shtml.
† Ibid.

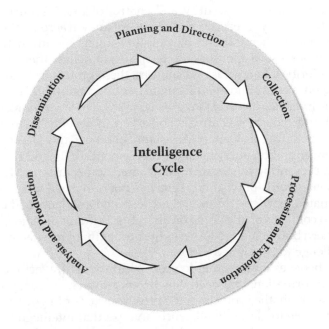

Figure 2.3 The intelligence cycle.

The intelligence process steps involve activities that often warn us of threats before they become imminent—making them "early warnings" and "indicators," which then enable leaders and managers to make timely tactical decisions.* The U.S. intelligence community has two primary challenges: determining the capabilities that an opponent can muster, and fathoming the intentions of the opponent to use those capabilities against us—the who, what, when, where, and how. As shown in Figure 2.3, this is an ongoing, round-the-clock process.

The keys to good U.S. intelligence are cooperative arrangements among the various U.S. agencies and bilateral and multilateral exchanges with friendly governments. But collection is only the beginning of a successful intelligence effort toward preparedness; more critical is how analysis turns data into useful information and then into an understanding about what opponents or the enemy is planning.† There are limitations and constraints, requiring the prioritization of resources. When the Soviet military

---

* U.S. Intelligence Community, http://www.intelligence.gov/2-community.shtml.
† U.S. Intelligence Community, http://www.intelligence.gov/2-business.shtml.

was no longer a threat, security and control of Russia's nuclear arsenal became the primary threat concern because of known accountability issues. Development of chemical and biological weapons by any nation or any group without a state sponsor and the means to deliver them also are significant priorities. In contrast to countries, these groups operate much like an intelligence entity and are difficult to track and monitor.

In an interview with Alonzo Pena, a 28-year law enforcement professional and federal executive who served in several law enforcement agencies, including as Deputy Assistant Secretary and Deputy Director for U.S. Immigration and Customs Enforcement, DHS, and the first DHS attaché representing the Secretary of Homeland Security in Mexico, Pena shared some words of wisdom.* Pena has not only been where the action is, he initiated, participated in, and orchestrated and launched operations needed to combat volatile crime on all fronts. Without question, Pena sees the southern border along Mexico as the border that presents the most risk and challenge to the United States.

Pena believes that in order to protect infrastructure facilities, personnel, and information, you need "intelligence-driven" security measures, regardless of whether you are in the private sector or in government. You need to be able to gather intelligence, analyze that intelligence, and then use it to determine what you need to do to protect your assets from adversaries or threats. The private sector needs to develop its own "intelligence gathering and analysis" capabilities so that they can adapt as quickly as threats and effectively mitigate today's risks.

Another important security component is the timely sharing of information between the private sector and government. One stumbling block to sharing information is a lack of confidence or a distrust that the information will not be reliably protected. Building trust takes time but it is essential to the timely sharing of information, which is just as important as having "intelligence." Everyone needs intelligence. It is what enables

---

* Alonzo Pena, interview by Elsa Lee, May 22, 2014, San Antonio, Texas. Pena is a graduate of Pan American University in Edinburg, Texas, the U.S. Customs Service Graduate School of Management, Advanced Executive Leadership Training from the Federal Executive Institute, and the Senior Executive Fellowship Program at Harvard University's John F. Kennedy School of Government. He is most recognized for establishing and directing the now highly successful DHS Border Enforcement Task Force (BEST) initiative, which brought together the combined efforts of hundreds of state, local, and federal officers responding to critical incidents and security threats that arise on the highly volatile southwest border. Today, Pena is the president and founder of DMEP, a professional and independent consulting firm providing a full range of expertise in all aspects of safety and security solutions domestically and internationally.

you to make strategic decisions about your business and how to best safe-guard your assets, particularly if you are a critical infrastructure owner.

TERRORISTS' OPERATIONAL METHODOLOGY

Modern-day terrorists linked to Al Qaeda or inspired by Al Qaeda follow a template for attacks. They learned their methods from the Al Qaeda manual, Web sites, or other "how-to manuals" that they circulate among themselves and on the Internet. Several decades ago, terrorists were recruited and trained through face-to-face contact but only after being sponsored and vetted by someone in the group. Control was tight and centralized, and each one had a role to play in an attack. There are many differences between today's terrorists and those of pre-9/11. There are as many differences in their methods as there are global regions and terrorist nodes. Many of them are loosely affiliated with Al Qaeda and trained through methods that make their detection difficult—through the Internet; extensive marketing campaigns; exchange of underground manuals; or face-to-face meetings in mosques, prisons, or any other gathering places where they can feel comfortable to plan and plot. Each terrorist group or affiliate may have autonomy over its own *recruitment, training, support, planning, target selection, attack methods,* and *decision-making authority.*

An example of a terrorist centralized command is Hezbollah. It is a Lebanese umbrella organization of radical Islamic Shiite groups and organizations. It operates in a traditional structure of centralized command where activities and operations are controlled by the top leadership. Hezbollah opposes the West, seeks to create a Muslim fundamentalist state modeled on Iran, and is a bitter foe of Israel. Hezbollah, whose name means "party of God," is a terrorist group believed to be responsible for nearly 179 attacks since 1982 that have killed more than 1,535 people, according to the Terrorism Knowledge Base.*

Hezbollah popularized suicide bombings as an effective terrorist tactic. In the 1980s, it allegedly carried out attacks at the U.S. Embassy, U.S. Marine Barracks, and French Barracks in Beirut, ultimately leading the United States to withdraw from Lebanon. Over the last 20 years, Hezbollah has professionalized its military capabilities, joined Lebanon's political process, and has even enmeshed itself into the social fabric of Lebanese society. In August 2006, Hezbollah became a minority partner

---

* MIPT Terrorism Knowledge Base, http://www.tkb.org/IncidentGroupModule.jsp.

in the Lebanese Cabinet, with two serving ministers and a third endorsed by the group, and it holds 14 seats in Parliament. Hezbollah's political wing also runs programs that provide schooling, medical care, and welfare to Lebanese Shia. Because of its involvement in politics and social services, countries like Russia do not consider Hezbollah a terrorist organization.*

In general, terrorist groups share expertise and revel in each other's success—often watching videos afterward and taking notice of what worked and what did not. Most terrorist planning cycles include the following steps:

1. Broad target selection
2. Intelligence and surveillance
3. Specific target selection
4. Preattack surveillance and planning
5. Attack rehearsal
6. Actions on objective
7. Escape and evasion

The selection of a target for actual operational planning often includes the following factors:†

- Does success affect a larger audience than the immediate victim(s)?
- Will the target attract high-profile media attention?
- Does success make the desired statement to the correct target audience(s)?
- Is the effect consistent with the objectives of the group?
- Does the target provide an advantage to the group by demonstrating its capabilities?
- What are the costs versus benefits of conducting the operation?

These groups work in networks of compartmented cells to increase the success of the mission if an individual or cell is compromised. The groups are well known to each other, but to prevent compromise of the network, only one member may know someone in another cell. Groups like Al Qaeda have been trained in military, special operations, and intelligence tactics. So while they may not operate under the banner of one

---

* University of Maryland, National Consortium for the Study of Terrorism and Response to Terrorism, "Terrorist Organization Profile: Hezbollah," http://www.start.umd.edu/tops/ terrorist_organization_profile.asp?id=3101.

† U.S. Army, *A Military Guide to Terrorism in the Twenty-First Century*, TRADOC G2 Handbook no. 1, 2007, http://www.maxwell.af.mil/au/awc/awcgate/army/guidterr/app_a. pdf, app. A.

nation, they employ tactics as if they did. One of Al Qaeda's trainers was Egyptian–American Ali Mohamed. In Peter Bergen's *An Oral History of Al Qaeda's Leader,* Mohamed, a former U.S. Army Green Beret, explains what his training role was at a training camp in Afghanistan.*

> I was capable of making explosives from a pile of aspirins. The science is in knowing how to separate the acids and then mix them with other substances. I also learned how to make explosives with the mercury of thermometers. I even managed to make nitroglycerine, the handling of which is very dangerous. Very often as a result of copies of manuals intended for the American Green Berets! (U.S. Special Forces manuals provided to Al Qaeda by its main military trainer, the Egyptian–American Ali Mohamed, who was a U.S. army sergeant at Fort Bragg, South Carolina, the headquarters of the Green Berets between 1986 and 1989.) [I arrived in Afghanistan in March 1990 and left in] October '91. My group used my services on several occasions because I had a clean European passport and could therefore travel and contact certain people. I went to India, Egypt, and Turkey as part of my work.†

Another recruit details the methodology about their surveillance training and working independently without knowing other cell members.‡

> We started [surveying] small things, like bridge, like stadium, like normal places in which nobody is, and then in the second stage we went to police stations, for example, and in my group we were trained to go to Iranian consulate and Iranian cultural center in Peshawar.
>
> The trainer [Ali Mohamed] explained how to make surveillance of targets and how to collect information about these targets. We trained how to use different cameras, especially small cameras, and how to take pictures in the guesthouse in which we were living. After taking pictures we go back to our place and we develop that film, using a machine, fixer and developer and water.§
>
> During the training, Mohamed explained [to] us that this job is the first part of [the] military part. You collect the information about this certain target, and whenever you finish your work, our group, we just leave, we send our reports to our bosses and we leave. Those people they go through this report and they read all the information, and everything. Then they make some decisions how to attack that target, and then they

---

* Peter L. Bergen, *An Oral History of Al Qaeda's Leader: The Osama bin Laden I Know* (New York: Free Press, 2006).
† Peter Bergen, with copyright permission granted.
‡ Bergen, *An Oral History of Al Qaeda's Leader.*
§ Ibid.

send another group who supply everything so as to attack that target. Whenever that third group finish[es its] job, [it] has to leave. At the end the fourth group who can do the job come so as to do the final job.[*]

An early Al Qaeda recruit and Portuguese convert to Islam was Paulo Jose de Ameida Santos. He met bin Laden in 1991. After his training he was dispatched to Italy to assassinate Zahir Shah, the 77-year-old king of Afghanistan who lived in exile in Rome. It appears this was the first time Al Qaeda engaged in international terrorism.[†] Santos posed as a journalist, gained access to the highly guarded villa, and stabbed the king in the heart with a dagger, but a tin of cigarettes saved the king. Santos served 10 years for the attempted assassination. He confirms what has been known for years about working in cells with specific independent yet supporting missions:[‡]

> We had been divided into several groups. There was a technological group. I did a test to become part of that group, but the person in charge, who was an Egyptian electronics engineer, did not like what I did and failed me. They put me in the analysis group where I had to read all the newspapers and give my analysis about what to do.[§]

These accounts support the fact that terrorist cells operate independently in an effort to protect each other or the plot itself. Therefore, if terrorist activities such as "surveillance of an attack target" are not discovered while they are in the planning stages, the attack is not likely to be preempted or stopped on the day it occurs because a different set of role players will be on the scene. There is no chance of recognizing them if their first time on the scene is "to carry out the bad deed." Nevertheless, the potential exists to gather "intelligence" or "critical information" from terrorists' reconnaissance activities if we are vigilant and lucky enough to detect them early while they are in progress.

Sometimes the most reliable intelligence performed by federal government agencies comes from clandestine operations—the secret undercover gathering of information. For these operations there are many aspects that need to work well together to be successful, and if the clandestine capability does not exist, it can take several years to create that capability. Where an indigenous capability is either inadequate or nonexistent, intelligence sharing with friendly governments with an existing capability

---

[*] Bergen, *An Oral History of Al Qaeda's Leader.*
[†] Ibid.
[‡] Ibid.
[§] Ibid.

becomes imperative but dangerous. We never know to what extent "trust" exists or whether the information being provided to the United States has been effectively vetted, but in the absence of any other reliable capability, the United States may have to consider this option.

Because we are dealing with terrorist threats in a way that we never had to before 9/11, constant education is critical. The terror networks we are dealing with can be highly organized and centralized, or can be highly decentralized, but the networks are well connected across many regions worldwide. Sometimes critical intelligence comes from investigative journalism. In Steve Emerson's *American Jihad: The Terrorists Living among Us,*[*] a picture emerges on just what kind of threat Ali Mohamed was. He volunteered to serve as a source for the Federal Bureau of Investigation (FBI) to report on illegal activities of cross-border Mexicans to move the focus away from his "terrorism role." By working for the FBI, he was insulated and protected from any scrutiny from other agencies. He also tried to serve as a source for the Central Intelligence Agency (CIA) at the same time but was not successful. In another case, unbeknownst to the FBI, the man who was at one time responsible for moving bin Laden from Afghanistan to Sudan and setting up training camps in New Jersey and Connecticut was using them while operating as their source.

LIMITATIONS OF EARLY WARNINGS

When threat warnings surface, they are almost always too broad in nature—not enough to identify the details of the threat, where it will strike, or what, "if anything," can be done to prevent it.[†] The sources that report threats sometimes cannot be vetted or the information cannot be verified because of legal limitations. Intelligence and law enforcement investigators are not authorized to investigate without cause; or the information did not contain sufficient details to prevent the act. In nearly all investigations that followed a terrorist attack, information surfaced indicating there were warnings of the attack. Suspicious individuals were observed at the target site and were reported to law enforcement or the intelligence community channels. Again, details are found to be too broad

---

[*] Steven Emerson, *American Jihad: The Terrorists Living among Us* (New York: Free Press, 2002).
[†] National Commission on Terrorist Attacks (hereafter, 9/11 Commission), *Final Report of the National Commission on Terrorist Attacks upon the United States* (hereafter, *9/11 Commission Report*), 2004, http://www.gpoaccess.gov/911/pdf/sec11.pdf (accessed March 2008).

in nature to prevent the act. This happened not only with the 9/11 attacks in 2001,* the 2000 *USS Cole* attack,† the 1996 Khobar Towers attack,‡ but also with the 2013 Boston Marathon bombing and the 2014 campus rampage shootings in the United States.

Broad threats cannot be analyzed to any reliable degree of success to provide details about a specific time and location of an attack. What we can count on with absolute certainty, however, is that regardless of which government, law enforcement, or intelligence agencies announce a terrorist threat warning, the responding agency will always receive criticism for the manner in which it was announced, handled, or mishandled. This is unfortunate because it is a no-win situation. If they make an announcement based on limited details, they get criticized for not providing enough details. If they do not make an announcement because the information is too sketchy to be of value, they will get criticized for not sharing it publicly.

"They are overreacting" is what critics say about the government if no terrorist attack is witnessed after an alert or warning has been publicly announced. This occurred in the summer of 2007, when then Secretary of Homeland Security Michael Chertoff announced that he had a "gut feeling" that terrorists were planning to attack the United States in the summer.§ Reporters thought it was an odd statement. In his defense, the truth about most terrorist attacks is that when people notice that something is wrong or is out of place, their stomachs will always tell them before their brains do. This is true even of people who apparently have no intuitive or instinctive abilities whatsoever. This is what people who have witnessed precursors to disasters have said in the postincident debriefings. Experts say that the funny feeling in the pit of the stomach or the feeling of hairs standing up on the back of the neck is the body's way of telling us that something is very wrong.¶ The body gets a shot of adrenaline because the brain determines that there is danger. The subconscious

---

* 9/11 Commission, *9/11 Commission Report*, 347.
† CargoLaw.com, "*USS Cole* Attack," http://www.cargolaw.com/2000nightmare_cole.html#disaster.
‡ Rebecca Grant, "Khobar Towers," *Air Force Magazine Online* 81, no. 6 (June 1998), http://www.afa.org/magazine/june1998/0698khobar.asp (accessed February 2008).
§ ABC News, "Chertoff Explains 'Gut Feeling' about Terror Attack," http://abcnews.go.com/WN/LegalCenter/story?id=3367404 (accessed March 23, 2008).
¶ Scott Flint, "Learn to Trust That 'Gut-Feeling': It Just Might Save Your Life," http://www.selfgrowth.com/articles/Flint2.html (accessed March 23, 2008).

mind, which operates 10 times faster than the conscious mind, picks up on signals of danger that the conscious mind has not yet processed. The queasy stomach feeling is simply the body's first reaction to adrenaline entering the bloodstream. At that time, the digestive system shuts down to allow more blood to flow to the muscles so that you can take the physical actions needed to survive if you have to bolt for survival. Apparently, there is nothing magical about this phenomenon. It is not paranoia or imagined fear. It is real, and survival often depends on it.

"The threats are not specific enough," private sector businesses often say about DHS threat information provided through critical infrastructure information-sharing networks. Before the *USS Cole*, Khobar Towers, and 9/11 attacks took place, general warnings were circulated within the intelligence community in the United States, and unilaterally between the United States and allied nations, but nothing specified a date, time, or location.

No matter how significant the "threat warning" or how skilled the intelligence analysts were, threat warnings issued did not prevent the attacks, and here are some reasons:

- People suspend belief and imagination.
- People generally don't think "it" will happen to them.
- The warning is too ominous to take specific action to prevent it.
- The warning gives a false sense of control.

Before the Twin Towers were attacked, engineers, builders, and tenants strongly believed that nothing could bring the Twin Towers down— not wind, not airplanes, not fire, not earthquakes. "The effect of a bomb on the Twin Towers was likened to that of a flea on one's leg.* The general consensus was that those buildings were indestructible. They were built to withstand almost anything. To try to blow up these buildings was seen as pure folly."† The size of the bomb required would be so conspicuous, it would not be able to be smuggled in. It was not imagined that the bomb would come from the air. The prevalent mind-set never allowed any other thought process to dominate, such as the possibility of another attack or that an airliner could possibly be used as a weapon to attack the Twin Towers.

---

* Edward Jerlin, "My Twin Towers Experience," http://www.geocities.com/ejerlin/ (accessed March 23, 2008).
† Jerlin, "My Twin Towers Experience."

POST-9/11 ERA THREATS AND WARNINGS

Boston Marathon Bombing

In 2013, two pressure cooker bombs exploded at the Boston Marathon near the finish line killing three people and injuring 264 others (Figure 2.4). Within days of the attack, the FBI released surveillance photos of two suspects soon identified as brothers Tamerlan and Dzhokhar Tsarnaev who claimed their motivation for the attack was America's involvement in the Iraq and Afghanistan wars. Russia's Federal Security Service (FSB) had warned U.S. authorities in previous years to track and monitor their activities. They were considered to be potential terrorist threats.

During 2002–2003, Tamerlan and Dzhokhar Tsarnaev and their two sisters immigrated to the United States from Kyrgyzstan with their parents Anzor Tsarnaev and Zubeidat Tsarnaeva, and applied for and received an immigration benefit. In the years that followed, all six family members became lawful permanent residents of the United States. Two years before the Boston Marathon bombings, Tamerlan Tsarnaev and Zubeidat Tsarnaeva came to the attention of the FBI based on information received from the FSB. In March 2011, the FBI received information from the FSB alleging that Tamerlan Tsarnaev and Zubeidat Tsarnaeva were adherents of radical Islam and that Tamerlan Tsarnaev was preparing to travel to Russia to join unspecified underground groups in Dagestan and Chechnya. The FBI-led Joint Terrorism Task Force in Boston (Boston JTTF) conducted an assessment of Tamerlan Tsarnaev to determine whether

Figure 2.4 Boston Marathon bomb scene pictures taken by investigators show the remains of a pressure cooker improvised explosive device. A lid to one of the pressure cookers was found on a roof of a building near the scene. (FBI photo.)

44

he posed a threat to national security and closed the assessment three months later having found no link or "nexus" to terrorism. In September 2011, the FSB provided the CIA with information on Tamerlan Tsarnaev that was substantively identical to the information the FSB had provided to the FBI in March 2011. In October 2011, the CIA provided information obtained from the FSB to the National Counterterrorism Center (NCTC) for watchlisting purposes, and to the FBI, DHS, and the Department of State for their information. Upon NCTC's receipt of the information, Tamerlan Tsarnaev was added to the terrorist watchlist. Three months later, Tamerlan Tsarnaev traveled to Russia, as the lead information stated he was preparing to do. However, Tsarnaev's travel to Russia did not prompt additional investigative steps to determine whether he posed a threat to national security.[*]

Elliot Rodger's Killing Rampage

In 2014, Santa Barbara City College student Elliot Rodger stabbed three people to death at his apartment before plowing through the streets in his car shooting into Friday night crowds, leaving seven people dead and several injured in the Southern California seaside town of Isla Vista near the University of California, Santa Barbara.

Although reports about the incident are still sketchy as I write this chapter, it does appear there were several warnings. Rodger's family and therapist warned police that Rodger intended to go on a killing rampage but when police questioned Rodger three weeks earlier, there was no evidence to merit a search, arrest, or involuntary mental health hold. Rodger had posted what was described by his family as disturbing videos on YouTube and this in fact prompted the calls to police. Santa Barbara County Sheriff's Office deputies interviewed Rodger but apparently found no reason to detain him. "He was able to make a very convincing story that there was no problem, that he wasn't going to hurt himself or anyone else, and he just didn't meet the criteria for any further intervention at that point, according to the Sheriff."[†] Rodger then reportedly wrote about the police visit in a 141-page manifesto, expressing relief that his apartment was not searched and his stockpile of weapons or writings on

---

[*] April 2014 U.S. Department of Justice Report, "Unclassified Summary of Information Handling and Sharing" (accessed May 30, 2014).

[†] Michael R. Blood and Tami Abdollah, "California Rampage Shows Gaps in Mental Health Law," May 28, 2014, http://abcnews.go.com/US/wireStory/california-rampage-shows-gaps-mental-health-law-23903109 (accessed May 30, 2014).

his revenge plans were not found. The document also allegedly outlined his plans that were eventually carried out in Santa Barbara. The manifesto was e-mailed to family and therapists just before the shooting. However, there might have been other clues. In addition to disturbing videos on YouTube, Facebook blog posts by Rodger carried themes of loneliness and rejection by women.* He had also reportedly been receiving treatment for years from psychologists and counselors. In this instance, sufficient details were provided, but existing laws prevented law enforcement officers to do any more based on what they saw and assessed.

Chinese Cyberattacks against U.S. Companies

In 2014, for the first time ever, the U.S. Justice Department indicted five officers from the Third Department of the Chinese People's Liberation Army (PLA) for computer hacking, economic espionage, and identity theft, among other crimes. The victims named in the indictment were Westinghouse; SolarWorld; U.S. Steel; Allegheny Technologies, Inc.; Alcoa; and the United Steel, Paper and Forestry, Rubber, Manufacturing, Energy, Allied Industrial and Service Workers International Union (USW), members of various critical infrastructure sectors and at least for some period of time early on were unaware that they were being spied on by foreign government collectors.

According to the Justice Department, the PLA has been engaged in criminal activity against these companies since 2006 conspiring to hack into U.S. businesses, to maintain unauthorized access to their computers, and to steal information that would be useful to their competitors in China—activity intended to gain the economic advantage. Some charges include: stealing senior USW employee e-mails to learn sensitive business strategies related to trade disputes with USW; installing malware on U.S. Steel company computers allowing the theft of hostnames and descriptions of computers, including those that controlled physical access to company facilities and mobile device access to company networks; creating a "secret" database designed to hold corporate "intelligence" about the iron and steel industries, including information about American companies; and stealing thousands of files including information about SolarWorld's

---

* Phillip Rucker and Robert Costa, "Sheriff: Calif. Shooter Rodger Flew 'Under the Radar' When Deputies Visited Him in April," *Washington Post*, May 25, 2014, http://www.washingtonpost.com/national/sheriff-calif-shooter-rodger-flew-under-the-radar-when-deputies-visited-him-in-april/2014/05/25/88123026-e3b4-11e3-8dcc-d6b7fede081a_story.html (accessed May 30, 2014).

cash flow, manufacturing metrics, production line information, costs, and privileged attorney–client communications relating to ongoing trade litigation, among other things.

Insider Threat

In a *Federal Times* article, Nicole Blake Johnson says, "DHS cyber security efforts have recently shifted to rooting out insider threats. To this end, it may invest in continuous monitoring of systems and harden the access controls on administrator accounts. At the same time, DHS is keen to consolidate its data centers and upgrade its network infrastructure to handle demand from new endpoints. Government IT acquisitions in 2014 will be driven by the need to protect assets from an expanding range of threats. According to the *Federal Times*, DHS agencies are purchasing network scanners as part of the department's $6 billion cybersecurity investment, and while the current focus of this strategy is on guarding against external attacks, insider threats are increasingly on the radar." Not only must they do this to protect their assets and investments, the security of the homeland, and protection and availability of our critical infrastructure, they must also comply with presidential directives that mandate they protect infrastructure from dangerous insiders. Decades ago, insider threats really entailed espionage-related cases. Today, it can include individuals who bring any harm to an organization's assets: people, information systems, buildings, and mass killings, or the leaking of information to unauthorized people, such as Edward Snowden did with classified national security information.[*]

Whether you are trying to protect your organization from insiders or outsiders to meet national security or homeland security goals or become more resilient, you must have a mechanism in place for threat awareness, risk mitigation, and constant evaluation of your threat posture.

CREATING YOUR OWN THREAT-WARNING CAPABILITIES

Owners and operators of critical infrastructure need to adopt similar practices as the national security–level resources and establish their own methods for "first line of defense" capabilities or early warning. They need to develop their own "information collection" practices.

---

[*] Nicole Blake Johnson, "DHS Cyber Efforts Shifts to Insider Threats," *Federal Times*, December 16, 2013, http://www.federaltimes.com/article/20131216/DHS/312160014/DHS-cyber-effort-shifts-insider-threats (accessed May 30, 2014).

They must also develop good analytical and threat assessment capabilities. Seeing threats on a closed-circuit television (CCTV) monitor does not qualify as an early warning. If you are seeing a terrorist threat on your monitor it is already too late to move your assets elsewhere, and now you have to go into reaction mode.

Establishing information gathering and analysis that mimic those of "national security" resources to meet homeland security preparedness, risk mitigation, and resilience can be challenging for the private sector but it is achievable. Generally, when the private sector "collects information," it is for the purposes of protecting its market share or trade secrets from competitors, not for determining which country or terrorist organization is interested in spying against them or putting them on a terrorist target list. Private sector assessments, sometimes performed by human resources, are usually aimed at identifying and mitigating potential workplace violence by disgruntled employees. The scale of damage that an employee can inflict rarely eclipses that which can be inflicted by Al Qaeda or affiliate terrorists groups. So, they should rethink who performs the assessments and think more broadly about the threats.

Through checklists, templates, and repetition of new practices, a newly adopted method of collecting and assessing information would soon become second nature. At first, it will seem difficult because the tasks that need to be performed will feel awkward. Perhaps it will require using skills or behaviors (legal and ethical) that stretch people out of their comfort zone. But it must be done because the federal government cannot carry the load of terrorism prevention alone. Additionally, the information provided through private sector–DHS partnerships will be too strategic to drive private sector decisions about capital expenditures for security that may or may not be needed.

In the threat assessment process of risk management, all information must be brought together to determine if there are imminent threats or just general broad threats. The analysis must determine if the threats are realistic and if they are directed at the organization. Fundamentally, we should all understand how threats work, what constitutes a threat, and how to address them at work and at home. At the organizational level, all organizations need to periodically perform threat assessments. If not, they risk operating in the blind, so to speak, and being completely surprised when an attack breaks out in their work environment. This could be a physical attack on their facilities or a cyberattack on their network. Threat assessment processes have to be bulletproof through high-quality information gathering and comprehensive threat analysis. People best suited for this endeavor tend to come from security, intelligence, and law enforcement professions. They have a keen sense of threats and a strong ability to naturally perform functions related to threat analysis—it is almost second nature to them.

PAINFUL LESSON: THE *USS COLE* ATTACK

The boat that attacked the *USS Cole* on October 12, 2000, in the Yemen harbor of Aden appeared ordinary. The two guys on the boat appeared friendly. Therefore, they aroused no immediate suspicion upon sight. The *USS Cole* intended to get in and out as quickly as possible when it went into the Yemen harbor to fuel. Given that no dates or specific locations came with the warning they had been informed of, that was the only logical precaution they could seem to exercise.

This attack is difficult to recall because it was not an attack against any ordinary Navy ship— it was one of the U.S. Navy's guided missile destroyers, and the resources needed for recovery were intensive. Imagine the scene: the *USS Cole*, a 505-foot destroyer, suffers damage—a 40-foot by 40-foot hole from the blast to the ship's hull, killing 17 sailors and injuring 39.[*] The first naval ship to arrive on the scene to assist the *Cole* was the Royal Navy Type 23 frigate, *HMS Marlborough*, which had full medical and damage control teams on board. The first U.S. military support to arrive was a small group of U.S. Marines from the IMCSF Company, Bahrain. Assistance also came from a U.S. Marine platoon with the 2nd Fleet Antiterrorism Security Team Company (FAST), based out of Yorktown, Virginia. The Marines from 4th Platoon, 2nd FAST arrived on October 13 from a security mission in Doha, Qatar.[†] The FAST platoon secured the *Cole*. The *USS Donald Cook* and *USS Hawes* arrived that afternoon, providing repair and logistical support. The *Catawba, Camden, Anchorage, Duluth,* and *Tarawa* arrived some days later, providing watch relief crews, harbor security, damage control equipment, billeting, and food service for the crew of the *Cole*. *Landing Craft Utility (LCU) 1666* provided daily runs from the *Tarawa* with hot food and supplies, and moved personnel to and from all other naval vessels supporting the *Cole*.

Two weeks before the attack, a popular satellite TV channel in Qatar broadcast an ominous message from Osama bin Laden. The broadcast

---

[*] Associated Press and Reuters, "U.S. Official Sees Similarities between *USS Cole* Blast and Embassy Attacks," http://archives.cnn.com/2000/US/10/23/uss.cole.01/ (accessed March 23, 2008).

[†] *Wikipedia*, "*USS Cole* Bombing," http://en.wikipedia.org/wiki/.

shows Osama bin Laden and his top lieutenant, Ayman al-Zawahiri. Zawahiri warned that it was time to "take action" against the "iniquitous and faithless" U.S. forces in Yemen, Egypt, and Saudi Arabia. Osama bin Laden looked on approvingly.* The Navy was criticized for possibly over-looking important information that could have foiled the attack that killed 17 American sailors. Officials always contended that the general warning provided to the United States of a possible attack on an American warship prior to the *USS Cole* attack lacked detail and did not specify the country in which to expect the attack, and therefore could not be acted on—except to exercise precautions, fuel quickly, and get out of there as fast as possible.

Since the early 1990s, there have been broadcasts of terrorist plans to attack the United States from bin Laden and other groups. In 2005, the British government warned that the United States could potentially see its own share of surprise attacks such as those carried out in London and Spain. British citizens were shocked that their own citizens—even doctors—were attacking them, and thought the United States had time and should take action to increase efforts to deter such attacks.

Let's stop for a moment to ponder a question. Has any U.S. company or government agency ever taken to heart the message of a terrorist group and successfully predicted where and when an attack would occur in order to preempt it? Can the private sector act on the strategic informa-tion provided by DHS through "information-sharing partnerships" cur-rently in place? The information provided by DHS at quarterly or annual meetings or through the DHS private sector pipeline is no different than warnings provided to the U.S. government by other nations or sources, such as the *USS Cole* warnings.

In 2004, targeting activities revealed that terrorists had conducted surveillance for years on the International Monetary Fund, the Prudential Building, the New York Stock Exchange, and facilities in Las Vegas, Nevada. The discovery of these activities would then imply that those facilities have received a warning.

THE CONSEQUENCES OF NOT UNDERSTANDING THREATS

The consequences of not understanding threats can produce grave conse-quences. Organizations could miss threats when the threats are heading

---

* Wikipedia, "*USS Cole* Bombing."

straight for them and thus will not get a chance to respond because the threat could be deadly and instantaneous. Factors that enable threats and produce risks include:

- Failure to properly invest in the right security technology and preparedness training
- Implementing insufficient security measures to protect assets
- Not knowing how to respond to threats when they emerge
- Not being able to recover and being put out of business for good

If the facility is high on the critical infrastructure list of services that the public depends on, it could have an adverse impact on the economy and society to such a degree that such recovery is not possible.

One of the critical gaps of preparedness is that no one within infrastructure sectors seems to be performing trend analysis as a way to more effectively secure them or as a way of creating an early warning system to infrastructure threats. In 2005, after the July London transportation system bombings, many instances of suspicious activities were reported in major U.S. city subway systems where "men" were observed taking covert photographs. In one incident, four men who appeared to be Middle Eastern were caught taking photos of the undercarriage of a subway train by a maintenance employee. When asked what they were doing, they left the scene in a hurry. The men appeared to be Middle Eastern but could easily have been Hispanic or any other race. The "look" is not a reliable way to profile a suspicious person. We as a society have faulty methods of identification. Our powers of observation are not reliable. There are numerous cases in which witnesses have identified the wrong suspects in lineups resulting in wrongly accused people being sent to prison. In the same city in 2005, on a different subway line, a man riding the subway, who appeared to be Middle Eastern, held a small camera at his waist in a covert manner and snapped many photos of the tracks and the scenery behind the train as the train was in motion. The individual was not interrupted; the witness stayed on the train until the individual got off the train. The witness rode with the individual from the start of the line to the end of the line. The man appeared nervous and looked around often to see if anyone had noticed him taking photos. The witness reported that he felt "a sick feeling in his stomach and reported that the hair on the back of his neck stood up," but remained calm, and when he exited he went straight to the nearest law enforcement officer on site at the station. The information was not well received, and the individual had to make several attempts to file a report on this activity.

It would have been invaluable to make an attempt to identify the people involved in these two incidents and properly investigate the matter but that did not occur. Law enforcement and terrorism task forces were either being overwhelmed with mass reports or the information was not always reported to the right office to be acted on. The two events described happened within a month following the 2005 London train bombings and were characteristic of terrorist cell intelligence collection methodology to plan an attack, probe or test our security measures and reactions, or a dry run.

These incidents could have been indicators of a possible attack in the planning stages but since they were not properly investigated, and the individuals were not identified, we will never find out. These behaviors are synonymous with intelligence gathering behaviors exhibited when "attack targets" are being identified and studied. They were also similar to behaviors observed in Spain and in London where attacks actually took place. It is quite possible that plans for attacking a subway system were shared among many networks worldwide and they were all racing against each other to see who would successfully attack first. There were two attacks in progress in London at the time of the transit attack. The second one did not succeed because the bomb-making techniques were sloppy, but the procedures for carrying out the attacks were identical. Why would this be the case unless the two were plotting unbeknownst to each other, and the second group saw no reason to abort its attack? As for the suspicious behaviors observed in the American city in 2005, it could very well have been for the purpose of planning a similar attack as those in Europe, or perhaps just probing behaviors to test citizen reactions and subway or law enforcement personnel's security measures.

LESSONS LEARNED: FIRST WORLD TRADE CENTER ATTACK, 1993

Ramzi Yousef, arrested for the 1993 attack of the World Trade Center, was also discovered to be linked to another terrorist plot in the Philippines. The plot was uncovered in January 1995 when a fire broke out in his apartment. The plot called for blowing up a dozen U.S. airliners over the Far East as part of an operation he called Project Bojinka. When 9/11 occurred, everyone was shocked and in total disbelief that four U.S. airliners were flown into buildings by men willing to follow an order and fly the planes to destination "death."

If everyone had better analyzed the clues, and our leaders and managers were not in denial that such an event could ever occur, we would not have been extremely surprised about the method in which the airplanes were used on 9/11. This was not the first time a plane was considered for a terrorist attack nor was it the first time a plane was hijacked in America.

LESSONS LEARNED: FIRST AMERICAN HIJACKING, 1961

On August 1, 1961, a 40-year-old American male hijacked a commercial airliner at Chico Municipal Airport, Butte County, California. Armed with a switchblade and a Colt 2-inch 6-shot blue steel revolver, he stormed his way onto the plane. A ticket agent tried to stop him from getting on the airplane without a ticket. "This is my ticket," the man said, pulling out his gun and shooting the ticket agent in the back. He then fired a shot at a stewardess and missed. Next he announced that he would begin killing as he turned the gun on a nearby seated passenger and fired. Again, he missed. He then headed for the cockpit. He stood over the pilot and copilot as they taxied the plane onto the runway, but they told him the plane could not leave until the cockpit door was closed. Through confusion or anger (or both), the man shot the pilot in the head. The copilot knocked the gun from his hand. The hijacker then pulled out a knife but was quickly overpowered by three passengers. Reportedly, none of the victims died in the attack. Prior to arriving at the airport, the hijacker had been chased in a high-speed pursuit by police. He was very late and would have missed his flight, but the plane was also very late in departing. The man only had a gun, a knife, and a car, and he was trying to get home to his wife after working away from home. It is not known why he did not consider other less drastic measures. It appears he had been inspired by recent news accounts of passenger planes in other countries that had been hijacked to Cuba. Perhaps he thought he would succeed. Decades later, it would take the 9/11 attacks to change the way airliner cockpit doors were designed to mitigate potential hijackings.

HOMELAND SECURITY ROLES AND MISCONCEPTIONS

The National Infrastructure Protection Plan (NIPP) states that private sector owners and operators of critical infrastructure facilities are primary security partners. These security partners are responsible for undertaking

"CI/KR protection, restoration, coordination, and cooperation activities, and providing advice, recommendations, and subject matter expertise to the Federal Government" for terrorism preparedness.[*]

There are many myths regarding homeland security roles and responsibilities. My interaction with federal government personnel and private sector security partners across the nation over the last five years reveals that much of the private sector is still not fully aware of its homeland security responsibilities or its linkage to the nation's critical infrastructure. This creates a dangerous environment filled with ambiguities and assumptions on the part of both the government and private sector. The government truly believes that the private sector understands its role and envisions that all necessary steps for terrorism preparedness are being carried out. The private sector hears what the federal government—DHS in particular—is saying about "needs" but is not actively listening and does not seem to understand how critical the private sector is to the nation's overall preparedness. On the periphery it appears that the private sector has measures for preparedness, but they tend to be "ad hoc" and generally are not adequate to make the organizations compliant with all existing DHS guidelines, including the NIPP.

Protection and preparedness against terrorism also require effective measures to response, resiliency, and recovery through business continuity plans, security plans, and emergency management processes followed by most local or state emergency operations centers, and the Federal Emergency Management Agency (FEMA) and FEMA's Incident Response Management. It has been interesting to hear the views of private and public sector individuals at security conferences when asked how they would respond to terrorist attacks. Members of the private sector (financial, energy, port, airport, commercial building, water, and transportation managers) often say that if they were to experience a terrorist attack, their security guards would know how to respond and they would rely heavily on them. The idea of prevention or deterrence is rarely mentioned and does not seem to be a thought that enters their minds.

Just after 9/11, security guards working at private sector facilities often said that responding to or stopping a terrorist attack was not within their scope of work nor were they trained for it. They believed if they witnessed anything that looked like an attack, they would call law

---

[*] Department of Homeland Security, *National Infrastructure Protection Plan (NIPP)* (Washington, DC: Department of Homeland Security, 2006), p. 2.

enforcement because law enforcement was trained to respond. Over the last decade, law enforcement officers have worked hard to respond not just to traditional crimes but also to leads and information related to potential terrorist-related activities. No doubt they want to do everything within their power to prevent 9/11s or recognize the obvious signs of a potential plot or attack as early as possible. The attack of the Boston Marathon was one example of how law enforcement has made improvements in the ability to investigate potential terror-related plots in a timely manner.

Security guard training has also improved in recent years. As an example, according to the New York State Division of Homeland Security and Emergency Services, it has "an Enhanced Security Guard Training Program intended to support and complement the existing security guard training and counter terrorism efforts in New York State by providing training and education designed to improve observation, detection and reporting skills, coordination with police and first responders, and security technology, and terrorism awareness."[*]

SHARING INFORMATION

As part of a strong commitment to improving communications between the private and public sectors, one of the things that must be addressed by law enforcement is the need for common access to a databank of known threats and to conduct trend analysis on those threats. Various public and private sector organizations have their own internal logs of incidents and events. It would be useful for the owners and operators within the 16 critical infrastructure sectors to have the ability to look through the window of other infrastructure facility incidents and learn about attempted attacks, probing activities, or surveillance, and share information. What a concept! It would cue them that the same suspicious activities may be going on at other similar facilities across the United States or even in the local area. Threats can change overnight. That is why threat information gathering, analysis, assessment, countermeasures, and reviews need to be continuous. The goal is to be able to see the threats before they become imminent, actively engaged against your facility, or inside your building creating catastrophe.

---

[*] New York State Division of Homeland Security and Emergency Services, "About the SPTC," http://www.dhses.ny.gov/sptc/.

One handicap that the private and public sectors share is the inability to perceive true threats to the company or organization. In 2000, an employee of a public sector company was reportedly caught breaching network security and accessing unauthorized files. The event took everyone by surprise because the individual held the highest government security clearance, had undergone extensive background screening, and had passed a polygraph examination. For years, the individual had been entrusted with the nation's secrets in a position where he focused on external threats.

Similarly, a Fortune 100 company overlooked the possibility of external threat because it was lulled into a false sense of security because of its high rate of happy employees. As such, there was no urgency to incorporate a recommended risk mitigation plan for workplace violence. Just three weeks after the recommendation was issued, an outsider, someone who had previously been turned down for employment, held workers hostage. The incident caused several businesses and streets to be shut down while police worked to get the incident under control. This closure not only affected the victim company but the surrounding companies as well.

It is not so important to ask why critical infrastructure is a target or when the next attack will occur. If you have studied and developed an understanding of religious conflicts and world politics, you would see the correlation between terrorism and such conflict and understand the why. The answer to when is in accordance with the terrorist's timetable, not ours. The question to focus on is how. How will we detect and respond, or how can we best be prepared? Having no sense of potential threats and therefore no plans in place puts facility owners in a vulnerable position on so many levels. They may find that they are not following DHS infrastructure protection guidelines, or learn that they are spending more than is necessary on security, or that the solutions they implemented may not be effective in mitigating risks. Without a focused look, owners could end up doing a lot of dangerous guessing and wasteful spending.

DHS leaders across the nation simply trust that the private sector will take steps to develop and implement plans to protect the infrastructure, but there is no way to validate that this is actually occurring. Unless a disastrous incident occurs, it is likely that no one will come to review or evaluate those plans. If an incident occurs, however, a facility owner's plan could end up being scrutinized as material evidence in a court of law. Even worse, lives endangered or lost. It is simply prudent to recognize the need to perform due diligence and assess and secure facilities by applying DHS guidelines.

CONCLUSION

Ignoring threat trends or even being oblivious to the possibility of threats in this day and age is not just risky business but also an irresponsible workplace management paradigm. Assessing threats is an essential part of managing risk. When the threat posture of an organization is known, it is possible to choose how much risk to take on. Risk can then be mitigated, eliminated, transferred, or managed. Taking proactive measures to mitigate risk generally results in regulatory compliance, reduced risk exposure, reduced liability, and stakeholder confidence in the organization's response measures. Additionally, a confident workforce is likely to successfully respond and minimize the consequences of a terrorist attack because people know exactly what to do and are able to go into response mode without freezing. On the other hand, an organization that has never exercised its response plan, has never taken proactive steps to understand threats and manage such risks, or whose workforce has not been trained or educated in security and threat identification or is unaware of the response procedures would have a high probability of a failed outcome to a terrorist attack.

3

National Infrastructure Protection Plan for Threats, Vulnerability, Risk, and Resilience

Government alone cannot protect our U.S. critical infrastructure from attacks and disasters. You too must do your part, get on with it!

Elsa Lee

OVERVIEW

Industry has many roles in homeland security. Industry is supposed to make sure that it has effective measures in place for emergency response in any crisis, protection of all assets from terrorist attacks, and DHS partner resiliency. Industrial facilities comprise an important component of the DHS's national protection plan. DHS plays a couple of roles in its interaction with industry: it is a partner to industry and it can assume an authoritarian role expecting industry to comply with its guidelines. It can be "directive" if a particular sector or organization is being negligent in securing facilities and making itself or the nation openly vulnerable to attack or disaster. Industry's role is namely to actively participate in its own protection, preparedness, and resiliency.

All organizations or businesses have varying levels of security knowledge. Some are more advanced than others. Perhaps you are a new high school or college graduate just starting your first job. There is a fairly good chance that you work in a facility that comprises our critical infrastructure sectors and for the first time in your life are being exposed to the importance of security. Some organizations' security teams are comprised of former military or law enforcement officers, or security and facility managers possessing superior security skills and an understanding of protective measures. Those who are employed in facilities operating in high hazard environments generally possess comprehensive knowledge about security, safety, and DHS requirements and expectations, and are pretty advanced in their practices. Because we all have varying levels of security experience and knowledge, we all operate under different standards. Therefore, responses to emergencies or disasters will also vary. In high-risk environments that are heavily regulated, there is no choice on procedures used. They are required to operate according to published and established standards and procedures. One example is the defense industrial base. The more than 100,000 defense contractors that support the military must abide by regulations, or they could make our nation's defense missions vulnerable.

DHS has many industry partners working together to develop standards and guidelines to respond to all phases of disasters and terror attacks. Many industries have developed their own standards and guidelines, which may be similar to or perhaps exceed DHS requirements. Methods used across all sectors may be from DHS guidelines, the military, or corporate security programs. Whether you use formal or informal procedures, you should always strive to have high-quality standards and compliance.

Security and education are important aspects of emergency management, which cover mitigation, preparedness, response, and recovery used by government and first responders (Figure 3.1).

Emergency Management Phases

Figure 3.1 Emergency management phases.

The private sector has many educational and training options for increasing its homeland security knowledge including industry certifications, college degrees, and Federal Emergency Management Agency (FEMA) courses. According to the Naval Postgraduate School and the U.S. Department of Homeland Security Center for Homeland Defense and Security, at this time there are approximately 424 colleges and universities offering homeland security programs across the United States; some college programs are funded by DHS.[*] ASIS International (ASIS) is a security industry association that promotes education, standards, procedures, and much more to assist industry in its homeland security role. ASIS is the largest organization for security professionals, with more than 38,000 members worldwide. Founded in 1955, ASIS is dedicated to increasing the effectiveness and productivity of security professionals by developing educational programs and materials that address broad security interests, such as the ASIS Annual Seminar and Exhibits, as well as specific security topics. ASIS also advocates the role and value of the security management profession to business, the media, governmental entities, and the public. ASIS publishes *Security Management Magazine* to help security professionals advance and improve security performance.[†] This publication offers valuable insight and well-written security articles on a variety of topics—something for everyone.

In Chapter 2, we looked at essential threat factors. In this chapter, we will identify threats, discuss methods for identifying threats and vulnerabilities, and determine risk and countermeasures through three models. This chapter is designed for organizations that have very little in place for preparedness and for readers who require security education related to DHS risk management and critical infrastructure and key resources (CI/KR) protection requirements. With today's threats to our nation from terrorism, it is clear that tactical and strategic approaches are needed to help protect and secure critical infrastructure. There is an abundance of information and resources to assist industry on preparedness—there is no possibility of getting just one set of simplified instructions. In this chapter, I have attempted to chart a path for understanding threats, helping industry see its threats, identify its vulnerabilities, and then suggest measures to secure assets to a level of preparedness and compliance using as many simplified and proven approaches as possible.

---

[*] Naval Postgraduate School and the U.S. Department of Homeland Security Center for Homeland Defense and Security, http://www.chds.us/ (accessed June 1, 2014).
[†] ASIS, "About ASIS," http://www.asisonline.org/about/history/index.xml.

Because threats are in a constant state of change, it is difficult to keep up with security measures to prevent, detect, and respond to all of them—or is it? Security measures that are in place and working effectively today may no longer be appropriate six months from now. Current measures need to be reviewed to see if they are adequate and effective against newly discovered threat activity. By assessing and updating the threat picture, an organization can determine if it is investing enough and focusing sufficient resources to keep up with the threats. The full extent of vulnerabilities cannot be known without a regular snapshot of the threat environment to assist in identifying the risk exposure.

Threats and vulnerability, among other elements, determine the level of risk exposure organizations face. The process of determining threats and vulnerabilities should be periodically performed, because the environment is constantly changing. After the threats and vulnerabilities are reviewed, measures and countermeasures should be considered and implemented.

This is a team process and not one to be performed by one or two individuals, even though this is usually the most common way it is done by organizations today. The importance of using members with different abilities in the organization to form the team that performs threat, vulnerability, and risk assessments is discussed in more detail in Chapter 7 ("Human Factors and Team Dynamics").

Risk management is needed to properly protect critical infrastructure against terrorism—as DHS requires and expects. Your risk management efforts should include business continuity, information technology (IT), security, and emergency services risk managers, who can collectively determine the best courses of action for solutions to respond to the threats. By involving diverse resources, the organization's moves demonstrate that it can execute a fully integrated approach that includes physical security, information systems security, and emergency response, which is absolutely necessary and critical.

Threats have many dimensions and aspects that are important, and once threats are identified they need to be weighed against known vulnerabilities so that risk can be determined and risk management decisions can be made.

Models for risk analysis, risk management, and risk economic assessment are available through DHS, Homeland Security Centers of Excellence (established in 2003), and private industry. DHS has invested heavily in developing frameworks to unify protective and preparedness measures for public and private sector users and for individual consumers. It has not, however, done a good job of educating the end users on the wealth of resources available through DHS. For example, the Critical Infrastructure Partnership Advisory Council (CIPAC) represents a partnership between government and CI/KR owners and operators, and provides a forum in which they can engage in a broad spectrum of activities to support and coordinate critical infrastructure protection.* The DHS Critical Infrastructure Protection Partnerships and Information Sharing program enables information-sharing efforts between the private sector, DHS, and other government entities. According to DHS, the protection and resilience of the nation's critical infrastructure is a shared responsibility among multiple stakeholders; neither government nor the private sector alone has the knowledge, authority, or resources to do it alone.† DHS's Homeland Security Centers of Excellence—university-based partnerships or federally funded research and development (R&D) centers—bring together leading experts and researchers to conduct multidisciplinary research and education for homeland security solutions, such as providing independent analysis of CI/KR protection issues. Today, even institutions not funded by DHS offer a variety of programs related to homeland security and intelligence. The University of Southern California has one such center. It evaluates the risks, costs, and consequences of terrorism, and guides economically viable investments in countermeasures that will make our nation safer and more secure. The research that they conduct is valuable and will be useful for the next generation of homeland security leaders, but it is not clear how current owners and operators of critical infrastructure facilities could tap into the research material to help transition it to a user level, and DHS has not advised infrastructure owners on how they can access the research. In addition to the research efforts, the Homeland Security Centers of Excellence also offer degrees in homeland security programs.

Academic and research communities play an important role in enabling national-level CI/KR protection and implementation of the National Infrastructure Protection Plan (NIPP), including the following:‡

- Establishing centers of excellence.
- Supporting the research, development, testing, evaluation, and deployment of CI/KR protection technologies.
- Analyzing, developing, and sharing best practices related to CI/KR protection efforts.

---

* Department of Homeland Security, http://www.dhs.gov/xprevprot/committees/.
† Department of Homeland Security, http://www.dhs.gov/st-centers-excellence.
‡ Department of Homeland Security, http://www.dhs.gov.

- Researching and providing innovative thinking and perspectives on threats and the behavioral aspects of terrorism.
- Preparing or disseminating guidelines, courses, and descriptions of best practices for physical security and cybersecurity.
- Developing and providing suitable security risk analysis and risk management courses for CI/KR protection professionals.
- Conducting research to identify new technologies and analytical methods that can be applied by security partners to support NIPP efforts.

THE DEPARTMENT OF HOMELAND SECURITY (DHS) RISK MODEL AND NATIONAL INFRASTRUCTURE PROTECTION PLAN (NIPP)

One of the best models for risk management and the one that the private sector should use as owners and operators of critical infrastructure is the NIPP, a framework provided by DHS. The NIPP is part of DHS's overall protection effort to ensure a steady state of protection within and across all sectors. This DHS model includes a step for the "consequences"—the negative effects on public health and safety, the economy, public confidence in institutions, and the functioning of government, both direct and indirect.

The private sector often makes decisions about security investments based on (1) what is known about the risk environment, and (2) what is economically justifiable and sustainable in a competitive marketplace or in an environment of limited resources. Having said that, the private sector probably already uses processes from its business continuity and emergency-planning strategies to identify what type of security expenditures need to be made and what it will need to do to comply with government regulations. DHS will not offer expenditure and budgeting advice for homeland security preparedness. The private sector must determine for itself if the security measures and technology it has in place are sufficient to protect its critical assets, and it must perform its own cost-benefit analysis to determine what—if any—return on investment can be expected. At any rate, it can continue to use successful risk assessment practices as long as it meets the standards and requirements of the NIPP.

DHS offers a model with detailed instructions for performing all the steps that it believes are warranted in the effort to assess and control risks to critical infrastructure. To properly apply the model requires electronic

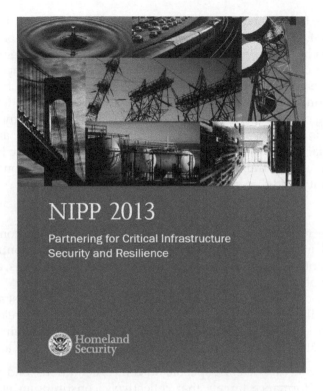

Figure 3.2 The National Infrastructure Protection Plan (NIPP).

or printed versions of the very thick and comprehensive NIPP document (Figure 3.2).*

It is important to understand how the NIPP applies to homeland security. To assist in this education, DHS and FEMA offer independent study courses on the NIPP, emergency management, and security awareness and practices (www.fema.gov). The courses, offered through the Emergency Management Institute, cover a wide range of topics, such as "An Introduction to Hazardous Materials" and "Fundamentals of Emergency Management." The courses can be taken for credit or simply for professional enrichment. Those completing the course for credit must take a final exam and will receive a certificate from DHS.†

---

* DHS NIPP Document, http://www.dhs.gov/publication/nipp-2013-partnering-critical-infrastructure-security-and-resilience (accessed June 1, 2014).
† ASIS, http://www.asisonline.org.

The DHS risk management framework in the NIPP can be applied on an asset, system, network, or function basis, depending on the fundamental characteristics of each individual sector. For sectors primarily dependent on fixed assets and physical facilities, a bottom-up, asset-by-asset approach may be most appropriate. A common approach based on a robust understanding of existing methodologies is needed to enable the setting of protection priorities across sectors. The first element of this approach is to establish a common definition and process for analysis of the basic factors of risk for CI/KR protection. In the context of homeland security, the NIPP framework assesses risk as a function of consequence, vulnerability, and threat:

$$R = f\,(C,V,T)$$

For sectors with diverse and logical assets, such as telecommunications and information technology, a top-down, business continuity, or mission continuity approach that focuses on networks, systems, and functions may be more effective.

Each sector can choose the approach that produces the most actionable results for the sector and work with DHS to ensure that the relevant risk analysis procedures are compatible with the criteria established in the NIPP. Following are a few of the NIPP's risk management framework activities:

Set security goals—Define specific outcomes, conditions, end points, or performance targets that collectively constitute an effective protective posture.

Identify assets, systems, networks, and functions—Develop an inventory of the assets, systems, and networks, including those located outside the United States, that comprise the nation's CI/KR and the critical functionality therein; collect information pertinent to risk management that takes into account the fundamental characteristics of each sector.

Assess risks—Determine risk by combining potential direct and indirect consequences of a terrorist attack or other hazards (including seasonal changes in consequences, and dependencies and interdependencies associated with each identified asset, system, or network), known vulnerabilities to various potential attack vectors, and general or specific threat information.

Prioritize—Aggregate and analyze risk assessment results to develop a comprehensive picture of asset, system, and network risk; establish priorities based on risk; and determine protection and business continuity initiatives that provide the greatest mitigation of risk.

Implement protective programs—Select sector-appropriate protective actions or programs to reduce or manage the risk identified; secure the resources needed to address priorities.

Measure effectiveness—Use metrics and other evaluation procedures at the national and sector levels to measure progress and assess the effectiveness of the national CI/KR protection program in improving protection and managing risk.

RESPONSIBILITY AND ACCOUNTABILITY PER DHS

The NIPP says owners and operators of critical infrastructure will be responsible for taking action to support risk management planning and investments in security as a necessary component of prudent business planning and operations. The NIPP does not dictate what specific actions to take for security measures or how much to spend, but expects that activities listed in the NIPP will be conducted. NIPP 2013 represents an evolution from concepts introduced in the initial version of the NIPP released in 2006. The updated NIPP is streamlined and adaptable to the current risk, policy, and strategic environments. It provides the foundation for an integrated and collaborative approach to achieve a vision of: a nation in which physical and cyber critical infrastructure remain secure and resilient, with vulnerabilities reduced, consequences minimized, threats identified and disrupted, and response and recovery hastened.

The NIPP 2013 is being issued in response to Presidential Policy Directive 21 (PPD-21) on Critical Infrastructure Security and Resilience and was developed through a collaborative process involving stakeholders from all 16 critical infrastructure sectors, all 50 states, and from all levels of government and industry. It provides a clear call to action to leverage partnerships, innovate for risk management, and focus on outcomes.

The sectors are all different and not all aspects of infrastructure are critical. What works for one sector may not work for the rest. Also, the cost of protecting one facility may be much lower than what is required at others. The threat of terrorism may not be equal across the entire infrastructure; some of the sectors may never see the early phases of terrorist planning (surveillance) or an attack. Terrorism nevertheless remains a constant and serious threat. As you read this book, plots are in progress and some terrorist cells may even be collecting information and identifying

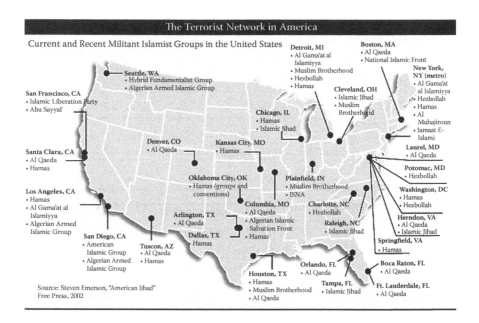

Figure 3.3 Islamic fundamentalist networks. (Excerpt from Steven Emerson, *American Jihad*, Free Press, 2002. With permission.)

their next target, while others are being successfully deterred by effective security programs or are being successfully identified and captured by police in the United States, Europe, Asia, Central America, and the Middle East. The average worker does not see the magnitude of the threat until it becomes visible through such arrests. Nor is he aware that terrorist cells have been living among us since the 1970s. This became known and publicized in 2002, as displayed in Figure 3.3. The map in Figure 3.4 provides an overview of the threats to the United States since 1970 and demonstrates how terrorists migrated from Europe and the Middle East to the United States over the decades.

NIPP AS A TEMPLATE

Now that we know that a first line of defense capability is possible through intelligence analysis and threat assessment, we can look at a third approach for effective threat and risk mitigation. If there is no preferred method for assessment in place or it is too difficult to select an approach, the NIPP is a

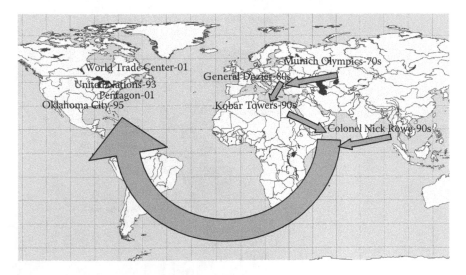

Figure 3.4   Terrorist threats to the United States, 1970s to present.

good one-stop shop for the many steps that lead to preparedness, including threat assessment. Without a clear understanding of threats faced, the subsequent security steps that follow for risk management could end up being performed in a sequence that is counterproductive or inadequate to achieve preparedness. The NIPP is designed primarily for the government sector of critical infrastructure, but DHS expects that the private sector can use it as a guideline to contribute to the national unified effort to secure and protect infrastructure assets that they are in control of. The NIPP provides an approach for integrating the nation's many CI/KR protection initiatives into a single national effort. This collaborative effort between the private and public sectors will result in the prioritization of protection initiatives and investments across sectors.

A PRACTICAL FRAMEWORK FOR TAKING THE NIPP APPROACH

Figure 3.5 illustrates the steps involved in organizing teams to develop and implement plans to mitigate risk. In assessing threats to eventually mitigate risks, the approach I would take would be to assemble a team consisting of all business units, physical security, IT security, risk

Figure 3.5   Security process model.

managers, security managers, and continuity and disaster recovery plan-ners. I would have a copy of the NIPP for each member. I would send a memo ahead of time on what to expect and schedule a required meeting. I would plan to meet during lunch, as it would make sense to meet for two to three hours. The meeting room would be a large room where everyone could sit in a circle. I would have note takers present and large easel pads ready (the type that can be torn and hung around the room). I would have one member knowledgeable on the NIPP briefly explain what it calls for. I would have another member briefly explain what emergency plans have been completed and their current status. I would also want to know if the plans have been rehearsed and tested or are they dusty. I would turn every section in the NIPP's table of contents into an action item or check-list to start with something manageable. I would task the group to com-pare the DHS action items to the current plans, then convene the group again after giving them time to report what actions they felt needed to be performed to complete the company's tailored NIPP checklist. I would assign a project manager and allow the team to help establish a timeline and goal date for completion. By stepping through the process this way, everyone gets a chance to buy into the whole effort instead of viewing this as a project that was dropped in their lap with no guidance on something that seems overwhelming.

A PRACTICAL FRAMEWORK FOR ASSESSING THREAT

The threat assessment process should never take place in a vacuum and should never be a low-priority task assigned to one person. The process is best served when performed by a team as a dedicated effort with a start and end date and clearly defined objectives, scope, and purpose.

The way an assessment is conducted varies across industries. Sometimes organizations are lucky enough to have employees with experience in assessing government, military, and corporate facilities. In such cases, all of that experience translates into having the ability to use combined methods tailored to the organization's needs.

For assessments conducted at nuclear weapons facilities, the procedures for all methods have to be performed by the numbers. For example, during the conduct of one assessment I am familiar with, when team members first showed up for the introduction meeting, they were met by the guards at the front gate … with weapons pointed at their heads. The team had been told exactly how to approach the front gate and what to do until their identities had been validated. All of their movements were by the numbers, precisely orchestrated and closely followed by the guards' gaze as instructed before their arrival. The guards were warned that there was zero room for errors. This experience is not like anything the average worker goes through in his or her everyday job. However, it was clear that the facility's owners and operators took their business seriously.

This meticulous attention to threats is not the norm across all sectors. Though it is inarguably the most important component of risk management, the process is often overlooked, misunderstood, and performed by inexperienced personnel. In government settings, threat assessments frequently focus on external threats—terrorism, espionage, and sabotage—while the private sector focuses more on human resources (HR)-related workplace violence and cyberthreats. This is changing, however, as cyberattacks become a more pervasive problem in the government sector. Threat assessments do not have to be like those performed at highly restricted defense facilities, but they need a dedicated and focused effort and need to become part of the organizational culture. The fact that few organizations have the resources to keep up with constantly changing threats or the expertise to perform assessments does not excuse an organization from performing them. It is true that anyone obsessed enough to do harm will find a way to do it regardless of how much security is in place, but there is much that can be done to discourage an attack. It happens through strategic security measures developed from realistic perspectives of threats.

Taking the time to compile and analyze threats and security event trends enables security teams to visualize the potential threat picture that can then translate into possible *early warnings*. In the national security arena, "early warnings" often come from intelligence resources, and thus "intelligence" is often considered to be the first line of defense. It affords time to respond protectively and further harden the security of assets or move the assets to a safer location. When threats are identified, they can be mitigated or discouraged through deterrence methodologies, more effectively from human intervention than technology.

There are many models for assessing risk. Figure 3.6 is a simple three-step model for mitigating the risk of both terrorism and natural disasters when time is critical and there is only a short period to perform essential steps.

In this model, Step 1 involves collecting information about the threats the organization faces and making sense of those threats. Are they imminent? Are lives in danger? Is the organization in compliance with applicable industry mandates? What is the worst thing that will happen if these threats are not addressed now? What is the deadline for completing Step 1? Is it in relationship to a DHS deadline? Did someone make a terrorist threat against the company? Are there other factors that warrant timely completion of the process? After threat information is collected, Table 3.1 can be used to identify and rank the threat information using the following criteria:

High—It has occurred one or more times at this location, and correlating security vulnerability exists.

Medium—Someone has articulated a desire to conduct the act, no correlating security vulnerability exists, and a threat or event has occurred at other similar facilities.

Low—No one has articulated a desire to conduct the act, no correlating security vulnerability exists, but the act has been carried out at other similar facilities.

Negligible—It has no possibility of occurring, and no correlating security vulnerability exists.

Figure 3.6 Lee's simplified risk model.

Table 3.1 Threat Ratings

Threat	Negligible	Low	Medium	High
Terrorism				
Suicide bomber (male)	X			
Suicide bomber (female)	X			
Truck or vehicle bomb		X		
Letter bomb			X	
Assassination	X			
Kidnapping	X			
Improvised explosive device		X		
Hijacking/airplanes	X			
Siege/hostage taking		X		
Remote triggered bomb		X		
Time-fused bomb		X		
Chemical attack	X			
Biological attack	X			
Radiological attack	X			
Nuclear attack	X			
Espionage			X	
Sabotage				
Vandalism				
Disgruntled person			X	
Cyberattack				
Civil unrest	X			
Telephone bomb threat				
Hazardous material incident			X	
Letter bomb		X		
Earthquake				
Flood			X	
Fire				
Tornado				
Hurricane			X	
Tsunami	X			

There are several methods, templates, and published opinions as to recommended methods and sequential orders for establishing preparedness plans. But assessing the threat is a crucial first step for establishing preparedness plans using either internal teams or outsourced professionals, and the input of each functional unit is important. At a minimum, the following resources should be included in the process:

- Legal
- Public relations
- Security
- IT
- Human resources
- Finance
- Risk manager
- Marketing

In order for the assessment team to succeed, it helps to understand what is being protected and from whom at the organization is being assessed. For example, the role of critical infrastructure in homeland security is to protect facilities from terrorists, disasters, and other threats that cause interruption to services that the public, businesses, the government, and our nation have come to rely on to sustain life and ensure everyone's well-being.

When a team comes together to begin the process, it is often a major period of discovery, surprises, resistance, and delays. Scheduling time to perform the effort becomes burdensome for one reason or another. There are shrinking resources. Existing resources are overextended in more than one job function. The effort loses importance and steam. It becomes overshadowed by other activities and gets tossed aside to the "we'll get to it later" pile.

When the team finally comes together and compiles a list of critical facility aspects that must be protected, they are surprised to see what shows up on their list. What usually happens in such meetings is that each business unit, for the first time, successfully articulates what is truly critical for it, and now everyone in the room is enlightened and on the same page. Sometimes this same discovery occurs when contingency or business continuity plans are being developed. The result is that the team discovers that some of the items they previously considered important are now hardly worth the money spent to protect them. The threat landscape of most organizations is formed from an amalgamation of data obtained from various internal and external sources, such as the example in Table 3.2. Threat assessments must be performed on a regular basis to

Table 3.2 Threat Information Sources

Source	Data Produced
Police	Criminal trends and statistics.
Fire department	Can report vulnerabilities in response measures, and an existence of chemical or fire hazards in the vicinity or close proximity of premises.
Neighboring tenants or residents	Threats to their premises.
Employees	Might report suspicious visitors or activities observed on the premises during business or nonbusiness hours.
	Might report suspicious telephone calls, e-mails, or faxes received.
Internal reports and logs	IT personnel may provide a snapshot of network probing or Web site–defacing attempts.
	Security forces may have reports of suspicious vehicles parked in the vicinity or suspicious individuals who approached the premises appearing lost or in need of directions.
Public relations	May have knowledge of strange queries or callers.
Legal	May know that at other times, someone was trying to make the company "look bad" or "make the company pay," possibly disgruntled persons.
Information technology	May know that someone was probing the network; may know of defacing attempts, hacking attempts, and anomalies on network traffic that alone mean nothing. But, in the context of all threats, put all the pieces of a threat puzzle together.
Newspaper and journals	May talk about a threat that already occurred at a competitor site.
Visitors and guests	May be imposters simply there to collect information for exploitation.
Security personnel	May see patterns in their daily logs at a particular time, which alone mean nothing to them but in the face of the threats collected indicate a serious threat.
Human resources	May have records of disgruntled employees or red flags (i.e., employees who only worked one day).
Finance	Strange activity relating to money, the movement of money, or theft of funds.

continued

Table 3.2 (continued)   Threat Information Sources

Source	Data Produced
Local, state, and federal government	Local and global threat trends.
Competitors	Suspicious things that they noticed in their companies that are outside the normal scope of threats they normally face.
Company Web site	May be defaced, leaving a footprint of the attacker.
Internet	Blog sites used by terrorists to share information or by other people talking about events that have happened or things they have seen.

accommodate the changing threat environment we live in. Table 3.1 is an example of just one subjective and qualitative method of rating threats—if no other preferred method exists.[*]

Step 2 involves performing data collection and analysis from some of the same threat sources and compiling a list of identified vulnerabilities. The results of the threats and vulnerabilities analyses should be protected and shared outside of the organization only on a need-to-know basis. In the federal and defense industries, such information is generally classified, not releasable to the public, and highly safeguarded. If compromised, it could be used to destroy an organization or cause severe damage to its financial well-being. Therefore, all documents gathered for this process need to be properly marked and controlled so they do not end up in the wrong hands.

When conducting organizational vulnerability assessments using the intelligence and other information we have gathered, it is best to create a table that provides information in a sensible format and identifies all the possible vulnerabilities. Regardless of how informal the assessment process is, a dedicated, diverse, and experienced team should be organized to conduct the analysis, and perhaps a separate team should be created to come up with a risk snapshot and countermeasures.

WHAT THE RESULTS SUGGEST

By analyzing Table 3.1, you will see that certain findings require what-if exercises to determine steps that are appropriate, required, or within the

---

[*] Elsa Lee, "Threat Assessments: Those Blind Spots Can Be Dangerous," *Risk Management Executive*, 2005.

realm of reality. For example, what are the details that caused sabotage to score "high?" What corrective steps were taken when this last occurred? Has it occurred or been attempted in similar facilities, and what did they do? Generally, sabotage can be mitigated through the use of closed-circuit television (CCTV), electronic access controls, signage, changes in procedures, training employees and security guards to properly detect and respond to sabotage indicators, and establishing relationships with local law enforcement and fire department personnel to obtain information on previously reported trends relating to the threat (official and unofficial). Although this is a subjective method for rating threats, it also provides important criteria for determining a threat level. Combining the threat and vulnerability assessments will help to focus efforts and resources for risk mitigation through effective countermeasures.

Trend analysis should be performed after Step 2, and it can be done by the most analytical person on the team, but ideally by a former law enforcement or intelligence resource. Trend analysis is viewing all the collected information to see if patterns of threat behavior emerge.

Terrorist Activity Indicators
- Did any information collected point to possible surveillance of the facility? Examples include people walking or pacing, taking notes, and taking photos.
- Were any suspicious vehicles observed several times in the vicinity?
- Did any employees receive suspicious calls asking "weird questions?"
- Have any uniforms from guards or others been recently stolen?
- Did any of the tenants colocated report suspicious activity?

Espionage or Insider Threats
- Are any documents or materials missing?
- Did anyone suddenly quit after being on the job for only a few days?
- Does anyone show signs of unexplained affluence but cannot explain why?
- Any network anomalies, such as unexplainable remote logons or file downloads?

Information and Technical Threats
- Was any of the company's information found on a blog site where someone made a threat?
- Did anyone try to attack the computer systems?

- Did any viruses come through and cause excessive downtime?
- Did the Web site get defaced?

From these questions, you can see that the team or the trend analyst can come up with many more valid questions to attempt to produce a picture of realistic threats faced. One could build this model of assessment and tailor it to the facility. When this process is completed, there are two possible steps to follow: (1) move onto Step 3 and determine risks, or (2) identify the threats among those discovered in Step 1 that require further investigation by the organization or the police. These threats would be subcategorized as imminent or "early warning," and reportable to DHS or law enforcement. The determination should be made by the person in the organization who interfaces regularly with DHS under critical infrastructure protection (CIP) efforts.

Step 3 involves taking the collected information and analyzing it to see what kind of risk picture emerges. DHS expects that each risk will be evaluated separately, including the consequences. We cannot possibly address all the findings that are likely to turn up in the data collection and analysis, or how long it would take to perform all the tasks and subtasks under each step. What the risk managers should be able to do with the simple model above is to apply more comprehensive techniques, if desired or necessary, by merging the steps above with other comprehensive methodologies.

HOW TO HANDLE DISCOVERIES
OF THREAT AND VULNERABILITIES

Certain aspects of assessment results may need to be shared with DHS. The method for transmission can be decided when the need to share arises, but the preferred way is through face-to-face contact, which provides a contact who can sign for the information. All documents should be marked on every page with "Company Confidential" at a minimum. Prior to reporting the information, contact with a DHS representative should be established to determine what template DHS prefers for reporting information.

Other assessment methods exist through DHS and academic centers where formulas for measuring risk are provided and the application of formulas is more comprehensive and less subjective than the simplified three-step model described in this chapter. There are more sophisticated methods and practices the public sector uses, but in the private sector, where the threat assessment process may be new, the three-step method is an easy way of identifying the threat to properly allocate resources to mitigate risk.

DETERMINING VULNERABILITY

Once the threat picture has been captured, the next step is assessing vulnerabilities against the known threats. The most common vulnerabilities found in past assessments I have been involved with include those listed in Table 3.3.

Figure 3.7 is one example of a critical infrastructure facility's detailed facility plans, which were found stored at a local public library as part of a published environmental study. The plans provided the layout of the facility and other information that could be used by terrorists to collect target intelligence. The plans were required to be there because they were an environmental agency document and had to be made available as public information. Since these details have to be publicized, it is important to be aware of what exploitable information is sitting "out there." The difference between this document and documents that may contain vulnerabilities and security information are the titles of the documents and the information in the documents. A security document detailing security, facility security procedures and operations, and risk and vulnerability

Table 3.3 Common Vulnerabilities Found in Assessments

Threat	Vulnerability
Suspicious males photographing a metro train	CCTV was broken and not working.
Suspicious male photographing a high-rise building	Employees did not notice him.
Suspicious person called in a bomb threat	None, an employee enacted a bomb threat response checklist.
Network intrusion attempted	None, the firewall prevented access.
Internal workers stole documents	No checks and balances to detect insider theft.
Facility plans found in the public library	None, item discovered in vulnerability assessment phase.

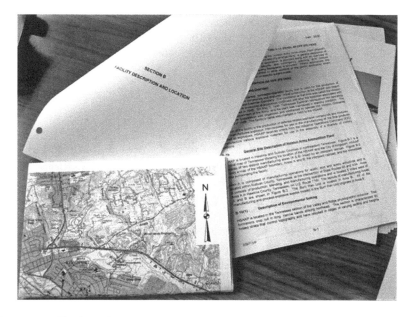

Figure 3.7 Facility plan.

assessments is exempt from the Freedom of Information Act (FOIA) rules and is not required to be publicized. The Critical Infrastructure Information Protection Act of 2002, in section 214 of the Homeland Security Act, exempts security-related information from being released to the public and classifies this as Protected Critical Infrastructure Information.

Once threats and vulnerabilities are identified, an assessment team would decide what the risk level should be and the best mitigation and risk management measures to recommend as well as the consequences of every recommendation. Threat, vulnerability, and risk assessment is a continuous process. The organization needs to have a baseline report of what the threat conditions are, otherwise, it has nothing to compare to and will not know what is normal activity compared to abnormal activity. It will not have the ability to go back in time and compare threat activity to see if it is normal or increased.

Sometimes the vulnerability in an organization stems from the hiring process. The screening is not conducted at all, or the methods of screening and performing due diligence are not reliable. Some companies are transitioning to more frequent checks even after people have been employed for a year.

Figure 3.8   Border crossing.

Sometimes America opens its arms warmly to people from other countries and adds to its vulnerability. Borders are easily crossed, especially in North America between the United States, Mexico, and Canada, as depicted in Figure 3.8. Nidal Ayad was employed at the Allied Signal Corporation.* Ayad, a Jordanian citizen who came to the United States, was fulfilling the American dream: he had a master's degree from Rutgers University, a good job, and he was married and had a child. Despite all of this, "he became the brains behind the 'witch's brew' used in detonating the bomb at the World Trade Center in 1993."† Within a short time, the adopted country also became the battlefield and the target.‡

---

* Judson Knight, "World Trade Center, 1993 Terrorist Attack Encyclopedia of Espionage, Intelligence, and Security," 2004, http://findarticles.com/p/articles/mi_gx5211/is_2004/ai_n19126798 (accessed March 23, 2008).

† Bruce Hoffman, William Rosenau, Andrew J. Curiel, and Doron Zimmermann, "The Radicalization of Diasporas and Terrorism," RAND Corporation, http://rand.org/pubs/conf_proceedings/2007/RAND_CF229.pdf.

‡ Hoffman et al., "The Radicalization of Diasporas and Terrorism."

SIMPLIFIED ASSESSMENT MODEL

Step 1—Take a hard look at threats regularly. The first time should be based on a thorough comprehensive effort. Thereafter, it can be in "snapshot" mode two to four times a year. Do disgruntled employees threaten your network? Do you have competitors that would like to take you out of business? Is your facility next to a known terrorist target? Do your employees leak confidential information? Is your facility being accessed by deranged individuals who appear to be ticking time bombs?

Step 2—After identifying threats, next look at vulnerabilities to determine how risky it will be to conduct business in the face of those threats and vulnerabilities. Are the vulnerabilities exploitable? What if they are not? Should you spend dollars to secure exploitable weaknesses, or simply eliminate or mitigate? What is the worst-case scenario if the identified threats caused damage to your business? Threat assessments often show that certain perceived threats were not valid. Most businesses would want to know this before continuing to fund the activity. What if the security programs' expenses were over the top and the value of the assets happens to be one-fourth the cost of the security expenditures? Or, what if the security budget is insufficient compared to the value of the material assets? Without going through a process of assessment—formal or informal—a business has no idea where it stands in terms of preparedness or whether it has a wasteful spending habit. There is no correct answer to this dilemma because organizations do not typically take into consideration that some assets have no monetary value, like employees. If the only thing at risk is human life, then security investment is still needed; all life is worth protecting.

Organizations are often very lucky. After threat assessments are performed and a picture emerges, people are immediately surprised at the threats and vulnerabilities discovered, and it is common to hear remarks such as "Oh my God! We were so lucky!" At one financial institution during a nonroutine check of the servers, the IT team discovered that they had four Web servers operating outside the firewall, in the open with unrestricted access to the public. The servers contained customer credit card numbers and Social Security numbers. These servers had been replaced by other servers, but someone forgot to disable them from the network, or at least secure them inside the firewall. They had been accessible by people on the Internet for four months. If someone had stolen the information that was stored on those servers, the organization would have suffered from lawsuits due to identity theft of customer information, penalties for failing to meet basic security requirements, negative publicity, and loss of customer confidence. After the company overcame the immediate shock, they found themselves in an ethical dilemma: What to do about the discovery? Report it to corporate management? Report it to the customers? Or never say anything about it? The answer for them was not to report anything until customers complained about identity theft, and then let the company's public relations and legal departments handle it. No one reported any incidents, so it appears this organization was lucky. This is not the right answer. It seems to be a common approach, though, to risk mitigation. Standard operating procedures in security and periodic vulnerability assessments could have prevented this event from happening in the first place.

Step 3—Review all your possible threats, vulnerabilities, and determine the risk you face with each one.

Step 4—Collect information that will serve as "intelligence" to drive your decision about what to do next. Intelligence is information relating to your threats. If your threat is terrorism, what terrorist group or individual appears to be a probable threat? What do you know about the threat's capability? Can the threat cause you serious damage? What type of damage? How likely is it that this threat will become a reality, and, let's say, "blow up" your building? Likely? Unlikely? After you have developed intelligence and analyzed it, make decisions about the next step and prioritize your actions.

COUNTERMEASURES

Countermeasures usually have to do with denying the threat access to the information or materials needed to exploit the vulnerability and allow the attack. After reviewing a list of identified threats and vulnerabilities, a team needs to determine the best way to deny their threats for what they seek. In many threat assessments that I have performed, we walked the employees or guards through the process of exploiting the identified vulnerability. We shot video after discovering certain vulnerabilities so that we could use the footage as training, but the videos were controlled as security-related information. We showed employees videos of their actions. Often, the vulnerability discovered involved human error, and the solution was not to buy more technology but rather to train more and build skills. Some of the ways that other teams have secured vulnerabilities include the following:

- Training guards to recognize and detect terrorist reconnaissance or terrorist intelligence gathering, and testing them through red team exercises.
- Training security managers with one-on-one "train the trainer" exercises so that they will then train the workforce on recognizing suspicious calls, suspicious probes, and suspicious persons watching the premises or other identified threats.
- Training the employees to recognize social engineering attempts by phone where a person calls in pretending to be the help desk but in fact is a threat trying to gain access to networks.
- Testing response personnel through simultaneous attacks at multiple access control points so that they will improve their response capabilities and the procedures for capturing and detaining a suspicious person until the authorities arrive.

The U.S. military is experienced in dealing with a variety of threats from terrorists to organized military forces. The military simulates collecting and gathering intelligence on vulnerabilities, operating like the enemy. To mitigate the terrorists' ability to gather accurate information, as a tactic used in conjunction with increased security and deterrent technology, the military also uses random antiterrorism measures (RAMs; not to be confused with risk assessment methodologies). This tactic includes plans that are used by security personnel and employees to change the security atmosphere surrounding a facility. RAMs alter the security "signature" to terrorists or their supporters who may be providing surveillance, thus presenting a terrorist group with a very ambiguous situation. RAMs also provide an alternative to trying to maintain the highest posture of security at all times, which can be costly. This puts the terrorist in a position to ask: "Do they know we are here?" "Have we been compromised?" "What is the impact of these new security practices on our ability to achieve our operational goals?"

Some examples of RAM tactics include the following:

- Checking vehicles at random; the number and timing are changed on an irregular basis but are planned for by security personnel.
- Frequently changing the facility or building entry points of employees and visitors.
- Requiring different requirements for visitors proving their identification.
- Frequently altering visitor access control procedures.
- Altering guard shifts and the number of guards at different posts so there seems to be no regular schedule to an observer.
- Changing procedures for deliveries (supplies, FedEx, etc.).

These procedures are only limited by the creativity of the team that develops them; but a tool for RAM has been designed by a research team at USC's Academic Homeland Security Center of Excellence for just such a purpose. Keep in mind, though, that too many changes may frustrate employees and cause them to find ways to circumvent security procedures. The key is to conduct operations where patterns cannot be determined by those who aim to exploit them.

A threat assessment can be used to evaluate the likelihood of terrorist activity against a given asset or location.

REPORTING INFORMATION

If criminal information is discovered in any of the aforementioned steps, the information needs to be reported as soon as possible to authorities. Controls need to be immediately established. The organization should convene to determine how the information or discovery will be protected from other employees, from suspects, and from the media. Only one person should be designated to speak with the media, and the information discovered has to be protected and controlled, as it may now be evidence. A possible scenario is that evidence will be collected and the crime scene is released from law enforcement so normal activities can resume. Another scenario is that law enforcement will confiscate the materials and take them to their evidence room, where they will remain until no longer needed. It is best to plan for the latter. It is important not to disturb evidence as soon as it is discovered to be evidence. Be aware that the media plays a role in covering threats and methods in which companies handle them thereby publicizing them. Establish a proactive approach;

call the media before they call you, and have a press release expert ready to prepare a release if the need arises. If you are trying to protect information, the media may unintentionally or inadvertently compromise your security, your plans, your weaknesses, your capabilities, and your limitations to protect assets. More important, that information must be protected under several Homeland Security Acts, as previously mentioned.

Decide ahead of time what is required to be reported and what is not. You do not want to publicize critical details if there is no requirement to provide such information. All vulnerabilities and secrets about your defenses must remain secret and controlled. All documents that describe your threats and vulnerabilities should be controlled, marked as "Copy of 1 of 10 assigned to __," and entered into a control log. Also include responsibility for control of information on the bottom of each page, and educate employees on the dissemination of information contained in marked documents. If you have a better way for document control, use your own methods, but make sure your methods enforce need-to-know controls and education. Companies and even lawyers from government agencies get confused about FOIA and what information is exempt from FOIA. If something does not feel right to you—you get a gut feeling—pay attention to it. Sensitive information, or whatever classification label you are using relating to critical infrastructure or your company's assets, must be protected. If there is confusion, seek several interpretations. The last thing you will ever want to know is that your disclosure caused an attack; this is the single most important message about release of information under FOIA. Some organizations make costly mistakes.

COST VERSUS INVESTMENT

Capital expenditures on security programs have always been viewed as a cost, not a moneymaking function. That paradigm must shift to align with realistic modern practices. There is a definite risk in not taking action; not increasing security measures will result in penalties and liability that will result in high costs, probably more than it would have cost to implement procedures and technology to protect the assets upfront. Everyone buys car insurance, home insurance, life insurance, and short-term disability policies. We pay on them for years, and there may be no return on these. Some people are lucky and never have to use them. The unlucky others who have to file insurance claims are sure glad they had a policy. It is time to view security measures as an investment, not a cost.

Penalties

In addition to having to be compliant with homeland security directives and mandates, organizations also have to worry about being fined by the Occupational Safety and Health Administration (OSHA) for negligent safety and security practices.* Identified in Table 3.4 are some of the penalties that can be imposed on corporations that are found to be negligent on safety and security. Citation and penalty procedures differ from state to state.

METHODS FOR SMALL BUSINESS SECURITY PRACTICES

Small businesses employ a large portion of the working population. They support all critical infrastructure sectors. They also must have effective risk management strategies. In 2013, *The Business Insider* reported 16 surprising statistics about small businesses:†

- A small business is 500 or less employees.
- There are 28 million small businesses in the United States.
- Approximately 75% of all businesses are single-employee businesses.
- Over 50% of the working population (120 million workers) work in a small business.
- Small businesses have generated 65% of new jobs since 1995.
- About 543,000 new businesses are started each month; 70% survive 2 years, 50% survive 5 years, 30% stay in business at least 10 years, and 25% stay in business 15 years or more.

Since we rely on small businesses to support our economy and we can agree that a good percentage of these businesses are in critical infrastructure sectors, should we not be concerned about whether they have adequate preparedness plans in place or whether they present a major risk to homeland security because of a lack of measures. Small businesses are comprised of entrepreneurs who are good at bringing their visions to life but not so much in other important details of the business. Unless

---

* The U.S. Department of Labor Occupational Safety and Health Administration (OSHA) is the federal agency charged with the enforcement of safety and health legislation for employees in the workplace.
† "Infographic: The State of U.S. Small Businesses," September 10, 2013, http://www. businessinsider.com/infographic-the-state-of-us-small-businesses-2013-9 (accessed June 1, 2013).

Table 3.4   Safety and Security Violation Penalties

Other than serious violation—A violation that has a direct relationship to job safety and health, but probably would not cause death or serious physical harm. A proposed penalty of up to $7,000 for each violation is discretionary. A penalty for an other-than-serious violation may be adjusted downward by as much as 95 percent, depending on the employer's good faith (demonstrated efforts to comply with the act) and history of previous violations, and on the size of the business. When the adjusted penalty amounts to less than $100, no penalty is proposed.

Serious violation—A violation where there is substantial probability that death or serious physical harm could result and that the employer knew, or should have known, of the hazard. A mandatory penalty of up to $7,000 for each violation is proposed. A penalty for a serious violation may be adjusted downward, based on the employer's good faith and history of previous violations, the gravity of the alleged violation, and the size of the business.

Willful violation—A violation that the employer knowingly commits or commits with plain indifference to the law. The employer either knows that what he or she is doing constitutes a violation, or is aware that a hazardous condition existed and made no reasonable effort to eliminate it. Penalties of up to $70,000 may be proposed for each willful violation, with a minimum penalty of $5,000 for each violation. A proposed penalty for a willful violation may be adjusted downward, depending on the size of the business and its history of previous violations. Usually, no credit is given for good faith. If an employer is convicted of a willful violation of a standard that has resulted in the death of an employee, the offense is punishable by a court-imposed fine, imprisonment for up to six months, or both. A fine of up to $250,000 for an individual, or $500,000 for a corporation, may be imposed for a criminal conviction.

Repeated violation—A violation of any standard, regulation, rule, or order where, upon reinspection, a substantially similar violation can bring a fine of up to $70,000 for each such violation. To be the basis of a repeated citation, the original citation must be final; a citation under contest may not serve as the basis for a subsequent repeated citation.

Failure to abate prior violation—Failure to abate a prior violation may bring a civil penalty of up to $7,000 for each day the violation continues beyond the prescribed abatement date.

De minimis violation—*De minimis* violations are violations of standards that have no direct or immediate relationship to safety or health. Whenever *de minimis* conditions are found during an inspection, they are documented in the same way as any other violation but are not included on the citation.

Table 3.4 (continued)   Safety and Security Violation Penalties

Additional Violations for Which Citations and Proposed Penalties May Be Issued upon Conviction

Falsifying records, reports, or applications can bring a fine of $10,000, up to six months in jail, or both.

Violations of posting requirements can bring a civil penalty of up to $7,000.

Assaulting a compliance officer, or otherwise resisting, opposing, intimidating, or interfering with a compliance officer while they are engaged in the performance of their duties is a criminal offense, subject to a fine of not more than $5,000 and imprisonment for not more than three years.

they are in the business of providing security-related services, they may lack or have inadequate security measures. These reasons include: (1) they do not have the resources, (2) they have not thought about it, (3) they do not know exactly what to do, or (4) they do not think their small business requires security. When you add statistics about small business survival to these security gaps, it is reason enough to be concerned about the level of vulnerability that they create in homeland security.

No matter how small, even a single-employee business should have security measures in place. In Appendix A, you will find a sample security plan for small businesses that can be used and tailored to business owners—at all budget levels.

MINI CASE STUDY 1

At one major financial institution, a security and continuity assessment was performed along with a review of emergency policies and procedures. Through these review processes, it was determined that this institution had never exercised its evacuation and emergency plan (the plan was in existence for over two years), so no one knew for sure that it would work. After the assessment and review were completed, a field exercise of the plan was put into motion and this is what it revealed:

- The plan did not identify the executive committee that would oversee the plan through rehearsal or execution. None of the institution's top managers had any idea that someone needed to take ownership of this plan.
- The plan listed the locations where employees would report in the event of an evacuation and emergency response due to a

disaster. While exercising the plan, it was discovered that some of the locations were in hazardous areas that placed the employees in harm's way.

- Access to the locations was not properly planned and arranged. Reporting to the locations was to occur in a sequential order and the keys to gain entry to the locations were in the hands of employees slated to arrive later, placing the earlier arrivals in unprotected and vulnerable positions.
- No one had interviewed the "wire transfers" employees to see what they thought about the designated areas or the plan, nor had they been introduced to the plan and the procedures.
- Many individuals who were listed as major role players within the evacuation and emergency plan were not aware of the plan or the fact that they were major role players.
- Alternate work locations in the plan were not safe and were not suitable for work activities.

If a disaster had required them to initiate the plan, and the employees reported to the alternate work locations and suffered from the potential hazards found there, the company could have faced fines for endangering the employees' safety. In the two years since the plan had been written, the areas either became unsafe, or they were never safe to begin with. Safety and security risks lurk all around us; physically assessing safety and security periodically in the workplace is an absolute necessity.

4

Risk Mitigation, Transference, and Elimination

It is apparent that "change" is critical to effectively manage terrorism threats and risk. Just as it requires seeing threats in a new dimension, it also requires seeing risk differently and determining the best ways to deal with it. The workforce has different strengths and capabilities. Some people are suited to assess threats, others are suited for data collection of vulnerabilities, and still others are suited to come up with countermeasures and solutions or creative ways to manage risk that we may not have thought about. It is not easy to come up with solutions because the very things that keep us busy every day prevent us from having any time to "take time" to see how we should best deal with threats. That is a problem; we do not have time "to think." So in some ways, this is not about "thinking" or finding a solution, it is about finding someone who can tell us how to do it based on expertise, experience, and a proven history of doing it for others. If we do not have time to learn and master a required skill or adapt current skills to see threats differently so that we can properly mitigate them, then we should bring in people who are already good at it.

Leadership consultant Peter Drucker says that leaders need to recognize when to stop pouring resources into an effort, if something is costing too much and it has served or not served its purpose. "When do you stop pouring resources into things that have not achieved their purpose? One tries it twice. One tries it a third time. But, by then it should be obvious

91

this will be very hard to do."* He calls this *creative abandonment,* a leadership principle that good leaders need to be able to exercise.

His leadership philosophy can be applied to the risk management process. Many organizations pour critical and costly resources into something that they would consider to be a solution. Organizations have to make capital expenditures annually to accommodate business or secure assets. This is a necessity for them. However, often they will buy more security apparatus or buy the latest and greatest technology. They might also continue spending money to fix old equipment that keeps breaking instead of replacing it—maybe it was expensive and needs to be "made to work" because an organization is stuck with it. If it is never going to work or will take too long to fix, risk is created because the equipment is not going to do what it is supposed to do or intended to do in a crisis. If there is a major security dependency on it, this is dangerous. Is it necessary to assume this risk? Is it smart? Does it make sense? Organizations will have to rethink how they conduct their risk decision-making process, especially if they are community partners or owners and operators of critical infrastructure (CI). Maybe there are some organizations in existence that can afford to gamble, but CI owners cannot. Organizational management must ensure that, at a minimum, it is following a risk management process similar to the one in Figure 4.1. This process is ongoing and never ends. It is a program, not a project.

Risk Management

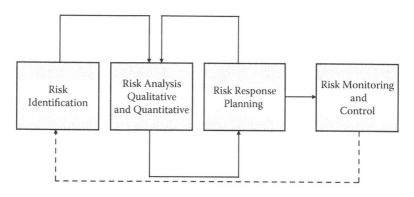

Figure 4.1 Simplified risk management process.

---

* Peter Drucker, "Peter Drucker on Leadership," http://www.forbes.com/2004/11/19/cz_rk_1119drucker.html.

RISK DECISION PRINCIPLES

The courses of action taken to manage risk require reviewing and understanding four principles:

1. Accept risk when benefits outweigh the cost.
2. Accept no unnecessary risk.
3. Anticipate and manage risk by planning.
4. Make risk decisions at the right level.

The center of risk management decisions should rely on six considerations:

1. Identify and characterize the threat.
2. Assess the risk of the threat.
3. Assess your asset values: what is important, what is valuable, and what is critical? (Don't forget the value of human life, which should outweigh other values.)
4. Analyze the vulnerabilities.
5. Identify and cost-analyze the countermeasure being considered.
6. Implement cost-effective security measures.

One simple but important lesson comes to mind. Several years ago, I received a parking ticket because the meter had expired. If I had parked farther away at a public parking lot, it would have cost $10. I decided to park at a metered slot near my meeting, and I dropped about $2 worth of coins in the meter, but when I returned the meter had expired and a parking citation had been issued—it cost me $35. So to park at the metered slot, the cost of parking turned out to be $37 plus two hours of labor afterward to deal with the problem. If I were to be paid $100 or $1,000 an hour for my services, then it is possible that the ticket actually cost $237 or $2,037 with labor factored into it. Was it worth the risk? Did I assess the risk of the meeting going longer than expected or forgetting to put more money in? Was the risk acceptable? Could it have been avoided? This is just one simple exercise to illustrate how hard it is for us to take time to see risk with a strategic perspective that really takes into consideration the value of our time and the true cost. The risk I faced could have been eliminated if I had better planned the time and parked just a block away. I could have possibly even transferred the risk if one of my coworkers had driven with me and we had taken his or her car.

In the security assessments that I performed over the years, there were many similarities in how people viewed risk. Not everyone had the ability to see intangible things. Here are some common trends observed:

EXAMPLE 1

The virus software and intrusion detection hardware requires updating, but if we change over now, the current products are not compatible with other components that we have in place. To replace the other components is cost-prohibitive. The decision made was to have a "work around" for the potential viruses to be experienced even if it did make the organization vulnerable to viruses, which could mean downtime from a few hours to a couple of days. A major procurement would occur in the coming 12 months.

EXAMPLE 2

"The suspect cannot ride in our car," said a security manager in one of our red team exercises. In one critical infrastructure assessed, a member of the red team (posing as terrorists) was detected and detained inside the gate of the facility. It was a hot day, and several guards surrounded him until someone could show up to tell them what to do. Others came over to help decide what to do. As controllers, and knowing what else was going on, we realized they had taken their attention off of the critical duties of providing security to protect this important facility, so we asked them why not just take him to the security building. Unbeknownst to them, we already knew that other red team members were busy with other breaching attempts that were being missed because of this activity. "We cannot let this person ride in our vehicles; our insurance policy will not allow it," they said. So we waited and waited, and at the end of the exercise, they realized they have to be able to weigh and compare risks, or additional greater risk will be assumed if something as simple as decisions about detainment were not part of the guards' training.

Once threats and vulnerability are known, organizations have generally four options to consider in addressing risk.

1. *Accept the risk*—Is the risk acceptable, or is the cost of managing it greater than the benefit? Management or decision makers may opt to accept the risk.
2. *Transfer the risk*—Many risks can be transferred to other parties (often at a cost), for example, insurance coverage or well-negotiated third-party and vendor agreements.
3. *Treat the risk*—take action to reduce the impact or likelihood of the risk, for example, policies and procedures, training, disaster recovery procedures, or implementation of physical or logical controls.
4. *Terminate the risk*—If the risk is too great or cannot be managed, the activity may be terminated to eliminate the risk entirely.

Many business owners often feel that they can mitigate risk through insurance policies, but that may not be entirely true. Insurers have changed the way they issue insurance policies and the limits of what they cover due to cost incurred in incidents like the World Trade Center attack and the Oklahoma City bombing. In the article "One Hundred Minutes of Terror That Changed the Global Insurance Industry Forever" by Robert P. Hartwig, senior vice president and chief economist at the Insurance Information Institute,* in the section titled "To Pay or Not to Pay: 'Act of War' and Terrorism Exclusions," he states:

> Ability to pay is distinct from willingness to pay. While insurers made it clear that they had sufficient resources to pay losses arising from the attacks, the question of whether the attacks themselves represented a covered cause of loss became a temporary sticking point for some companies. First, some insurers and reinsurers seem to conclude more readily than others that the attacks were compensable. A number appeared to be quietly wondering whether the attacks could be interpreted as an "act of war." Such an interpretation would have freed insurers from their liability to pay because *act of war* exclusions are found in virtually every commercial property and personal property insurance policy. The possibility of invoking the *act of war* clause was probably very tempting because President Bush and many other top administration officials repeatedly referred to the attacks as "acts of war." Political rhetoric and saber-rattling aside, insurers and reinsurers quickly concluded that invoking the *act of war* exclusion would probably not withstand a court challenge. This decision was reached after considering court precedent as well as observation of the fact that no formal state of war between the United States and any nation (including Afghanistan) existed on the morning of September 11, 2001.
>
> Rumors that there might be terrorism exclusions in some of the affected property policies were also quickly debunked. Nevertheless, for a period of time it seemed plausible, even likely, that terrorism exclusions might have been negotiated into the terms of the property policies sold to the owners of the World Trade Center complex. After all, terrorists had already tried to blow up the buildings in 1993 by detonating a truck bomb in a parking garage under the towers. Insurers paid $510 million to cover the costs of that attack. Insurers had also paid $125 million to settle claims arising from the 1995 Oklahoma City bombing. No such exclusions were in place, however. The fact that the industry was providing coverage against terrorist attacks for little or no additional premium

---

* R. P. Hartwig, 2002, "One Hundred Minutes of Terror That Changed the Global Insurance Industry Forever. Online: Insurance Information Institute," PDF file, http://www.iii.org/media/hottopics/insurance/sept11/sept11paper/.

is a practice that Berkshire Hathaway president and investment guru Warren Buffett would later deride as "foolish" and "a huge mistake." In the wake of the attacks, however, Berkshire quickly emerged as one of the few insurers to offer coverage against terrorist acts, but in exchange for tight limits and a sizable premium.

Further studies and personal experience have proven that conducting effective risk management and demonstrating proof of plans and procedures to mitigate risks can reduce insurance rates. My observations are that businesses have not adopted effective risk management strategies if they think their policy alone is going to cover catastrophes and, so far, there is nothing that guarantees that insurance policies will provide that.

How do you know if you are investing enough to protect critical resources that we rely on to sustain the daily activities that we seem to take for granted?

Many critical infrastructure and key resources (CI/KR) owners and operators recognize the importance of securing and protecting facilities from terrorists and other threats. They make sure their systems can be upgraded or retrofitted to sustain the growing populations that were not foreseen when they were first built. Many recognize that proper expenditures are needed to meet their objectives. They perform a good risk assessment to ensure the security expenditures support the risk. Others see it as "a cost" or "not their responsibility," "the government will take care of them," or worse, they overspend on improvements for security when the threat and risk are minimum, or they decide their risk can be mitigated through an insurance policy. Was getting an insurance policy really a risk assessment decision, or was it an easy way out that, hopefully, was not a gamble?

A few years back, an international engineering firm contacted my company for an assessment on its decision to mitigate the effects of a future computer system outage due to a 9/11-type of attack. After a review of their solution, we informed them that their solution was quite expensive because they were requiring a "zero" outage time for all their systems. Were all the systems really that critical? Did they have alternative procedures for some of the applications on other servers? Were the business units that used those applications really critical to the continued operations of the organization? After several discussions, we asked for their risk decision process analysis so we could review it. Guess what? They did not perform a risk analysis. Their vice president of information technology was the one who made the decision that all systems needed

Figure 4.2 Lucky or unlucky seven.

to have zero tolerance for outages; none of the business managers was involved in the decision and, of course, they did not complain about the solution. After an extensive education on the risk process, a new solution was identified that still provided the organization effective continuity if a disaster was to occur. The new solution saved them 50 percent in cost. That is a lot when the savings is over a million dollars. Of course, if you have the money to throw around, you could implement the full spectrum of technology solutions and mitigate all possible threat scenarios. I do not think many organizations today have that much money just lying around.

Many risk decisions are made on assumptions: it has never happened in our industry before, it happened once and there is no way it will happen again, and what are the chances. The sad thing is that management credibility rides on these assumptions and risks. It's like playing craps, and as in Figure 4.2, the roll could be the lucky seven at the beginning of the game or the unlucky seven that later ends the game.

RISK MANAGEMENT

In an interview with Phillip Van Saun, director of risk, security and resilience for the University of California, Van Saun shared what he felt were important aspects of preparedness plans.* Van Saun believes that government, large businesses, and even small businesses have a responsibility in disaster preparedness. He sees exercising as an important quality of disaster planning. Any business can model its disaster-planning process after a broader planning technique called microgaming. Microgames are mini hypothetical crisis-management sessions intended to boost team dynamics and communications. Van Saun is an evangelist for this technique and believes decision making in a crisis must be fast and frugal. "You can't always predict or prevent disasters, but you own the space of preparedness," he said. For startups and small businesses whose coffers are already tight, microgaming can be cost-effective when compared with the cost of formal training workshops. For example, if a startup with seven employees, each with an hourly rate of $30, met for 30 minutes over a company-hosted lunch ($30) twice a month to microgame any number of possible topics, the cost of microgaming would be only $3,240 per year. Of course, these meetings could induce follow-on policy development or action items that might incur incremental improvement costs, but the intention is to save time, effort, and money when what Van Saun calls "the intrusion of reality" such as fires and earthquakes actually do occur.

Van Saun, a former member of the Marine Corps Presidential Helicopter Squadron, also believes that the choice not to prepare is a choice of willful blindness. Indeed, he titled his primer on crisis management *Failure Is an Option*. In this book and in his presentations, Van Saun outlines six steps for a microgame: (1) Present the basic details of the risk to be addressed; (2) brainstorm possible solutions; (3) discuss challenges to a resolution; (4) determine possible moves given the realities of your culture; (5) select moves to respond to the problem; and (6) implement steps to mitigate the identified risks. In order to carry out the microgame, Van Saun recommends that managers gather their staff on a regular basis for small increments of time to work through the six steps. At first, a facilitator guides the group to identify and adjust for bias in the decision cycle, demonstrates how to ask good questions, engages the team in fast and frugal decision making, and closes with an analysis of what went well and what needs to improve. Once the group gets regular practice and builds these habits of mind, the role of the facilitator diminishes, empowering employees and team members to take the initiative themselves. According to Van Saun, this heightened state of preparedness and risk management

---

* Phillip Van Saun, interview by Elsa Lee, June 1, 2014.

can be incrementally developed when microgames are implemented over time and as the challenges presented become more complex.

LESSONS NOT EASILY LEARNED

According to the *9/11 Commission Report*, there are many threat cues that people are just not attuned to. This lack of awareness leads to threats being bold enough to find vulnerabilities to exploit, thus causing us to face high risk. The report showed that analysis, which should have been taking place, did not take place. Here are some of the highlights of lessons from the report:[*]

1. The CIA's Counterterrorism Center (CTC) did not analyze how an aircraft, hijacked or explosive-laden, might be used as a weapon. It did not perform this kind of analysis from the enemy's perspective ("red team" analysis), even though suicide terrorism had become a principal tactic of Middle Eastern terrorists. If it had done so, such an analysis would have pointed to suicide operative and large jet aircraft alerts.
2. The CTC did not develop a set of telltale indicators for this method of attack. For example, one such indicator might be the discovery of possible terrorists pursuing flight training to fly large jet aircraft or seeking to buy advanced flight simulators.
3. The CTC did not propose, and the intelligence community collection management process did not set, requirements to monitor such telltale indicators. Therefore, the warning system was not looking for information such as the July 2001 FBI report of potential terrorist interest in various kinds of aircraft training in Arizona, or the August 2001 arrest of Zacarias Moussaoui because of his suspicious behavior in a Minnesota flight school. In late August, the Moussaoui arrest was briefed to the Director of Central Intelligence (DCI) and other top CIA officials under the heading "Islamic Extremist Learns to Fly,"[†] language which did not cue them to events like 9/11.

---

[*] 9/11 Commission, *9/11 Commission Report*, http://www.gpoaccess.gov/911/index.html.
[†] 9/11 Commission, *9/11 Commission Report*.

4. Neither the intelligence community nor aviation security experts analyzed systemic defenses within an aircraft or against terrorist-controlled aircraft, suicidal or otherwise. The many threat reports mentioning aircraft were passed to the Federal Aviation Administration (FAA). While that agency continued to react to specific, credible threats, it did not try to perform the broader analysis warning functions described here. No one in the government was taking on that role for domestic vulnerabilities and exploitation by terrorists.

The methods for detecting and then warning of the surprise attack that the U.S. government had so painstakingly developed in the decades after Pearl Harbor did not fail according to the 9/11 Commission; instead, they were not really tried. They were not employed to analyze the enemy that, as the 20th century closed, was most likely to launch a surprise attack directly against the United States.

We should study the past to learn about changes that are needed in our behaviors and in our procedures to better mitigate terrorist attack risks. The following events are worthy of our own analysis to help us see attacks in a new light with this question in mind: Is my organization a target? What did facility owners miss in the months or years before the attacks that could have served as cues of an impending attack?

It is 12:17 P.M. on a Friday in New York City, and a van loaded with 1,500 lbs. of urea nitrate fuel oil has just exploded in the underground garage of World Trade Center Tower 1. The explosion blasts through four sublevels of concrete, killing six people and injuring 1,000, but fortunately for us it did not have the intended domino effect. Tower 1 did not topple over, bringing Tower 2 down and killing the intended 250,000 people on February 26, 1993. How can industry better anticipate such risks to properly mitigate them? Intelligence, early warnings, and threat analysis can address this area of risk. After this incident, risk management was performed and solutions were provided to prevent it from happening again, but it seems the focus was on only this type of threat, and other threat possibilities and risks were not considered.

On June 25, 1998, a dump truck carrying 20,000 pounds of TNT explodes outside the front barriers of the Khobar Towers in Saudi Arabia, killing 19 airmen and injuring many more. In the months prior to the attack, the unit had taken steps to implement security measures to diminish 36 of 39 vulnerabilities permitted up until that point. The other three were still being worked on. The highest ranking officer had spent most of his assignment implementing risk mitigation measures for Khobar Tower facilities, but three were not within his powers or control. Intelligence sources and an early warning, combined with a plan to act on trend analysis, may have helped them in addressing the other vulnerabilities, such as is the host government stable, and can we rely on their security and early warnings?

It is 3:45 A.M. on August 7, 1998, in Washington, DC. Any minute now, someone is going to receive a call. Two bombs have just exploded, killing 257 and injuring more than 5,000 people at the U.S. Embassies in Tanzania and Nairobi. There is blood and carnage everywhere. What could have prevented this attack? Perhaps, a timely interpretation of threats is easier to perform by people from "low-context-communicating" countries. Low-context communicators prefer to be less direct, relying on what is implied by communication.* The United States is a "high-context-communicating" country, where things can be taken at face value rather than as representative layers of meaning.†

At 8:47 A.M., September 11, 2001, citizens of New York feel the blow of another attack at World Trade Center Twin Tower 1. If not for the fact that an airplane was used like a guided missile, we could almost call it a barbaric act from another era. How could we have mitigated this risk? We all need to read the *9/11 Commission Report*. It is surprisingly comprehensive and straightforward about what could possibly have been done to mitigate this risk.

It is 3:11 A.M. on October 12, 2000, and someone in Washington, DC, will be getting a call in the next 2 minutes. A bomb has just exploded, creating a hole on one side of a U.S. Navy destroyer, the *USS Cole*, killing 17 people and injuring 39 others. Some say that sailors at the top deck had just given a friendly wave to the two men on the boat that delivered the bomb as it got closer. The two men on the boat allegedly returned the friendly gesture. Comprehensive risk analysis on a country's political climate is helpful (for example, is the host government reliable to provide security and early warnings).

Along with the 1993 World Trade Center bombing, the 1996 Khobar Towers bombing in Saudi Arabia, and the 2000 attack on the *USS Cole* in Yemen, the double U.S. Embassy bombing in Africa is one of the major anti-American terrorist attacks that preceded 9/11. Comprehensive risk

---

* Michelle Lebaron, "Cultural Diversity," 2003, http://www.beyondintractability.org/essay/communication_tools/.
† Lebaron, "Cultural Diversity."

analysis on a country's political climate and its propensity to help terrorists is helpful and provides a bit of "intelligence" to help guide decisions.

What do all these attacks have in common? They put people in high-risk situations in places where the "best of the best" risk managers and security experts need to put their heads together to develop the best risk management solutions. People who work at critical infrastructure facilities have to be "risk aware" and imagine all types of scenarios. Is there a dry run being conducted today for a possible terrorist attack? Are the cars or people who are seen on a regular basis on our premises but not from this company actually collecting information to determine vulnerabilities? Is your "response" being tested through devices being left for you to discover—backpacks with weapons, clay with wires made to look like explosives, or a knife or cutter left inserted into a book with a cutout in the center—as some people have reported finding.

5

Readiness Plans
Develop, Validate, and Update

A good plan today is better than a perfect plan tomorrow.

U.S. Army General George S. Patton

OVERVIEW

Do you have a preparedness plan? Some call it a readiness plan; others have various labels for it. Are you prepared for a terrorist attack? If an earthquake or tornado struck your facility, would you be able to activate a response and recovery plan? Do you have one or both? In some organizations, a preparedness plan might be found as a component of the organization's security plan, emergency response plan, business continuity, or continuity of operations plan. Is your organization totally prepared? Is your plan located on a bookshelf with a little bit of dust on it or in your head? Over the years of reviewing hundreds of private and public sector organization plans for terrorism response, I often found that most of the plans were outdated or not in existence. Management's answers for not having a documented plan for terrorism often went like this: "We don't need a written plan; all of our lead personnel know what to do."

This is a common response from many organizations that are not regulated or required to have a documented plan. It is true that if plans are regularly exercised, then detection and response procedures become second nature. But without some semblance of a documented plan or

103

checklist, in the heat of chaos during a disaster, critical items will be missed. How do you train new personnel on their responsibilities or procedures? What if lead personnel are not available or do not show up due to circumstances related to the disaster? How do their "alternates" know what to do? A documented plan would provide them with a place to go to obtain information on what to do or whom to contact. It needs to be physically available, not just on the network, in the event of a power outage.

Another common response is "We have a business continuity plan that addresses disaster response, and a terrorism attack is just like responding to a disaster so that plan will do just fine."

Most business continuity plans only address natural disasters. Yes, there are some similarities between responding to a natural disaster and a terrorist attack. In natural disasters, however, warnings are usually issued before they hit so personnel have time to take appropriate actions. The plans that do address human threats do not take into account weapons of mass destruction (WMDs)—chemical-, biological-, nuclear-, or radiological-related terrorist events requiring a whole set of response procedures like no other.

Another common statement is "We have an emergency evacuation plan that is practiced regularly, and that is all we need. If an attack happened, we would just evacuate anyway."

That is great, however, even an evacuation plan that is practiced regularly is only one component of a terrorism preparedness plan. It should also address security reporting and response to suspicious activities or events. What if the attack involved WMDs and you were informed that you were required to shelter in place for three to six hours or even for a few days? Will security staff know how and when to control access to the building to prevent further contamination? Has the building been evaluated to identify the best location that is least affected by the outside environment? Will employees know where to assemble to provide them with the best chance of survival? Do you have a communications plan to receive updates from the response teams? Who will know when and how to shut off ventilation systems if facility management is not available? At one evacuation relating to a chemical hazard, firemen responded in full gear—mask and all. No one knew how to get to the heating, ventilation, and air-conditioning (HVAC) room except for the building janitor and, eventually, someone found him and sent him in. He walked responders to the HVAC room, explained a few things, and then came back out and left. No one thought to give him protective gear, or even just a mask or a set of gloves before dispatching him to the "hazard zone."

Some businesses say, "We have insurance for disasters and have a rider policy to include terrorist attacks."

There may be small print in the policy precluding coverage to damage caused by a terrorist attack, as discussed in Chapter 4, especially the human life that might be lost. Employees would be devastated and morale would be affected if they knew the organization had not provided reasonable efforts for their safety and security to protect them from a terrorist attack and instead relied on insurance to mitigate the risk of loss (loss you hope is covered). There should never be an overreliance on insurance. Insurance laws on this topic are still relatively new and not the most reliable method for mitigating terrorist risk when a plan would be the better approach. Additionally, any company that is part of the critical infrastructure (CI) community must have plans developed and implemented.

Some have stated, "Terrorists wouldn't attack us because we are a 'widget' company. Besides, there is a federal building down the street that they would attack over us."

Based on the attack history of terrorists, a "widget" company more than likely would not be a terrorist target. But, does that widget company provide products to the government, military, or a critical infrastructure? If so, it could be identified as a possible target of opportunity or a secondary target. A terrorist's thought process is as follows: if the federal building seems to be too hard of a target and this company provides products to the government or a CI, and is an easier target, it is just as good of a target. If you do not provide products to the government or a CI, think about an attack on a federal building that may be nearby. If the attack was a large one or it included WMDs, how would that affect your organization? I am sure that businesses in the vicinity of the Twin Towers that believed they were not a target never expected to be impacted the way they were on 9/11.

Terrorism preparedness plans should be documented, well communicated, and rehearsed by everyone affected, and they must be able to guide a wide range of responses to different threat scenarios. General thoughts from planners on the purpose of a plan include the following: a plan is a tool to educate and provide instinctive response when it is exercised regularly; and another thought is that it is a checklist to provide guidance because rarely is the scenario you develop a plan for the event that actually happens. Both thoughts have merit. The human body may go into shock and freeze when faced with a terrorist attack, but confident people who know what to do are likely to minimize the impact of the incident, respond rationally, and assist in recovery efforts.

Large corporations that do not seem to be classified under any of the 16 critical infrastructure sectors need to adopt their own preparedness strategies—that includes planning, as if they were part of the critical infrastructure. They can utilize the resources and guidelines that the Department of Homeland Security (DHS) has assembled for private sector use. Hopefully, your organization is well ahead of the DHS requirements and plans are prepared, well communicated to employees, exercised, and efficient and effective for response.

HOW TERRORISTS PLAN

Al Qaeda dedicates extensive resources to planning and training through various means, including the distribution of publications as well as planning meetings in training camps and other locations worldwide. They plan carefully and extensively and exercise their plan before carrying out their attacks. Figure 5.1 shows Al Qaeda's training manual and other publications that are used to spell out how a terrorist should put a plan together. Al Qaeda conducts hands-on planning after all the information is gathered, assessments are made, and risks are evaluated. Sound familiar? They also have support cells that are dispersed throughout the world, and almost all are on standby to render the assistance needed to plan attacks. How would you compare your efforts against Al Qaeda's planning efforts?

| Al Qaeda's Biweekly Online Training Manual | Al Qaeda Training Manual | Magazine for Women Mujahideen | Al Qaeda's Biweekly Online Propaganda Magazine |

Figure 5.1 Al Qaeda training publications.

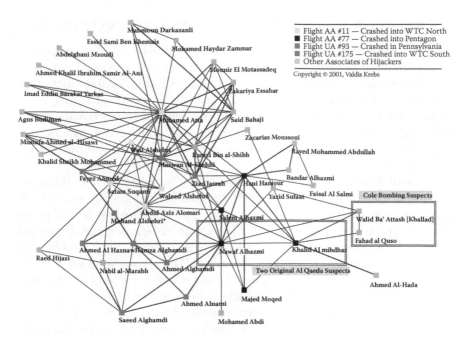

Flight AA #11 — Crashed into WTC North
Flight AA #77 — Crashed into Pentagon
Flight UA #93 — Crashed in Pennsylvania
Flight UA #175 — Crashed into WTC South
Other Associates of Hijackers

Copyright © 2001, Valdis Krebs

Figure 5.2 9/11 attack terror network.

Figure 5.2* is the work of Valdis Krebs, an expert on social network mapping who took public sources and began mapping the terrorist links after 9/11. The different shades of gray represent the event linkages. As illustrated in the map, a large amount of coordination was required to execute the mission. Obviously, this was not executed without a plan. Krebs has been mapping networks since 1988. His type of skills can be useful in protecting us from future attacks. To be able to respond effectively to an organization that puts this much energy into its attack-planning efforts, we need to put just as much effort into our plans for prevention and response.

---

* Valdis E. Krebs and INSNA, 2001, with the kind permission of *Connections* and the International Network for Social Network Analysis. Copyright ©2001, and http://www.firstmonday.org/Issues/issue7_4/krebs/#k1.

COLLABORATION WITH EXTERNAL ORGANIZATIONS

When developing plans for terrorism preparedness, external collaboration with other organizations is critical. This includes professional security and continuity-planning associations in your area, local industry and response organizations, city response planners, and neighboring businesses. They can provide insight on lessons learned, particularities with the local area's detection and response protocol, and correct any assumptions you might have on immediate response and whom you can rely on for support.

About four years ago, a business occupying a high-rise building in downtown San Francisco had just finished its emergency evacuation plan and was eager to exercise and validate it. The date was set; all plans were in place and disseminated. Management, key personnel, and all the employees were trained on how to evacuate, where to go, and how to report so accountability could be performed. The alarms went off, and the planned evacuation was in progress. Unbeknownst to this company, and by sheer coincidence, about two blocks away another high-rise was exercising its evacuation plan. Employees began arriving at their designated assembly area—a small grassy park about four blocks away that was easily identifiable and far enough away not to impede emergency response efforts. The assembly area began to fill quickly; in fact, people were overflowing into the streets. As managers began to get accountability, there were many people who were not on each group's list, and managers could not find some of the ones who were. Employees were reporting to someone who was doing accountability where they were located, but they did not recognize him or her. Finally, it dawned on one of the planners that not all the people gathered in this assembly area were from his company, and he wondered, was there another event going on that they did not know about? Employees were given the "all clear" to return to the building because of all the chaos. The planner went over to an employee he did not recognize to find out what was going on. He found out that two other large companies had identified the same assembly area. Not a problem, since it is unlikely that both buildings would be evacuated at the same time. The companies subsequently met and agreed to precoordinate their exercises in the future so they would not get so messy. Weeks later, while attending a city facility manager emergency response seminar, two planners were talking and laughing about the incident and were overheard by other building emergency response planners. To their amazement, several other high-rise buildings had the same assembly area. If they had coordinated through an organized effort or shared information with each other, this would not have happened. Again not a problem, since it is unlikely they would all evacuate at the same time. But what if a terrorist event involving WMDs, an explosion that caused structural failure, a fully engulfing high-rise fire, or an earthquake required more than the directly affected building to be evacuated. And what if all four scenarios happened at the same time? In several meetings with the other planners and the city fire chief, other adequate assembly areas in the city were identified and everyone agreed to incorporate changes and adjust their plans. In fact, the city plan had identified several assembly areas in case of a citywide disaster, and now both businesses and the city were on the same sheet of music.

In the northwestern United States near a small city, a consultant was asked to review a government facility's antiterrorism and response plans. The plans were not very robust: the responses to all hazardous events were to evacuate and wait for first responders and city government support, or move to their continuity site if the situation dictated and transportation routes were available. These plans were in place even though the facility had people from previous assignments trained in medical emergency response and hazardous materials due to their storage of those types of materials on-site. The consultant inquired and was informed that the city would take care of them, and if it was a terrorist event the federal government would be involved. The facility did not have the time to develop robust plans or train people, so it kept its plan simple. The consultant attended the city's monthly terrorism planning response meeting and met with some of the key planners. What he found out was contrary to the facility security and emergency planner's assumptions. He requested that the city and facility planner meet. The city plan indicated that during an event that affected the city, it would request support from the government facility since they had personnel trained in emergency response and hazardous materials. The plan also indicated that the federal facility was low on the city's response priority because the city assumed that since the facility had trained personnel, it could be self-sufficient longer than other facilities and businesses, and would not expect any city help for three to six hours or longer depending on the scale of the attack or other hazardous event. The key point of this actual story is that both entities developed assumptions of support or nonsupport in their plans without ever coordinating their planning efforts. The potential for chaos would have never been known until an event occurred or they had exercised their plans with all parties involved. It is important that organizations—both private corporate and public—are involved not only in the local business and city disaster or antiterrorism response planning efforts, but also in local business, city, and government terrorism prevention and detection planning efforts.

Sharing of plans, information, and experiences is vital to efforts against terrorism. Developing collaboration and mutual agreements with local businesses can expand the areas of awareness, detection, and intelligence—like a business community watch. Of all the sites assessed over the years, only about one-fourth of the organizations of the public sector critical infrastructure were taking advantage of this opportunity; none of the private organizations was known to be using this concept.

My interaction with DHS and private sector entities has provided a unique look into how government and business view terrorism preparedness requirements. Both audiences must work together, and a few work together efficiently and effectively, but others do not yet know that they have to work together. The latter—consisting mostly of private sector infrastructure owners—creates many gaps in critical infrastructure preparedness. Plans that should be in place are not. Some reasons cited in a Government Accountability Office (GAO) report as to why 100 percent of the plans are not completed by mostly the private sector is that key representatives from all sectors' agencies and their private sector counterparts have not yet established communication.* Some had good relationships because of a history of working together to solve money-laundering crimes or because of the need to prepare for Y2K, and simply kept building on those relationships. Educating the private sector was cited as one solution for promoting self-governing and self-preparing in order to have effective plans. Effective plans come from learning from and sharing with others, which require relationships and collaboration.

PREPLAN DEVELOPMENT PROCESS

Determine if your plan is drafted and final; if not, determine why. Gather threat and vulnerably assessments, risk assessments, and measures to mitigate the risks, checklists, and templates. Begin "plan development" and devise a strategy for its approach, or "plan to plan." One of the best ways is through brainstorming, as illustrated in Figure 5.3. Is the plan going to be

---

* Eileen R. Larence, "GAO Report," GAO-07-626T, http://www.gao.gov/new.items/d07626t. pdf.

Figure 5.3 Brainstorming.

a part of an existing plan or a separate plan? What members of the organization will be on the plan development team? How will the company or organization communicate, train, exercise, and maintain the plan?

The "human factor," among other things, is what gives companies the ability to imagine and plan for different disasters so that they can write good plans. The team that works on the plan—note that I do say "team"—has to be carefully selected in order to take advantage of this quality. Chapter 7 discusses people and various levels of imagination. Some people will be able to envision all the possible disaster or crisis scenarios quite easily. The plan development team or work group should be a diverse group of individuals who can provide different perspectives based on their experience and critical functions within the organization. External individuals such as law enforcement and emergency responders should be identified but only included when the discussions entail topics in which they have expertise vital to response procedures (to ensure they are in line with reality). When individuals are informed that they be on a plan development team, they usually are not highly motivated. It is seen as just another additional responsibility among the list of others they already have or a waste of time. In their view, the plan will never

111

be implemented. Where will the plan be reviewed and worked on? If the conference room where this will happen is not well lit, smells bad, or is too hot or too cold, choose another place or make changes to improve the room. People are already stressed with all the activities in the workplace; the last thing they need is to be distracted by the physical shortcomings and negative energy of the room.

Once the team is identified, gather them and begin development based on all data gathered. On days that team members meet to work on the plan, perhaps make it a casual dress day(s) so that people can be comfortable—one less distraction. Many of the people who were involved in threat assessment, vulnerability assessment, and risk management in earlier phases will probably end up being on this team or most should provide input.

The team or work group may be very large at first but will later break into small groups to develop components of the plan. Several times during the development process, the whole group should come back together again to validate what has been structured. Some team members will be members of different subgroups because of their specialty skills (e.g., security managers, lawyers, and facility engineers).

The very first meeting is one of the most important. It sets the stage for all participants. Develop the meeting objectives and an agenda, and stick to it. Communicate it to all participants ahead of time. Start with the following:

- Identify a person experienced in facilitating meetings.
- Identify a recorder.
- Schedule a conference room large enough to accommodate all persons comfortably and schedule plenty of time to allow for an extended meeting so the next group will not disrupt you.
- Ensure that all those involved rearrange their appointments and turn off cell phones.
- Instruct invitees on the importance of not delegating attendance of this meeting to subordinates.
- Schedule a corporate executive to kickoff the meeting—this demonstrates organizational support—and request that the same individual occasionally check in and make an appearance at other scheduled meetings to show continued support.

One method for jump-starting the process is to make it fun. It is not what you know that makes or breaks your plan but being able to apply what you know in a way that will work. People provide valuable input when they are excited about something. Adding a few elements of creativity into the process that are different than what the participants are used to enables their brains to work differently. If people involved in developing a plan feel that it will never get management support or be exercised or used, they will not put in the effort and will consider it a waste of time.

Find a different way to relate to this important document. Studies show that people learn or adopt practices when the following apply:

- They have to—after they have suffered a terrorist attack or survived a disaster.
- When the process is fun and interesting.
- When creating an environment where everyone feels that upper management supports the effort.
- When it is elevated to a high level of importance.

Have an icebreaker to put people at ease. Have little trinkets you can give to people every time someone comes up with a good brainstorming idea. Pass them a trinket in a spontaneous, unexpected way; pull it out of a sack when it warrants giving away. Do not make such a big deal about the different method in which the meeting was conducted. People will walk away from the meeting feeling as if they were a part of something important and bigger than they are. They will also appreciate that there were surprises—the unexpected trinkets. The trinkets can come from a bag of trade show goodies that usually pile up somewhere in the company or anything else that is not expensive or excessive. This method of conducting the meeting is, as mentioned, just an icebreaker; in Chapter 8, there is more information for implementing change and building a strong team to tackle any task or respond to terrorism.

PLAN DEVELOPMENT

It is important that we understand certain flaws that make plans ineffective. Some common flaws that are consistent across industries include:

- Employees and key personnel often do not know the plan exists.
- Plans tend to exist perpetually in draft mode.
- Comommunication trees are often out of date.
- The procedures that people are practicing do not match the plan.
- Plans are developed in a "vacuum" by one or two persons.
- The plan is great "on paper," but it has never been exercised to validate or to identify gaps.

113

Corporations with global locations and employees abroad need a plan with a preset list of procedures in the event of a terrorist attack at their location, as well as how the headquarters will respond to an attack at one of their overseas facilities. Events can quickly become volatile, requiring immediate evacuation out of the country without the possibility of getting assistance from a U.S. Embassy, the U.S. State Department, or any other government agency. Who can you rely on to assist with such a requirement? In such cases, DHS usually cannot advise those corporations on what to do. This requires extensive research and planning on the corporations' part when they are in the brainstorming stages of plan development. It is not uncommon for a large company to turn to DHS and say, Now that the train or subway has been attacked in (fill in the blank country), what should we tell our people? Should we tell them to stay in their office and shelter in place? Should they stay away from public transit? There is general information available through the Department of State that can be interpreted and adjusted to assist the corporation in developing its plans for these situations, but information may not be very tactical in nature, and Web sites may not be updated in a timely manner.

For plans to work as intended, certain fundamentals are essential:

- Plans must have executive "buy-in" and support.
- Plans need an adequate budget for proper maintenance and exercising.
- Plans must be documented in a clear, concise manner that is easily understandable by anyone who reads them.
- Employees and personnel with key responsibilities in the plan must have training.
- Plans must be exercised to be validated and to ensure the plan is going to work.
- Plans must be kept updated.

Remember that plans are a vision of how an effort will be managed. Plans also require guidance. Some guidance will be included in the plan and other guidance is developed to support the plan, such as the following:

- *Policies*—The general rules to be followed and enforced within the plan.
- *Procedures*—The formal methods for "how to" perform tasks that comply with the policies and the plan.
- *Practices*—Enhancements to the procedures but not replacements for them.

Terrorism preparedness plans—whether they are stand-alone plans or are part of another plan such as business continuity or emergency plans—have to be in compliance with DHS standards (i.e., the National Infrastructure Protection Plan, or NIPP) for private sector critical infrastructure and key resource facilities. DHS has dedicated many resources in human capital and funding to developing frameworks and models for preparedness plans across many domains—for how government will work with government before, during, and after an attack or disaster, and how it will interact with the private sector (critical and noncritical organizations), citizens, and families. Everything needed to put the preparedness plans in place resides on the DHS Web site, although DHS has not done a very good job of publicizing and reminding the end users of the vast resources available.

OVERLOOKED PLAN ITEMS

One recommended document to use as a template for plans is the NIPP. It may seem that I am championing this plan and overlooking anyone else's great plan. That is not the case, but if we are to all use similar standards for preparedness, and if critical infrastructure owners already use the NIPP, then all of us need to have similar—if not the same—response measures and capabilities. Every organization is different and has different requirements, and there is not one template to use as a guide for all industries. Thus, the NIPP is not the only one to choose from among guides or templates. All plan templates I have seen or developed required customizing, but they retained the critical and basic components to meet the organization's culture and requirements.

Internal Communications Considerations

The planning process must include discussions on employee communications—how to communicate, when to communicate, and what to communicate. People need time to prepare mentally and emotionally for change or for whatever is coming. Be sure to incorporate a good communications plan that addresses communications before, during, and after an incident. The communications should meet employee safety requirements and include details about people with special needs. Be sure to also determine the different communication methods that can be utilized and consider how you will communicate when the power is out and the public address system or phones are down. Do you have a backup for this? Are there emergency backup generators, and is the public address system included on the grid or does it have its own backup power? This is of paramount importance because people may need very specific direction and instructions.

Your plan must also address how security will communicate with building occupants and key personnel during an attack or an emergency. Consider an alternate method of communication with key personnel within the building using two-way radios. Also include a component for the communications plan for when electronic devices are not available or, even more important, if cell phones and two-way radios are prohibited from being used. This can happen during a bomb threat situation or when a bomb has actually been identified in your facility, because bombs can be electronically activated accidentally by cell phones and two-way radios (when you key the mike).

Internal communications between security personnel should be included in the plan. The use of two-way radios is common, with the telephone as a backup. Even though they are more expensive, encrypted radios should be used if the budget accommodates to prevent intelligence-gathering efforts conducted by criminals and terrorists.

External Communications

The mechanism for communicating among federal, state, and private sector responders just prior to and after an incident is still not efficient today.

A major component of the preparedness plan should incorporate how industry will interact and communicate with DHS—starting with assigning the right people with "people skills." There is a good outreach effort on the terrorism prevention front between government sector councils and private sector owners of critical infrastructure and key resources. They meet annually, quarterly, or more frequently, but this is not adequate to enable integrated communications between both sectors in a recovery situation.

Crisis and Media Communications

In the planning process, discussions must occur that identify communications to the media and family members—how to communicate, when to communicate, and what to communicate.

Employees, family members of the employees, stakeholders, and the media need to be kept aware in a crisis or a panic situation before rumors set in. Improperly handled communication could affect employee morale, destroy the organization's reputation and bottom line, and result in negative publicity. Everyone needs to know that something is being done other than what they are observing on television. In most situations, the first time we find out how communication impacts recovery is after a disaster or in the conduct of realistic exercises. The solution is to prepare ahead of time through planning—identifying a team to handle crisis communication, developing a plan that identifies potential problems and solutions, training the crisis team, and exercising the plan with the team.

A crisis communications plan requires facility executive managers to be involved as soon as a crisis hits—not just any manager but management personnel at the top level who can make a decision on behalf of the organization. This part of planning needs to include what the line of authority or chain of command will be in a response effort. What if the president and CEO are involved in the incident and are incapacitated or, worse, hospitalized? Who is next in line?

When selecting the right people for the crisis communications team—note again that I do say "team"—they need to be formally trained and experienced in crisis communications and conflict resolution. In most companies, crisis communications is the responsibility of the public relations department, and in some cases I have seen it tasked to the human resources department. To prevent conflicting statements and rumors and provide continuity, a single person should be selected as the spokesperson; you should also identify alternates in case the primary person is not available. This is commonly overlooked. The designated spokesperson needs to have the ability to be in direct communications with the top management decision-maker who is available.

It is best to identify primary and alternate locations to set up a media communications center and equip it with the tools needed to communicate: phones, computers to prepare news releases, fax machines, and an Internet connection. All this is needed to communicate to employees as well as the media. For the media, it is best to plan on at least two news updates a day. Tell the whole story—openly, completely, and honestly. For employees and family members, a call center should be available for them to get critical updates. New technologies today allow for updates to be provided via 1-800 numbers that employees and family members can call into to get the latest information. Remember, though, that these must be kept

117

updated, and the information provided must not have any inconsistencies or conflicting guidance—none. There is nothing worse than an employee or family member calling into a number for four hours and hearing the same message. Provide as much accurate information as possible, keep them informed, and demonstrate the company's concerns through your statements and actions. Designate one person for this effort—a detail-oriented person who can multitask.

The last task in developing your crisis communications plan is ensuring that policies are in place for employees and that education is provided on how to deal with the media. A company recovering from a disaster does not want the added pressures of having critical information breached, having to retract statements, or having rumors become like reality, especially when they are about who is to blame, how many people were injured or killed, and who they were.

Over the years, many corporations and government agencies have suffered the consequences of ineffective crisis communications plans—public blame, a lack of confidence by customers and employees, and financial losses. These were caused by representatives and employees providing speculations; pointing the finger at who was to blame; refusing to answer media inquiries, leading the media to make their own assumptions, releasing information that violates individuals' privacy, or even using a crisis to pitch products or services. You will find that by developing and training employees via an effective crisis communications plan, there will be fewer interruptions during recovery efforts and more cooperation and understanding by employees and the public.

Cybersecurity Planning

Cybersecurity plans have never been as important as they are today. Our personal and professional lives as well as our national security could be gravely impacted if cybernetworks are severely compromised. They are under attack on a daily basis by foreign governments, hackers, attackers, and terrorists to name a few. Cyberattacks threaten all components of the security hierarchy mentioned in the previous chapters. In 2013, my company Advantage SCI hosted a counterintelligence seminar in California. The attendees comprised government and private sector members of nearly all sectors. Two presenters were former Federal Bureau of Investigation (FBI) agents discussing cyberthreats. The astounding fact that shocked everyone in the room was that FBI agents were busy on a daily basis issuing "victim notifications" to businesses whose systems had been attacked. These businesses were either government contractors or owners of critical infrastructure facilities. What this means is that a foreign intelligence service was in their network—and in some cases for years—without the business being aware of it. In many instances, recovery from such an event is not possible without: (a) the FBI's help; (b) loss of computer use due to the boxing up of all your computers to be processed as evidence that will hopefully result in indictments, as discussed in Chapter 2 with regard to the Chinese military; and (c) the need to wipe out the network and build a new one from scratch. In one instance the cost of such a replacement was reportedly several million dollars.

DHS and other organizations provide guidance to create a safe, secure, and resilient cyberenvironment for the homeland security enterprise. Stakeholders at all levels of government, the private sector, and international partners are expected to work together to develop the cybersecurity capabilities that are key to the U.S. economy, national security, and public health and safety. Two main objectives of DHS are

- protecting our critical information infrastructure today, and
- building a stronger cyber ecosystem for tomorrow.

Plan Response for Bomb Threats

Bomb threats are by far the most common method used by terrorists and others seeking to cause alarm and disruption. Generally, terrorists do not begin a campaign with bomb threats, but the potential exists that it would be used as a ploy to gather intelligence about response capabilities. However, the disruptive effects of actual terrorist bombings may be amplified by subsequent bomb threats. Bombings also inspire hoax threats. Therefore, all organizations must have well-established protocols for dealing with bomb threats.

First, it is essential that the threat be relayed to the responsible persons, whether it is initially telephoned to the police, transportation company headquarters, switchboard operators, stationmasters, toll-free help lines, reservation centers, or any other number. Everyone should be trained to obtain as much information as possible from the caller and promptly forward it to the appropriate authorities. A sample bomb threat checklist can be found in Appendix B. This checklist should be located next to anyone's phone whose number is published. Using a checklist is important in gathering valuable information for investigations. It has been proven that no matter how much training is provided for response to a bomb threat phone call, people forget under a crisis situation. Using a checklist provides them with a quick reference list of information to gather and particular sounds to be aware of in the background and document, especially immediately after the call.

Second, a protocol for evaluating the threat is needed. Actions can range from watchful waiting to local searches to shutdowns and immediate evacuations. Evacuations will be rare. Authors and callers of bomb threats are rarely bombers. Still, even when threats appear to be hoaxes, as almost all are, they cannot be ignored. A reasonable assessment must be made and appropriate action taken. The desire to avoid needless disruptions must be balanced against the threat to public safety. Guidelines based upon actual experience (and defensible in a court of law if things go wrong) are helpful in taking the pressure off local decision-makers.

During an exercise last year, a bomb threat was called in to a manager's office to evaluate training requirements and procedures. Once the caller informed the manager it was a bomb threat, the manager immediately dropped the phone, stood up, and yelled out in the office, "Bomb threat. Everyone get the [expletive] outta here!" And the manager proceeded to run for the exit, leading the pack.

Addressing Loading Docks and Mailrooms

Mailrooms and loading docks are vulnerable to the delivery of chemical "weapons" and bombs, especially if you are not fortunate enough to have high-tech equipment for inspecting incoming packages. A vulnerability of a loading dock is that it usually receives large vehicles capable of delivering explosives. Human visual inspections may not be enough to detect true threats.

What should you address in your security or antiterrorism plan? Your plan should address measures to deter, detect, and respond to the threat. To deter a threat, many organizations avoid locating their mailroom in the same building as the one in which the other employees work, as opposed to conveniently putting it in the basement. Likewise, loading docks receiving deliveries should not be located in the same building as the critical functions of the organization or where most of the employees work.

Access control should be limited and restricted so delivery vehicles are not allowed to veer from their course to another area. Inspections of vehicles by security must be thorough, including the undercarriage and inside. Many facilities establish procedures so vehicles do not enter unless the person expecting the package notifies security that a delivery is coming and provides them with information on the company and driver delivering. These are just some examples. During terrorist or criminal intelligence gathering and surveillance, these simple procedures may be enough to deter and give the perception that your facility is difficult to attack.

Keeping informed of the latest trends on attempts and actual attacks using mailrooms is critical in conducting your threat and risk assessments as well as in improving your ability to detect threats and developing good plans.

PLAN VALIDATION AND MAINTENANCE

Plan validation and plan updates are part of your plan maintenance program. Validation (commonly known as *exercising your plan*) should be addressed in your plan. It should address, at a minimum, the procedures for conducting exercises and include an exercise schedule. Without validating your plan, how do you know if it works? Many organizations consider their plans validated when they do an annual review. This is not a plan validation and neither are tabletop exercises, as depicted in Figure 5.4. A tabletop exercise is one of the steps that leads toward plan

Figure 5.4 Tabletop exercise.

validation. A plan is fully validated when it is either successfully executed in a "real-time crisis" or after being exercised in a scenario-driven exercise. Chapter 9 provides more information on exercises.

Plan validation is performed upon completion of policy integration, program awareness, and training steps. To conduct an effective exercise, the following checklist is provided. These are the items you must perform.

- Develop exercise objectives that are comprehensive, approved, measurable, and support your plan goals.
- Schedule exercises on a regular basis—determined by your industry (at least annually).
- Develop appropriate metrics to meet or exceed exercise (tabletop, walk-through, or full) objectives.
- Ensure auditors are included in the validation process.
- Ensure executives, upper management, crisis management, and security managers are included in the validation objectives approval process.
- Document exercise results and any changes.
- Capture required plan revalidation items and include them in the next scheduled exercise.
- Conduct a postexercise meeting as soon as possible upon completion of the exercise, and include all the key participants, facilitators, and evaluators, as well as any role players, to identify what went well and what needs improvement.
- Develop an exercise "results" report that identifies the type of exercise and includes those activities, successes, shortcomings, and individuals and teams involved (internal and external), and how each addressed the objectives.

Exercise the plan; plan validation, or exercising, is a key measure of the success of your security and response program.

PLAN UPDATES

Plan updates are a critical piece of any plan maintenance. All organization plans, policies, and procedures require updating. This is often overlooked, especially with security and response plans since they are not used on a regular basis. Plans must be kept updated to be effective. You should have scheduled updates at least annually, updates performed when there are major organizational changes that affect policies and procedures or key personnel, and updates after exercises or after an event has happened requiring you to implement your plan. These updates are intended to make improvements to procedures from gaps identified during these events. In your plan development, you should describe your update review process, change control, and update procedures.

PLAN TO SHARE INFORMATION

Information sharing between the public and private sectors is difficult. Almost nationwide, there is the question of what to share, with what frequency, and how to act on the information shared. There is one primary frustration between the two sectors: expectations on both sides. The private sector expects timely and actionable intelligence. Neither side can define *timely* and *actionable*. But "timely" is not capable of being measured in hours or days. This creates a definite problem because the private sector most of the time defines "timely" as tactically sufficient to put decisions into action. They expect DHS entities to provide specific information and tell them within minutes of an incident that the incident is imminent and they should now take action. The government, however, can only provide the private sector broad-based information of strategic value. When DHS discovers a terrorist plot or monitors a plot in progress, it is usually from a distance. For example, this type of "plot" monitoring involves plots that emerged in Europe, but there is no telling when, in the future, it will hit the United States—if at all. What can the private sector do with that information? Sometimes the private sector stumbles upon information that gets submitted to the right office, and sometimes the private sector–public sector share networks as envisioned by everyone.

Understanding how DHS works will help us develop better plans so that areas where the private sector has to be self-sufficient can be addressed in the plan. This is how the process works when DHS learns that a specific attack is being plotted inside U.S. borders. They cannot track it or investigate it unless there are substantial actions by the terrorists for which the terrorists can be held accountable—conspiracy is not adequate. The actions have to be specific enough to demonstrate and prove "intent." The reason that the terrorist planners of the Fort Dix 2007 attack plot were able to be brought to prosecution was that they had taken substantial actions to put the plot of killing Army soldiers into motion, and the authorities were able to link specific actions to them. The alleged plot included conducting surveillance of the Army base and purchasing

123

multiple firearms, including assault weapons, handguns, shotguns, and semiautomatic weapons.* In other words, it was more than just intent or a plan in someone's head. The private sector needs to gain an understanding of these limitations; they will be much less frustrated when they know the rules and laws by which DHS must operate.

DHS can provide strategic information that can be used to "prepare and protect" over the long run, but generally nothing may fall under immediate actions. The private sector needs to understand that although fusion centers are in place and DHS attempts to share as much as possible, the private sector also needs to develop its own capability to do the following:

- Gather threat information and analyze threats.
- Integrate their protective approach to include a unified effort among their physical security, information technology (IT) security, and emergency response teams.
- Invest in whatever they feel is appropriate to protect critical infrastructure; DHS will not direct this effort or specify how much should be budgeted for this effort.
- Train and be prepared.

The NIPP is a mandate and guideline published by the DHS designed to ignite a national unified approach for integrating critical infrastructure protection initiatives through partnerships between the private sector and federal, state, local, and tribal governments. Make sure your corporate plan adheres to what is required in the NIPP.

The method of assessing, prioritizing, ranking, securing, and protecting our nation's infrastructure was first spelled out in the June 2006 version of the NIPP—about two years after sectors voiced confusion. Those who had plans in place simply had to update them, but there were many others who had not even started the lengthy process. Those that did not have plans were waiting on someone to provide them with a template. Some of the sectors claimed that they were members of a sector that was too diverse in its composition to establish relationships (for example, the food and water sectors). Some sectors did not understand the criticality of their role. They did not know if they were small role players, major producers of the information in the plans, or consumers of the plans—meaning

---

* A group of six radical Islamist men, allegedly plotting to stage an attack on the Fort Dix military base in New Jersey, were arrested by the FBI on May 7, 2007. They were subsequently charged with planning an attack against U.S. soldiers.

someone is going to prepare the plan for them, and they are still trying to figure out who that someone is.

There is a hierarchy of role players who have to put these plans together: government agencies, private sector owners and operators, and representatives of a broad base who interact with critical infrastructure.

The relationship that exists between national-level DHS resources and the private sector can often be confusing and create misconceptions, wrong expectations, and a lack of understanding of roles and responsibilities within the two groups, further contributing to a lack of plans in many organizations.

WHAT THE DHS SAYS ABOUT PROTECTED CRITICAL INFRASTRUCTURE INFORMATION

The Protected Critical Infrastructure Information (PCII) Program was established because of the Critical Infrastructure Information Act of 2002 (CII Act). It creates a new framework that enables members of the private sector to—for the first time—voluntarily submit confidential information regarding the nation's critical infrastructure to DHS with the assurance that the information, if it satisfies the requirements of the CII Act, will be protected from public disclosure.

The PCII Program seeks to facilitate greater sharing of critical infrastructure information (CII) among the owners and operators of critical infrastructure and government entities with infrastructure protection responsibilities, thereby reducing the nation's vulnerability to terrorism.

To implement and manage the program, DHS has created the PCII Program Office within the Office of Infrastructure Protection (OIP), National Protection and Programs Directorate (NPPD). The PCII Program Office will receive critical infrastructure information and evaluate it to determine whether it qualifies for protection under the CII Act.

Why was the program created? An essential element of ensuring homeland security is the protection of the nation's critical infrastructure by federal, state, local, and private sector efforts. Critical infrastructure is comprised of the systems, assets, and industries upon which our national security, economy, and public health depend. It is estimated that over 85 percent of the critical infrastructure is owned and operated by the private sector. Recognizing that the private sector may be reluctant to share information with the federal government if it (information) could be publicly disclosed, Congress passed the CII Act in 2002 with provisions

125

for protection from public disclosure. The security and protection of the nation's critical infrastructure are of paramount importance not only to the federal, state, and local governments but also to private utilities, businesses, and industries. There are several benefits for private sector participants in the PCII Program:

- Proprietary, confidential, or sensitive infrastructure information can now be shared with governmental entities that share the private sector's commitment to a more secure homeland.
- CII is protected.
- Information sharing will result in better identification of risks and vulnerabilities, which will help industry partner with others in protecting their assets.
- By voluntarily submitting CII to the federal government, industry is helping to safeguard and prevent disruption to the American economy and way of life.
- Private industry is demonstrating good corporate citizenship that may save lives and protect communities.

PCII may be used for many purposes, focusing primarily on analyzing and securing critical infrastructure and protected systems, risk and vulnerabilities assessments, and assisting with recovery as appropriate. The NPP Directorate plays a critical role in securing the homeland by identifying and assessing threats and mapping those threats against vulnerabilities such as critical infrastructure.

6

Prevention, Detection, and Response Factors across Sectors

Trust, but verify.

President Ronald Reagan

OVERVIEW

As the public becomes more educated on terrorism and what this nation has to do to be prepared to defend itself against terrorism, the public will be less inclined to ask what government is doing to protect us. They will arrive at the conclusion that everyone, including them, has a role in contributing to preparedness. Then there will be an expectation—from a wider audience than just the Department of Homeland Security—that companies, organizations, and government agencies responsible for critical infrastructure are taking proactive measures to ensure preparedness and protect the infrastructure from attacks. The world is not large anymore, and U.S. interests are geographically dispersed throughout the world, so our people, businesses, and government can still be attacked almost anywhere. It would seem, then, that now is the time to relook at how we practice security and what we are building in the way of preparedness and deterrence. Deterrence can work when the stage of imminent threats is not already at our door. If threats are imminent and warning messages have been issued, it may be too late to launch a deterrence campaign. The threat is in motion, and now the targets, whoever "they" may be, are at somewhat of a disadvantage. They must grasp how they are going to be attacked, and then react to it as quickly as possible and hope that the *detection* component of their preparedness program will be reliable as quickly as possible. When you need this kind of reliability, you have to put more dependence on "human factors"; technology, as advanced as it is, does not do a good job of being intuitive, curious, and investigative.

Preparedness is the overarching umbrella of security. Preparedness is the "desired state" in which we want our national homeland security program. When we as a nation have effective and efficient prevention, detection, and response capabilities in place across the spectrum of industry, government, and the public, we will have preparedness. If we would "humanize" preparedness and the components that come under it, it would be something like Figure 6.1.

Prevention, detection, and response are three broad categories of preparedness, and each has many subcomponents under them from closed-circuit television (CCTV) to virus controls to guards. I chose human, physical, and cyber because those are what DHS is using in its homeland security national plan—and at some point, we as a nation of contributors to homeland security all need to be on the same page, communicating in ways that we can understand one another. It is easier for us to adopt DHS language than for DHS to adopt the language of millions of companies and organizations. Although there are many configurations of security and preparedness components, Figure 6.1 is the simplest concept to grasp and includes business continuity and information technology (IT)

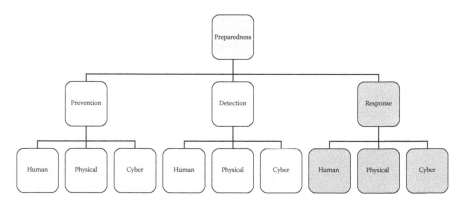

Figure 6.1 Preparedness components.

security along with physical security, and we should be able to see where they fit into this preparedness structure. Activities under "prevention" will generally consist of installing locks and access controls, installing CCTV, hanging up "No Parking!" and "Restricted Area" signs, installing perimeter fences, and using roving and posted security—efforts *to protect and deter.*

"Detection" consists of human, technical, or cyber abilities to detect and give off "warnings" that there are threats focused on our facility or that, possibly, others are getting ready to attack us. The detection component includes detection by means of humans, technology, animals, marine life, and insects. Regardless of how much technology you have in place for security, you should first rely on people for security-related actions rather than on technology. No amount of technology can replace the human factor to want to investigate further, leverage instincts, and use reasoning abilities to further investigate an event. Typical observations or inner dialogue a human would engage in to conclude or deduce what other actions may be warranted are as follows:

- I see you.
- I recognize you.
- I don't recognize you.
- I don't trust you.
- I must validate who you are.
- I need more information.
- I have a "gut feeling."
- I must ask more questions.

INNOVATIVE PREVENTION APPROACHES

"Reverse psychology" is a very economical and creative way which, under certain situations, can be used as a deterrence measure. We can enhance existing security technology, policies, and procedures through the introduction of desired perception. It's nothing new. People do not have to be psychologists to relate to the use and meaning of reverse psychology.

The use of propaganda and psychological operations (PSYOP) is a similar concept having to do with tricking or influencing people. The United States has used these methods, as have many other countries. One extreme example is from a report of a military operation from earlier decades where U.S. operatives left foot-long condoms on the Ho Chi Minh

Trail, presumably causing North Vietnamese Army (NVA) soldiers to hide their women as well as themselves. Other countries, however, have been less circumspect, often stumbling into embarrassing gaffes.*

Manipulating perceptions is a tactic used by many countries. During World War II, the Japanese dropped leaflets on American forces, trying to demoralize the enemy with the hardy perennial "Your girl is getting mounted by the strapping buck back home." To illustrate this theme, however, the Japanese used graphic pornography—a relative scarcity on the front lines. The effect of this tactic, says military historian Stanley Sandler, "did the opposite of what it was supposed to. It raised morale. Our guys loved it. They'd trade them like baseball cards—five for a bottle of whisky."†

One example of a large-scale deception operation occurred during WWII. *Fortitude* was the code name given to the decoy (or disinformation) mission mounted by the Allies to deceive the Germans about the date and, above all, the place of the landings in the famous D-Day invasion during World War II. The Germans were convinced that the British and American attack would come in the Pas-de-Calais area, and it was important not to disillusion them. They therefore had to be made to think that a whole group of armies was present in Kent, opposite Pas-de-Calais.‡

To deceive the German observation planes, which Allied antiaircraft defenses did their best to avoid, the local estuaries, creeks, and harbors were crammed with dummy landing craft. A giant oil-pumping head made from papier-mâché was erected, while large numbers of inflatable rubber tanks (Figure 6.2) were positioned in the fields. Plywood vehicles and guns lined the roadsides. For the benefit of the Germans, a team of technicians maintained constant radio traffic between totally fictitious units.

Fortitude succeeded beyond anyone's wildest dreams. Long after June 6th, Adolf Hitler remained convinced that the Normandy Landings were a diversionary tactic to induce him to move his troops away from Pas-de-Calais, so that a decisive attack could then be launched there. He

---

* "Dr. David Champagne, the 4th PSYOP Group's Civilian Afghanistan Expert, Who Says He Fell in Love with the Country as a Peace Corps 'Hippie,'" January 13, 2002, http://peacecorpsonline.org/messages/messages/467/2023161.html.
† Ibid.
‡ Ernest S. Tavares, Jr., Major, USAF. A Research Report Submitted to the Faculty in Partial Fulfillment of the Graduation Requirements. "Operation Fortitude: The Closed Loop D-Day Deception Plan," Maxwell Air Force Base, Alabama, April 2001, http://stinet.dtic.mil/oai/oai?verb=getRecord&metadataPrefix=html&identifier=ADA407763.

Figure 6.2 *Operation Fortitude* inflatable rubber tank.

therefore kept his best units prepared there, until the end of July, desperately scanning an empty horizon while the fate of the war was being decided in Normandy.*

Table 6.1 lists several concepts used by government, military, media, industry, and people to make others believe what they feel is necessary to achieve a goal or objective. Ordinarily, it is not something that could be relied on for a sustained period of time—eventually, the adversary would know he or she was being tricked. But it is an option that is thought of when there is a limited budget—it's just a matter of using the imagination—and lawyers to make sure that the activity will not create a liability.

A European counterintelligence officer once asked me a rhetorical question: If you could secure a facility with two good layers of security and add a third layer—bomb dogs, mean-looking ones—would the dogs add a comfort level? Of course, I said. Then he said, what if the dogs cost $35,000 but you only had $3,000; would you consider buying noncertified dogs even though all they could do was walk on a leash as though conducting a formal search? I did not answer the question because this is the type of question that, if I were to say, "Yes, I would use such dogs," I would not want to tell anyone. That information would have to be tightly—*tightly*—controlled. That would be considered *need-to-know* information only if my best approach was to use deception.

---

* http://www.normandiememoire.com/NM60Anglais/2_histo2/histo2_p5_gb.htm.

Table 6.1 Decoy and Deception Methods

User	Description	Purpose
Military	Psychological operations	Used by soldiers to persuade and influence perceptions and encourage desired behavior; the truth credibly presented in a manner to convince a given audience to cease resistance or take actions favorable to friendly forces.
Military	Decoys and deception	A "trick" used to gain an advantage in the battlefield.
Government, corporations	Disinformation	Preemptive dissemination of false information deliberately and often covertly spread (through planting of rumors) in order to influence public opinion or obscure the truth.
Military, government, media	Propaganda	A concerted set of messages aimed at influencing the behavior of large numbers of people; the message can be completely truthful but manipulated in some way to downplay or highlight something to selectively produce an emotional rather than rational response to the information presented.
Private sector	Honey pots	Used often by IT personnel to determine and identify network attackers.
Ordinary people	Reverse psychology	The use of a conversation where advocacy of one course of action persuades another person to do the opposite.

Any decision to use deception or PSYOP should be carefully studied and discussed with lawyers. If tactics are considered or used, they should be tightly guarded and disclosed only to a small number of people who need to know because the average American has a difficult time keeping secrets. As the number of people who know your tactic increases, there is a strong likelihood that the use of this method will be leaked. Then you would have to worry about the likelihood that your security weaknesses and protective measures would be disclosed leaving you openly vulnerable. Once security weaknesses are exposed, people are forced to make major expenditures to revamp security or immediately secure the vulnerabilities.

Because there are many things that can go wrong, it is important to evaluate all implications of a decision to employ these types of measures and consult with your legal advisors.

INNOVATIVE DETECTION TECHNOLOGY

There is much interesting research being conducted today. Government has researched the use of bees to detect explosives. By studying bee behavior and testing and improving on technologies already on the market, Los Alamos National Laboratory scientists developed methods to harness the honeybee's exceptional olfactory sense where the bees' natural reaction to nectar, a proboscis extension reflex (sticking out their tongue), could be used to record an unmistakable response to a scent. Using Pavlovian training techniques common to bee research, they trained bees to give a positive detection response, via the proboscis extension reflex, when they were exposed to vapors from TNT, C4, and triacetone triperoxide (TATP) explosives and propellants. If the bees can be trained to contribute to homeland security, can't every member of society be trained as well? Are we going to let the little ones do all the work?[*]

Rats are also known to clear a minefield faster than highly trained canines. The mine-clearing process is a two-stage effort; the rats comb a grid and clear an area. Then the canines come in behind them and validate. The rats sniff out the landmines and, after detecting one, they start to scratch the ground, alerting their handlers. "Basically, it's the same principle as with dogs, but because of their weight a dog could get blown away[;] rats do not have such problems and rats also do not get bored so easily."[†]

In 2007, a government agency began exploring research involving *chembots*, robots built of shape-memory materials that are capable of morphing into a new shape so that they can squeeze into openings smaller than their original form and reconstitute themselves on the other side, thus making not only a detection capability but a "kill capability," as well. A robot that is a real weapons system could be useful in saving human lives in dangerous operations where explosives or hostage situations are involved.

INVESTING IN RESPONSE CAPABILITIES THROUGH PARTNERSHIP

The adoption of the National Incident Management System (NIMS) from the Homeland Security Presidential Directive (HSPD-5) Management

---

[*] DOE/Los Alamos National Laboratory, "Detecting Explosives with Honeybees," November 2006, http://www.physorg.com/news83944407.html.
[†] Nikola Pavkovic, "Rats Are Called to Defuse Land Mines," http://mprofaca.cro.net/rats.html.

of Domestic Incidents has found many agencies, organizations, municipalities, corporations, and businesses unprepared to address strategic implementation, coordination, and training issues, affecting our nation's response to incidents.[*] The NIMS is the system by which all first responders would come together and respond to an incident. Many exercises have taken place through DHS funding and sponsorship where local, state, and federal governments, and the private sector tested their ability to respond to an attack. Exercises have involved simulated network attacks, pandemic outbreaks, and U.S. port facility attacks.

One such exercise was planned to address the concern that a poorly designed government response to the next terrorist attack could disrupt America's economy and society as much as or more than the attack itself. This concern is particularly relevant in the context of an attack that may be harmful but not catastrophic. In the event of a future attack, government officials will be under enormous pressure to respond swiftly, more than likely with limited information about the status of the attack or what to expect next. In today's news cycle, the public—and the situation—will demand a swift and decisive response perhaps before exactly what is happening becomes clear. Confusion, indecision, or false starts at government's highest levels will be magnified and may have long-lasting ramifications. Getting it wrong will be easier than getting it right. As the Hurricane Katrina experience has demonstrated, a lack of situational awareness, a lack of understanding of current plans, and an absence of effective decision-making tools can lead to disaster.

In the summer of 2001, a group of senior-level officials participated in an executive-level simulation. The exercise simulated a U.S. National Security Council meeting at which senior officials were confronted with a smallpox attack on the United States. The exercise illustrated the issues to be addressed in the event of a bioterrorism crisis, including the challenges facing state and local governments, the role and responsiveness of the federal government, and the likely friction spots between federal- and state-level responders and responses. Since it occurred before the September 11 terrorist attacks and the subsequent anthrax attacks, the exercise generated an enormous amount of interest in both the public policy community and the media. Among those briefed were then Vice President Dick Cheney; then National Security Advisor Condoleezza Rice; then Federal Emergency Management Agency (FEMA) Director Joe Allbaugh; more

---

[*] National Incident Management System, http://www.nimsonline.com/nims_training/ NIMS.

than 80 members of Congress; senior government officials and leaders, including approximately 20 ambassadors to the United States; and senior government officials from Asia, Latin America, and Europe. In addition to raising public awareness of the bioterrorism threat, these briefings contributed to the Bush administration's decision to manufacture 300 million doses of the smallpox vaccine.*

Companies often work in their own world, primarily concerned about their customers and their own operations and bottom-line impacts. The companies that I have worked with in the last four years across industry had security programs in place and vaguely understood the requirements for homeland security preparedness, but something was missing. The layers of security between humans, physical and cyber, must work well together in order to contribute to homeland security, but they are not yet smoothly integrated in private companies, and this is an area that DHS would like to see improve. This will be crucial, particularly in the response and recovery phases of an attack.

The national hierarchy plays a major role in preparedness, but there are limitations and inadequacies that impact its ability to prevent terrorist attacks. The analytical component of the intelligence community, fusion centers, and police forces is similar to private companies' independent security approaches in that the government entities do not all talk to one another and do not have mature skills in "predictive analysis." That is the type of analysis needed in order to attempt to predict where the next attack would take place.

Over the last few years, federal and state governments have begun the process of engaging Americans on a broad scale to help authorities detect activities that might be associated with terrorist planning. In July 2010, DHS launched a nationwide awareness campaign called "If You See Something, Say Something"™ hoping to educate people about the importance of observing and reporting anomalous behavior and other indicators of suspicious activity. On its Web site, DHS offers a simple explanation: "homeland security begins with hometown security. An alert public plays a critical role in keeping our nation safe." It is a simple concept that has caught on, especially in large metropolitan areas where the security of transportation systems is a big concern. There are weaknesses, of course, in this fractured method of "mass training." Deciding what constitutes suspicious behavior is one such dilemma. DHS advises everyone to call 911 if they see something happening and therefore, according to the Web

---

* Center for Strategic and International Studies, http://www.csis.org/hs/simulations/.

site, "the public should report only suspicious behavior and situations (e.g., an unattended backpack in a public place or someone trying to break into a restricted area) rather than beliefs, thoughts, ideas, expressions, associations, or speech unrelated to terrorism or other criminal activity. Only reports that document behavior reasonably indicative of criminal activity related to terrorism will be shared with federal partners." Still, there's a lot of room for interpretation. Guidelines from one state says this about suspicious activity: "The key thing to remember is that your judgment is the most important element in determining what is suspicious …" Every jurisdiction I examined offered its residents subjective indicators—from a "cold penetrating stare" to "sweating inappropriately" to an "odd smell." Even less subjective indicators rely on individual interpretation: "Taking pictures or videotaping in areas of no interest to the general public," or "someone filming or taking excessive photos of transit operations and equipment." How many people take photos of the famous San Francisco cable cars? How many photos does a terrorist need?

Clearly, there are many inadequacies that impact homeland security in government, in businesses, and within society. Collectively, we do not fully understand what is expected. Coordinating the preparedness effort is cumbersome and difficult for any one entity to manage. Yet, that seems to be the job of DHS.

The private sector needs to be aware of the shortcomings that exist and have surfaced in homeland security simulation exercises, because in the event of an attack, the private sector will be expected to know how it fits into the overall coordinated response effort. This effort is supposed to be managed under the NIMS system, which we should all be trained on. We are expected to understand our roles as business owners or critical facility operators during a crisis. If you have not yet taken the training, you can find it on the FEMA Web site. One of the absolutes that will be encountered in any response that will compound the unknowns, is that we will not know the who, what, where, or when of the event until we experience it. Remember that the event does not have to be a terrorist attack; it can be a natural disaster, a train wreck, a chemical spill, or an active shooter going on a killing rampage. Also, it is not known which jurisdiction the attack or event would occur, adding to the mystery of whom we would look to and to whom we would respond. One good example of this is the February 2013 ex-cop shooter Christopher Dorner who left a trail of victims and an indelible mark on the psyche of Southern California law enforcement.

CASE STUDY: CENTER FOR HOMELAND DEFENSE AND SECURITY (CHDS) ALUMNUS LEADS REVIEW OF SoCal SHOOTING SPREE

Ten days of terror by rogue ex-cop Christopher Dorner in February 2013 left a trail of victims and an indelible mark on the psyche of Southern California law enforcement.

A little more than a year later, Center for Homeland Defense and Security alumnus Rick Braziel, retired chief of the Sacramento (California) Police Department, has led a Police Foundation team comprising former law enforcement leaders in assessing the lessons learned and establishing a definitive timeline and history of the multiagency, multijurisdictional murder spree.

"It was a sentinel event that needed an independent review," Braziel said recently, returning to the center for a presentation to the Executive Leaders Program.

After writing a Facebook manifesto, Dorner killed four, including three police officers, and wounding three more. The report shows Dorner planned and strategized the attack in advance. The manhunt ended with the culprit's burned body found in a cabin near the resort area of Big Bear Lake, California.

"Police Under Attack" was released in May. The 102-page report outlines the facts of the case, gathered from the disparate agencies involved, and provides lessons learned not only for the law enforcement profession but also for the homeland security enterprise in general.

Complementing the document is a multimedia report featuring in-car videos and radio transmissions as they happened. Another section features memorials to the victims.

"You get a full appreciation of what really happened over those 10 days in Southern California," Braziel said. "Instead of just reading a report, you can see who the victims are. We wanted people not to just read about Christopher Dorner, we wanted them to experience these events."

In doing so, the report comprehensively sets forth the facts and chronology of the case, something often muddled in news media reports as the situation rapidly progressed over a far-flung geographical area. Ensuring accuracy in the report meant months of communicating with the individual agencies.

"No one agency had all the facts on Christopher Dorner," Braziel observed. "There were a lot of perceptions and a lot of myths, but no one agency even came close to having all the facts because it covered such a large geographical area and included multiple jurisdictions. So the Foundation report becomes truly the only collection of all the facts related to the case."

Beyond cementing a definitive timeline and factual history, the report offers lessons learned. Among them:

- Law enforcement personnel at all levels should become thoroughly aware of all aspects of the National Incident Management System (NIMS) and be able to adapt it to shifting circumstances.
- Agency heads should use NIMS and its three key constructs: Incident Command System, Multiagency Coordination System, and Public Information. The lack of full commitment to each of these three areas led to problems between agencies, the report said.
- Large agency leadership across the country must view multijurisdictional events as opportunities to collaborate and be inclusive with smaller agencies.
- Fusion centers are strategically placed throughout the United States and should be equipped and serve as preidentified unified command centers.
- Technology should be utilized to create a virtual environment providing real-time access to dispersed personnel. Regional communications among the responders from frontline officers to commanders, and vice versa, was among the top challenges as Dorner rampaged through several law enforcement jurisdictions, the report said, illustrating the need for a "rapid and effective communications system" for first responders in the region.

"While you think as a chief your message is being delivered the way you intended to your line employees, it is filtered," Braziel observed. "Every chief in the agencies involved had their message filtered to one degree or another. The same was true in reverse. The line employees and detectives mistakenly thought the chiefs and sheriffs were informed about all aspects of the case and efforts to find Dorner when in fact not all information made its way up the chain of command. In critical incidents like that you cannot rely on your traditional methods of communication. You have to figure out how to be faster than the media. It's a major undertaking that is next to impossible when you are competing against the speed of social media, but you need to try."

For one, classroom debate on NIMS gave Braziel deep familiarization from a multidisciplinary perspective. And, the ability to critically examine issues and offer constructive feedback is a skill cultivated at the center.

His hope is that the report can be applied in any homeland security discipline by any professional. And, he believes the type of students that CHDS attracts will find it immediately beneficial.

"The Dorner case is about a rogue former cop, but the lessons learned can apply to any terrorist event or any natural disaster, small or large," Braziel said. "This story needs to be generalized across all disciplines in such a way that if I were in a CHDS class with public health folks, fire folks, military folks, they would all see what their role would be in the lessons learned."

In the planning stages, a company may find that it has a specific liaison to interact with when things are normal and quiet. Yet, in a response effort when the incident is at hand, everyone goes into crisis mode, government representatives may be shifted around and switched out, and a company may not know whom it is supposed to be dealing with during the crisis. You can expect the scene to be chaotic. Knowing that this variable will affect response coordination and reporting, using the NIMS system as if you are a pro needs to be factored into your plan and procedures.

The reason that the DHS exercise lessons learned and the NIMS system are mentioned in this section instead of in a later chapter on training and exercises is because this information is a critical variable with tremendous potential to impact your response and recovery procedures. Furthermore, if no one in your organization has been trained on the NIMS, it is a survival essential for someone to be trained in the system. A catalog of NIMS courses are available online at www.FEMA.gov.

OTHER CONTRIBUTORS TO HOMELAND SECURITY

Though DHS's focus tends to be on the private sector responsible for 85 percent of critical infrastructure, there are other categories of businesses that are also vulnerable to terrorist attacks. Though no one has published a total number for U.S. businesses, indirectly linked to critical infrastructure are third- or fourth-party providers to infrastructure; we know there are many. We also know that there are many businesses that are vulnerable because they are colocated with or within close proximity of critical infrastructure, also referred to as *proximity threats*. We know that there are many iconic firms in the United States and abroad that are of terrorist interest to Al Qaeda networks or Jihad extremists because of their global symbolism of the United States.

If these businesses are not proactive, they could become targets of terrorists in future attacks or enablers to future 9/11s. For these businesses, there is no requirement to be a part of the national unified effort to put measures in place to secure and protect assets from terrorism. This category of business also includes thriving small businesses, which create two out of every three new jobs in America and account for nearly half of America's overall employment. They play a vital role in helping the U.S. economy thrive through the jobs they create.

While the concern is not that small businesses would stand out as front-runner targets, it is that, from their sheer volume, they could impact the U.S. economy, and one can easily surmise that many are probably linked to critical infrastructure. If that is the case, it is unlikely that any regulatory role-player is overseeing what security measures they have in place to ensure that all the links of infrastructure preparedness are cohesively protected. This category of private business is seemingly excluded from any government effort to protect facilities from terrorism. As a result, such businesses must rely on themselves and hold themselves accountable for preparedness. The federal government concentrates its funding and assistance on prioritizing the risk assessment and securing critical facilities most vulnerable and of high target interest, and providing for equipment and training of first responders. The level of assistance afforded to private sector critical infrastructure owners and operators tends to be mainly relationship-building, information-sharing, and providing guidelines on security programs related to homeland security.

RESPONSE CONSIDERATIONS

Information is one source of many problems and challenges to homeland security. Everyone will be seeking information in a response stage, and it will not be forthcoming. People need to know how first responders work. For example it may take firefighters two to three hours to get to the top floor of a high-rise, or traffic gridlock may delay first responders and people may have to self-treat or shelter in place longer than planned. The decision to shelter in place will need to be determined by the people in the event. Only they will know what the variables are—whether to leave right away, or go to high ground, or go upwind, or run perpendicular. It will depend on many factors that perhaps a firefighter can go over during a fire drill. Hopefully, you have met your local fire department and they have reviewed some of your emergency procedures.

As this nation strives to form, norm, storm, and perform as if we had all been partners for years in responding to terrorism, the media can play a contributing role as everyone's communications partner. There are certain roles that media may have to take on because all responders will be engaged in the event. Media may need to assume a first responder role, in which case there may need to be an extra person on the crew. By educating journalists on the profile of an attack, depending on when the media arrive, the timing could be such that secondary explosions have not gone off yet. Most attacks have multiple explosions. Journalists may be in a position to see other terrorists before they execute their attacks; they should be vigilant and watch for other acts that have not yet come to fruition. A second bomber will not have the look of other citizens in the area: ordinary citizens will look shocked and disoriented, whereas the suicide bomber may appear nervous and possibly heavily layered, but not likely to be in shock. We discovered this to be true in the April 2013 Boston Marathon bombing tragedy which is detailed next, fully extracted from the U.S. Senate Committee on Homeland Security and Government Affairs hearing, July 10, 2013: "Lessons Learned from the Boston Marathon Bombings: Preparing for and Responding to the Attack."

MINI CASE STUDY: BOSTON MARATHON BOMBING, APRIL 15, 2013

At 2:50 P.M. on April 15, 2013, two bombs were detonated 12 seconds and a few hundred feet apart on Boylston Street—outside the "secure zone" on public sidewalks just a short distance from the finish line of the Boston Marathon—an area teeming with marathon spectators and shoppers. Three people were killed at the scene and almost 300 injured; many of the injured lost limbs.

Fortunately, extensive preparedness measures to support the marathon were already in place. It is one of the largest annual events in the Boston area. An 80-person Multi-Agency Coordination Center (MACC) was already operating in the Massachusetts Emergency Operations Center. At the MACC were representatives from Boston's first responder community, public safety personnel from other municipalities on the race route, and key state and federal public safety agency personnel, including the FBI and National Guard. Additionally, on hand were hazardous materials response and explosive ordinance disposal teams, and State Police helicopters. A Medical Intelligence Center was set up to keep track of patients, coordinate resources, and share information. There was also a heavy police presence, medical emergency support personnel, first responders, and volunteers.

The emergency response to the bombing in Boston has been touted as textbook. But, as the FEMA Deputy Administrator stated afterward, "the fact that the response was so well executed wasn't an accident—it was a result of years of planning and coordination." The Boston Marathon was considered to be a "high risk" event, according to the interagency Special Events Working Group, which is managed by the DHS Office of Operations Coordination and Planning. Since 2002, Boston has taken advantage of the Homeland Security grant program to invest heavily in emergency preparedness education, training, equipment, and supplies. Additionally, tabletop exercises were conducted every year to practice responding to various scenarios. Area hospitals were prepared. On April 15, all injured were triaged, transported, and evenly distributed to emergency rooms in an orderly manner. As Dr. Art Kellermann observed, "Every hospital that received casualties had a well-crafted disaster plan that had been exercised prior to the event. Boston's healthcare providers reacted swiftly because they knew what they were supposed to do. That's how disaster plans work."[*]

Preparedness paid off in Boston. Within 22 minutes, all spectators and nearly 300 injured were cleared from the scene, the 19 critically injured all survived, and the terrorists were killed or captured within 102 hours from the time of the initial blasts. As Boston Police Commissioner Edward F. Davis, III testified, the success was "the direct result of dedicated training, relationships already in place, an engaged and informed public, and an unprecedented level of coordination, cooperation, and information sharing on the line by local, state, and federal agencies."

It is clear with the Boston Marathon attack that the media may be an enabler of communication. If they have a satellite feed into their network stations and first responders have no communication, media may have to be prepared to offer a hand to ease the response or recovery efforts. Planning this as part of their response effort may be a critical, if unexpected contribution to the overall effort.

The media will have some influence on how much shock the people in the event will experience. As such, they should rehearse scenarios and consider how they would cover events without promoting panic, and

---

[*] Dr. Art Kellerman is an emergency physician and holds the Paul O'Neill–Alcoa Chair in Policy Analysis at the RAND Corporation. His quote was part of his testimony to the U.S. Senate concerning key findings on the event from RAND Corporation research.

they may want to plan what headlines they would come up with for their next printing. What if they report that it was a "dirty bomb," but in fact it was not? What if it turns out that the attack involved a TATP (triacetone triperoxide) bomb?* Would the media know the difference? Having this basic education will be essential to preventing panic and an after-effect of people abandoning the area and not wanting to come back to work because they "erroneously" fear that radiation was dispersed in a dirty bomb—when in fact it was a TATP bomb. If we can educate people on basic terrorism methodology and terminology, they are likely to act in a less panicked and more proactive way.

PREPAREDNESS SNAPSHOT

Ultimately, preparedness will produce three components of activities, tasks, or focus for the purpose of achieving homeland security objectives. Incidents or threats will prompt workforces to take actions at every stage. If *prevention* measures fail, *detection* measures need to be relied on to prevent experiencing the attack or threat. If detection fails, one will be forced to go into *response* mode. That is what we want to avoid at all costs. There is much crossover between the three categories.

Figure 6.3 illustrates three pillars of preparedness with some of the measures that take place under each category. Each pillar builds on the next: if one pillar falls, the second and third should still serve their purpose. But if one and two fall, the third will have to be initiated, and there will be no reserves—we will be at full capacity containing, responding, and recovering.

All phases of preparedness consist of continuously gathering, analyzing, and assessing information: attending local TEWGs,† the FBI's InfraGard,‡ Homeland Security Advisory Council meetings, and security events. These efforts are part of a continuous process needed for developing and updating plans, policies, procedures, and practices for preparedness across industries and government, and for staying aware of threats.

---

* Officer.com, http://www.officer.com/web/online/Investigation/TATP—The-Terrorists-Choice/18$30796.
† Terrorism Early Warning Groups (TEWGs) constitute a multilateral, multidisciplinary, networked effort; see http://www.markletaskforce.org/documents/TEW.pdf.
‡ InfraGard is an information-sharing and analysis effort serving the interests and combining the knowledge base of a wide range of members. At its most basic level, InfraGard is a partnership between the FBI and the private sector. See http://www.infragard.net.

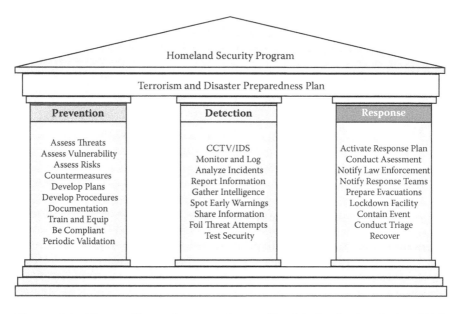

Figure 6.3 Three pillars of preparedness. (Graphic by Jessica Farias. With permission.)

Since the process of risk management is continuous—through periodic assessments and updates, and procedural improvements—monitoring for new laws and mandates that affect the organization is critical, and someone needs to be assigned that responsibility. Every month, the *Security Management*[*] journal publishes the latest laws, upcoming laws, and court rulings that affect the security industry, critical infrastructure, and workforces around the world as well as what mandates must be complied with. ASIS is an international organization with thousands of resources to create the most robust library ever on security and related topics.

HISTORICAL CASE STUDY

In the Khobar Towers attack of 1996 in Saudi Arabia, the leaders reviewed threat reports and put in place 36 of 39 protective measures after they had conducted threat and vulnerability assessments. Everything that could be

---

[*] ASIS, *Security Management*, http://www.securitymanagement.com.

physically done given the money and people resources and creative solutions was done. The number of fixes is mentioned not to show that one or two of the unfixed protective measures were responsible for the attack, because I do not think that they were, but rather to show that people were proactively doing everything within their power and humanly possible to prevent, detect, and respond to a potential attack. Their facility was not really their own to revamp to their satisfaction of preparedness. They could not, for example, move the front perimeter to increase the buffer zone (they did not own it and were not free to do so) or add Mylar film on the windows that cost millions of dollars because it was on a future schedule of procurements. They were living in a country where they had to depend on the host country's security and law enforcement to some degree. To mitigate the possibility of being attacked or being surprised, two sentries were posted on the roof of the building at all times two months before the attack; their job was to alert the others if there was any appearance of an impending attack.

On June 25, 1996, many of the residents of Khobar Towers were in their rooms. The outgoing commander was writing promotion recommendations in Building 133. Members of the 58th FS (unit in the attack) were packing in Building 127 and Building 131. The commander sat at the desk in his room, writing a note to the incoming commander who was to replace him. Beyond Khobar Towers, the final Muslim prayer call of the day was just ending.*

Staff Sergeant Alfredo R. Guerrero, a security policeman and shift supervisor, went up to the top of Building 131 to check in with the two sentries posted there. Once on the roof, Guerrero and the other policemen observed a sewage tanker truck and a white car entering the parking lot. They watched the truck drive to the second to the last row, turn left as if leaving the lot, slow down, stop, and then back up toward the fence line. It stopped directly in front of the center of the north façade of Building 131. The truck's driver and a passenger jumped out and hurried to the waiting car, which sped out of the parking lot.†

> The three security policemen were already in motion. They radioed in the alert and started the evacuation plan to notify each floor of Building 131 in waterfall fashion. A roving security police vehicle heard the alert from the rooftop sentries and rushed to wave people away from the

---

* Rebecca Grant, "Khobar Towers," *Air Force Magazine Online* 81, no. 6 (June 1998), http://www.afa.org/magazine/june1998/0698khobar.asp (accessed February 2008).
† Grant, "Khobar Towers."

building. They had managed to notify only those residents on the top three floors before they were shaken by an enormous blast. Before the wing operations center could activate Giant Voice (the sirens), the bomb went off.

The bomb that did the damage was not like the package bombs in Bahrain or the Riyadh car bomb, containing only a few hundred pounds of explosives. It exploded with the force of 20,000 to 30,000 pounds of TNT. The sewage truck shaped the charge, and the high clearance between the ground and the truck gave it the more lethal characteristics of an air burst.

As the blast waves hit Building 131, they propelled pieces of the Jersey wall barriers into the first four floors. The outer walls of the bottom floors were blown into rooms. With no structural support below, the facades of the top three floors sheered off and fell into a pile of rubble. Walls on the east and west ends were blasted four feet from their original positions, causing floors in several bedrooms to collapse. Building 131 did not collapse because it was made of prefabricated cubicles that were bolted together. Had it been built in a more traditional manner, it might have caved in from the blast.[*]

In the assessment and risk management scenarios, leaders had thought that the size of a bomb that could be used in an attack against Khobar Towers would be about 200 pounds. This was a huge miscalculation.

In May, just a month before the attack, the residents reported a suspicious act:

One particularly serious incident did occur in May. A car proceeding on the street along the eastern side of the compound did something unusual. The driver crossed the dusty median and banged the car against the solid concrete of the Jersey wall barrier. Then the driver backed up the car, nudged it against the barriers again, and drove away. Residents of Building 127 in Khobar Towers spotted the activity and reported it to wing security police. In response, the wing staked down the barriers along the perimeter.[†]

This appears to be a classic—*classic*—example of a dry run on the part of the attackers: to test the attack steps and see if the attack plan will work. A dry run!

In this attack, warnings and signals were indicating that prevention measures were not going to stop an attack. Detection measures were where help was most needed, perhaps asking the Saudis to provide

---

[*] Grant, "Khobar Towers."
[†] Ibid.

more random police patrols or moving all residents to the back rooms of the building, if possible. No one can think of all the possibilities, but this is one area where every perspective needs to be provided and brain-stormed. By reviewing past attacks, we can see what human factors are at play and leverage those planners with natural abilities for attention to details to help out. Generally, ESTJs (those possessing extroversion, sensing, thinking, judging) and ISTJs (those possessing introversion, sensing, thinking, judging) are needed for this part of planning—two of the personality profiles from the Myers-Briggs Type Indicator. The Myers-Briggs Type Indicator may be critiqued as good or bad, but this is one area where we may apply the concept or use of the Myers-Briggs test.* ISTJs (thinking introverts) function well in jobs requiring accurate record keeping of facts. ISTJs are quiet and reserved individuals who are interested in security.

---

* MBTI.com, "Myers-Briggs Personality Type Indicator," http://www.e-mbti.com/istj.php.

7

Human Factors
and Team Dynamics

THE HUMAN FACTOR

This chapter captures behavioral science aspects crucial to various aspects of homeland security and critical traits that are conducive to success. Today, relationship building is an important skill in the workplace. It is necessary to effectively interact, communicate, manage, and lead others. This skill becomes even more critical in the homeland security arena, particularly within the information-sharing component of preparedness between the private and public sectors. Preparedness and resiliency require the private and public sectors to leverage information-sharing networks so that timely responses in any situation can be carried out. In protection and response efforts, responders need a timely flow of information, that is, the movement of information internally, externally, up, down, and between public and private sector partners. But in a crisis, information may not be relayed in a timely fashion because of chaos and inaccurate details.

When it comes to security, most organizations often overlook the human factor—people. All security measures begin and end with the people. People develop the plans and strategies. People enforce and implement the plans and strategies. Yet, companies overlook this human factor and often develop a false sense of security simply because they have fences around their buildings, functioning high-tech closed-circuit television (CCTV) systems in place, security guards on patrol, and written response plans. None of the fancy bells and whistles will mean anything

149

if the people/employees are not factored into the preparedness plan and properly trained and tested. Instead, management places emphasis on nonhuman elements:

- Is our new system simple enough to preclude disruptions to operations or hindrances? If it is too complex, the human factor will take over—people will mentally turn it off. They will leave the doors propped open and take shortcuts that defeat the purpose of the security system.
- Did the employees get properly trained on this system? If there is no power and no backup power, can employees revert to human procedures and still respond effectively?
- If the incident requires human decision-making skills or social skills, does the technology in place have the ability to use judgment and make decisions? If not, do the people have sufficient knowledge to make critical decisions? How will they respond if a variable that had not been planned for suddenly surfaces?

HUMANITY IN CRISIS AND HERO MODE

Israeli citizens, military, and police are all trained to deal with crises by the numbers—it is automatic. For example, a terrorist went on a killing rampage, shooting, wounding, and killing teenage students at a school in Israel. Police were on the scene, but they took 20 minutes to intervene. An off-duty soldier putting his children to sleep in a nearby neighborhood heard the shots and ran to help. He ran past police, but not before demanding and obtaining a police cap so as not to be mistaken for a terrorist. He then entered the building and neutralized the terrorist with two shots. The human factor is best illustrated in this story and worthy of admiration—that a person would have the presence of mind to think strategically and tactically in the heat of a massacre, respond by the numbers, save students (and police), clear the building, attend to the wounded, and then say that he was not a hero and was just performing his duty is beyond words.[*]

The human factor also demonstrates to us that law enforcement and first responders, regardless of how well trained they are, may still freeze in the face of a crisis. Quite often, however, a leader will emerge. This

---

[*] David Shapira, http://web.israelinsider.com/Articles/Security/12702.htm.

is what happened when a bomb threat at a public school in the United States brought everything to a halt. Students were evacuated and held in an unprotected, wide-open area. The sun was hot, and temperatures were rising. First responders trickled in and out, but no one seemed to be in charge, nor did they seem to know what to do. Finally, after a few hours of standing around, an elderly woman who worked in the cafeteria took charge of the situation and rallied the first responders: "Here's what we're going to do. Let's move the children away from here. Call in the buses, and let's move them to protective ground in the shade. Someone is going to go in and clear the building and bring back water"; she feared the children were reaching dehydration levels. Once the building was cleared, she handed control back over to the first responders and returned to the cafeteria to prepare meals.

FEMALE TERRORISTS: THE HUMAN FACTOR GONE WRONG

The givers of life are not expected to walk into a building strapped with a suicide vest under their garb with the intention of blowing up themselves and everyone else in a selected location. The human factor is most visibly apparent in these situations. Security forces are really uncomfortable and unsure of what actions to take when dealing with activities that involve women as suspects. In my 28-year career of performing red team and simulation exercises posing as a female terrorist, there was only one instance in which a male was not outwardly affected by gender dynamics and took the proper immediate action—he denied me entry and handled the situation professionally, correctly, and with assertion. I later learned that he treated males the same way. Male and sometimes female security personnel show hesitancy, delay, and discomfort when dealing with women. This "human factor" must change, or our vulnerability to terrorism will increase as women become increasingly engaged in threat activities. Over the past few years we have become more accustomed to hearing about women in terrorist roles. Nevertheless, bloody attacks perpetrated by women still surprise and fascinate us. British-born Samantha Lewthwaite, dubbed the White Widow because she was married to one of the suicide bombers who killed 52 people in London in July 2005, is a good example. Young, white, beautiful, and the mother of three children, she would not attract attention as a possible terrorist. She blends in and does not fit our mental profile; we find it difficult to imagine her as a killer.

151

Yet, she is suspected of participating in the September 2013 Westgate Mall massacre in Kenya during which an estimated 67 people were killed; she is considered a very dangerous, considerable threat.

Recognizing the human factor in teams, joint committees, working groups, and security and emergency response partnerships is something that everyone must do to properly work within this dynamic realm. New information continues to emerge regarding dimensions of human interaction and behaviors. The research and theoretical models offered by social scientists, organizational behavior consultants, and management experts point to a compelling need to incorporate new ways of thinking and interacting in an ever-changing work environment. Today's work environments are structured very differently than they were in earlier decades, requiring different methods for communicating more effectively. In these potentially remote, virtual, or global offices, the staff is likely to be culturally diverse, adding yet another dimension to human interaction and increasing human factor concerns.

HUMANS IN CONFLICT

Having a sense of a team's individual and cumulative personalities and leadership styles helps predetermine what the team's crisis management abilities will be when it is faced with a crisis. While at one time, personality and leadership tests were more developed and were used only for research studies, there is tremendous value in applying these concepts to private and public sector teams. These tests provide team members with a framework for organizing and assigning roles based on natural and predisposed dominant traits. The results will produce a map of strengths that are often missed and not utilized when they are necessary. There are functional and dysfunctional roles that emerge in a crisis and in normal operations. By buying into the concept of personality assessment testing on a peripheral level, a team can begin to apply human factor models that can be perhaps more rewarding than other training. It is not only fun, but it is also revealing and practical/applicable. The language that people use, how they sense the environment around them, and how they learn says a lot about them. What type of language do you use? Does your language reflect a collaborative tone? Do you say "those people" or "our friends" over on the other side of the table (or river, ocean, etc.)? Do you create settings that foster trust and collaboration by your choice of words, or do you send the wrong message and put people on the defensive even before you have had a chance to introduce your message? Many leaders, managers, and supervisors are disliked by their subordinates, and often it is because these top-level executives have not had proper training or coaching. Do you have a mean look on your face? Or do you have a look that conveys, "I don't know how to handle this situation," "I'm uncomfortable," or "I am at the verge of reacting in the only way I know how, that is, to throw a tantrum?" In the end, people who react this way tend to do it because they have not learned "coping skills," giving off displays of immaturity that shut people off or make them feel uncomfortable, thereby closing the door to any dialogue. Dialogue is important if we are to find solutions to our problems.

Another human factor that needs to be monitored in the workplace is "conflict." Conflict can be addressed positively, and it can be viewed as an opportunity to make something better. Sometimes conflict can be sparked by emotions, or by stress, fatigue, hunger, low blood sugar, sleep deprivation, and alcohol- or drug-altered states. At other times, it is caused by personality differences, competition, and challenged beliefs and values. The model in Figure 7.1, developed by Kenneth Crow of DRM Associates,[*] is useful in understanding how conflict will impede progress, if not managed properly; or it can lead to collaboration, if managed properly.

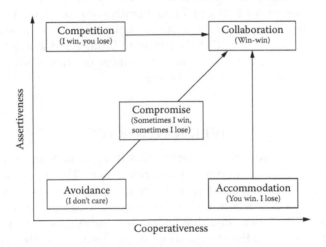

Figure 7.1 Collaboration model.

---

[*] Kenneth Crow, DRM Associates, 2002, http://www.npd-solutions.com/collaboration (accessed January 2008).

In Figure 7.1 above, there are two axes. The horizontal axis of *Cooperativeness* and the vertical axis of *Assertiveness* represent different approaches for dealing with conflict. A low degree of assertiveness and cooperativeness represents avoidance of an issue, or the approach of "I don't care." If both opponents (teams or individuals) feel the same way, they are communicating a mutual feeling of *Avoidance*. A high degree of cooperativeness and a low degree of assertiveness represent *Accommodation*, or the approach of "You win, I lose." A high degree of assertiveness and a low degree of cooperativeness represent *Competition*, or the approach of "I win, you lose." People generally believe that compromise is the ideal method of resolution. It represents a moderate degree of both assertiveness and cooperativeness, and says, "Sometimes I win, and sometimes I lose." This, however, is not the ideal solution to conflict. *Collaboration* represents the basis for a mutually beneficial approach or a "win-win" outcome where everyone walks away a winner and feeling good. The key to the win-win approach is to arrive at solutions that can mutually satisfy the needs of all sides rather than focusing on competing solutions that involve trade-offs or are mutually exclusive.

Once people understand that they just need to explore the options, they will find that arriving at collaboration simply takes practice, and in time it becomes easier to adopt a collaborative approach. Collaboration is what is needed to manage risk in the workplace. This would be especially helpful in settings where DHS is trying to build relationships and partnerships internally, with external government entities, with the private sector, or in accordance with a timeline.

OVERCONFIDENCE

In 2005, a call came into a security consulting firm from a member of the media looking to interview a security expert. The media representative engaged the administrative assistant in casual conversation while the company worked to accommodate the request. During the conversation, the representative remarked that he had just interviewed the manager of a major mall—one of the largest shopping malls around. He said that the manager of the mall felt his mall was safe and everyone was prepared to properly respond to a terrorist attack if one were to happen. The assistant asked the media representative if that manager knew what the hundreds of thousands of daily visitors to the mall would do in the event of an attack. Would that manager know that people, in general, react one of four ways to stressful situations (which a terrorist attack would definitely qualify as)? The first group will take a leading role—formulate a plan and tell others what to do; the second group will follow the leader and do what they are told to do; the third group will be catatonic and not be able to function at all; while the fourth group will respond with radical, uncontrollable behavior that will disrupt everyone and create more chaos than already existed. The media representative was surprised by the question and the concise explanation of what might ensue, and realized that he had asked the mall manager the wrong questions. If he had asked the correct questions, he felt certain that the answer would be that the mall might not really be as safe and prepared as he thought because they had not considered the human factor in the security equation. They had only really considered the physical security issues—what the security guards would do.

The human factor of security can also be seen in the aftermath of many recent U.S. disasters. The fire that razed The Station nightclub in West Warwick, Rhode Island on February 21, 2003,* killing 96 people, could have been less fatal/catastrophic if a few basic awareness principles had been followed. The evacuation plan for the building was inaccurate and not posted in full view of the crowd. If the people who were at the nightclub had been aware of the evacuation plan and knew where the exits to the building were, they may have been able to get out of the building before they were overcome by the fire. Instead, there was merely chaos leading to a catastrophic outcome.

When the initial events of Hurricane Katrina were captured and televised, one could never have guessed that such behaviors were being displayed by Americans inside U.S. borders. The scene looked as if it had been videotaped in a Third World country. The catastrophic losses from this hurricane might have been tempered if there had been more basic education and training given to the residents who lived in the area and more businesses had continuity plans. This was a defining event in our history and revealed what humans are capable of doing when desperate. One of the most noteworthy observations was that we cannot predict how people will react in such a catastrophe and how deeply they will fall into a state of shock in which all rational thinking goes out the window. They are no longer able to use reason or make critical decisions for survival, much like the Twin Tower evacuees who deferred their evacuation decision to the group they were in. We all need to be mindful of this phenomenon

---

* "At Least 96 Killed in Nightclub Fire," February 21, 2003, www.cnn.com/2003/US/Northeast/02/21/deadly.nightclub.fire/.

because we will not be able to count on certain people in a response or recovery event. On the one hand, we will have some citizens who will be told to evacuate now! On the other hand, others will be told to stay and shelter in place: *Do not get in your cars and drive to ...* (fill in the blank).

During the anthrax scares that followed 9/11, some of our nation's emergency rooms received tens of thousands of calls from panicked citizens. This flurry of activity overwhelmed medical responders and severely disrupted emergency care operations.* One can only imagine the scene at hospitals if the callers had simply shown up at these emergency rooms instead of calling in. If they had, could our hospitals have handled this volume, or would they have known how to manage such a crisis? According to some first responders, in the event of a disaster or broadcast of a Code Red alert prompted by a terrorist attack, the affected population would be expected to know whether or not to shelter in place and possibly self-treat until help could arrive, which could be more than three days later.

It is vital that companies, both large and small, create a security program that includes education and training for their employees, introducing the human factor to the security environment. Employees are the windows to the company and can be of significant help in detecting and deterring risks if they receive proper education and training. The education process should include the participation of all employees from the top down; it should also include getting input from all employees for how the plan or program can be improved and what they see as their role in security. Employees need to feel that they are a part of the overall plan or program in order for them to invest themselves in the process and be a viable part of their own security, as well as an important part of the organization's security. All employees must also know the possible threats that they may face and how they should respond to those different threats. By educating and training all employees, companies are taking an active role in creating a "team" approach when it comes to security. This will increase awareness and, therefore, increase detection of threats, allow employees to deter threats, and limit the need to respond to threats—all of which reduce the overall cost of security. The more a company educates and trains its employees, the greater chance the company and its employees will have of responding to and surviving an attack. An added benefit is that employees who are trained to be prepared value their company

---

* Elsa Lee, 2002, notes from attendance at UCLA International Institute Seminar on "Dangerous Exotic Bugs."

for having the employees' interests at heart, thus making them more confident and productive, and helping them to possess peace of mind. This attitude would promote human behaviors consistent with an alert and concerned workforce.

HUMAN TECHNOLOGY

Another aspect of the human factor in security is situational awareness. People in general tend to move from one place to another without being aware of their physical surroundings or what the people around them are doing. Through education and training, people must learn that they need to heighten their awareness. When they walk out of their house or go to their car in a parking lot, they must remember to survey the area around their house or their car. They should take notice of strange behavior, people out of place, and things that just do not belong. They need to make conscious decisions about how to proceed if, in fact, they *do* see something strange. Fancy technology can only notify us that something is happening, but only people can make decisions and react. It is important to remember that security is everyone's job—it does not just happen. It requires "living aware" and being super-observant.

During the evacuation of the Twin Towers, there were 15 minutes between the two attacks. This attack response required people to use their powers of observation and perception to make survival decisions quickly. It was reported in a National Institute of Standards and Technology (NIST) report of human behavior in the egress of the Twin Towers on 9/11 that some deaths were attributed to a delay in the decision to evacuate. The debriefings of survivors revealed that some deferred to group decisions instead of deciding on their own whether to stay in place or evacuate.* Many who were present during the 1993 World Trade Center attack relied on memory: it was safe back then to stay in place, so therefore it would be safe to stay in place again this time. Some people were not allowed to evacuate; they were told to go back to their offices. Some ignored the instruction and moved through thick smoke as quickly as possible, even though it seemed to them they were heading to the fire. Over three-quarters of those who were moving through smoke turned back instead of evacuating. The evacuation decision making varied. Some acted and evacuated immediately because the building shook. Others

---

* http://wtc.nist.gov/pubs/NISTNCSTAR1-7ExecutiveSummary.pdf.

waited for information. Seeing the explosion triggered a decision to evacuate in others. Some evacuated based on "something I felt," a survival instinct prompted the decision. Situational awareness seemed to be a key determinant as to who lived and who died.

Past studies have shown that people will not move through smoke, but the Twin Towers evacuation demonstrated that people will keep moving, even as conditions worsen. This incident also demonstrated that, in an emergency, floor wardens need enough information to be able to make safe decisions when the power shuts down and authorities are not able to communicate with them.[*] The floor wardens should not be "just anybody" or the lowest person on the corporate food chain; they should be people who have the ability to make rational decisions under stress when direction is not available or when things are not going according to the plan.[†]

The final report of the evacuation of the Twin Towers on 9/11 is a compelling study demonstrating that the human factor is often overlooked and underappreciated, yet it may be the only factor that we can each rely on to survive in the face of adversity. Understanding what people do in fires and how and why their actions may conform to or differ from the assumptions used in designing and planning for life safety in such large buildings will help shape future plans and increase the survival rate in future events and attacks. The most frequent reason given for turning back by those who did so was the smoke; others said they turned back because of crowdedness, locked doors, difficulty breathing, not being able to see, and fear. It took people 2 to 30 minutes to become aware that something required them to leave Tower 1, and 10 minutes to 4 hours and 14 minutes in Tower 2. Another disturbing element about this human factor is that people will consider this behavior as "I'm just minding my own business," but if a situation arises requiring them to intervene or report details about the incident, 90 percent of the people will report faulty information.

SUPERDIVERSITY

Not everyone has the skills, knowledge, or abilities to foster, build, and expand on relationships. People come in all shapes and sizes, and their personalities, skills, abilities, experiences, and capacity to work and

---

[*] http://wtc.nist.gov/pubs/NISTNCSTAR1-7ExecutiveSummary.pdf.
[†] Ibid.

interact with others successfully and effectively are shaped by many factors. These include where they come from, where they were educated, how much education they have, what technical skills they possess, and many other factors that we take for granted. When these differences are discerned as diversity, and diversity as a strength, problems can be solved more quickly than if no diversity was recognized in the group. These simple dimensions of the human race are generally not of importance unless the person is going to work in a critical position of trust and responsibility. Personal attributes or traits are very important in law enforcement, in military special operations, and in the intelligence community where people are faced with tremendous and critical responsibility and authority. Applicants for these career fields are tested in various ways to ensure that they are suited for the profession, that is, have the cognitive or psychological and emotional abilities to "carry a gun" or "hold the keys to the kingdom."

Tests are not necessarily reliable predictors of an employee's abilities, behaviors, or performance. However, much research indicates that under certain circumstances, these tests are helpful tools because they can reveal which personalities are suited for certain tasks. For example, we already know that people are either introverts or extroverts, left-brained or right-brained, creative or scientific, and highly technical or highly artistic. Opposites tend to attract each other until they get to know each other so well that the things they initially liked about each other, such as spontaneity and liveliness, later become the very things that are disliked most. Suddenly, they are loud and obnoxious or poor planners.

What is helpful about such personality assessments is that if we know who in our group is the technical introvert, maybe we could leverage that person's natural propensity for technical details and other strengths to write the important procedures for an emergency plan. Often, teams are not skilled to think in this manner, and the person assigned to such a task ends up being someone whose brain is not inclined to spell out details, follow a methodical approach, or project-manage the effort, and it ends up taking this person perhaps two months longer than it would have if a resource better suited for this task had performed it. There are active listeners, rational listeners, and multitaskers who are creative and go-getters but whose brains are overloaded with sometimes too many tasks being worked on to provide full attention to a single important project. There are also the creatively inclined and technically inclined types. Who will pay attention when you explain that he or she is responsible for meeting a DHS compliance requirement deadline or some other important task?

DIVERSITY AS A PROBLEM SOLVER

The value of diversity is often unappreciated in the workplace. Diverse teams will always outperform nondiverse teams in problem solving and in dealing with the unknown because of the uniqueness of their collaborative ideas, skills, and abilities.

Becoming skilled in the art of team selection can enable management and organizations to build teams of relatively similar or dissimilar members who together can accomplish things that amaze themselves as well as others.

The joint efforts by team members with differing talents will advance the solution of a single, undivided, perhaps indivisible problem, with one picking up where another got stuck by offering a new approach based on new heuristics for this stage of the problem reached thus far by the approaches and heuristics of others. A group with weak but diverse heuristics could accomplish things beyond the capabilities of even groups with strong but similar heuristics.[*] *Heuristic* means of or relating to exploratory problem-solving techniques that utilize self-educating techniques (e.g., the evaluation of feedback) to improve performance or improve what another individual or group has produced or solved.

A 2004 University of Michigan study[†] found that diverse individuals chosen randomly offer different perspectives that could result in better solutions than nondiverse individuals in a group. The same applies to a group comprising the best problem solvers. "If the best problem solvers tend to think about a problem exactly alike, then it stands to reason that as a group, they may not be very effective at coming up with the best solution."

In the 2004 study, diversity was not necessarily meant to indicate identity diversity—differences in race, gender, age, or life experiences—but rather differences in how problem solvers encode problems and attempt to solve them. According to the researchers, a person's value to solving problems depends on his or her ability to improve the collective decision.

"In an environment where competition depends on continuous innovation and introduction of new products, firms that take advantage of the power of functional diversity should perform well."[‡] The study of diversity clearly illustrates the importance of diversity in teams. By applying the concepts in this study, teamwork dynamics could be shifted into the

---

[*] http://www.garyjones.org/mt/archives/000165.html.
[†] University of Michigan, 2004, http://www.ur.umich.edu/0405/Nov22_04/23.shtml.
[‡] Ibid.

realm of private and public sector collaboration and enable the private sector to build a more comprehensive response program.

THE HUMAN FACTOR AS A TOOL

No one can predict when the next terrorist attack will occur. No one has access to limitless budgets to buy all the security technologies on our dream sheet, so what do we do? Does all the security technology in existence really work? It seems that as technology becomes more prevalent, we rely less on our human abilities. With the advent of CCTV, intrusion detection systems, computers, and the Internet, we have completely abandoned the importance and advantages of an employee's abilities. Why? What does it cost to employ the human factor as a weapon? There are many people in the work pool with natural abilities for security.

The human factor can help implement better security programs without breaking the bank or contributing to this country's—or an organization's—deficit. The loss of our ability to employ the human factor as a defense "technology" has resulted in the worst attacks to the American people by "the enemy"—terrorists have used the human factor to their advantage and our detriment. They have attacked destroyers armed with missiles. They have attacked the mightiest symbol of America's defense—the Pentagon! What does a Muslim leader really mean when he issues fatwas? Who can translate? Maybe someone who really understands what the fatwa might mean, another Muslim perhaps? Is there a Muslim who will help us, and if so, where should he or she go to safely provide useful information to help protect us against future attacks? How do we overcome intelligence failures and prepare for the next attack? If someone has the mental and emotional intelligence and the ability to identify the possible location and methods that could be used by future threats, should we seek him or her out? We cannot rely simply on our own counterterrorism abilities.

Some professions already recognize the value of the human factor and use it to their advantage. The recruitment, selection, testing, and training processes of certain intelligence professions are unique and different from anything that the average employee in a corporation goes through. Applicants for jobs in these professions are tested to see what their limits to stress and fear will be. Factors such as reliability, dependability, and trustworthiness must be determined as accurately as possible if the persons are going to be entrusted with the nation's top secrets. The

161

ability and manner in which an individual handles stress must be known before he or she is hired. Will they cave in under pressure if captured by an enemy? In the counterintelligence profession, the training received coupled with constant round-the-clock monitoring of threats produce individuals who are very adept at seeing and even sensing threats. This becomes second nature to them. Counterintelligence and human intelligence (HUMINT) personnel operate in the field independently, and often alone. They need to be able to quickly make decisions at all times. These people have an appreciation for the human factor—it is required in order to keep them alive every day on the job. Understanding other cultures and customs and learning to work completely immersed in them is critical. That means they have to be flexible and adaptable, with personalities that can stretch across a broad range of activities, scenarios, and circumstances (not unlike Oscar-winning actors). This is a valuable attribute, as they can quickly switch gears without hesitation. One day they are out on a high-speed chase driving 140 miles per hour, thinking about every turn to be made before they get to it, all the while hoping that they will stay in control of the deadly weapon at their fingertips. The next day, they might be in a fusion center rendering assistance with special analysis and reporting. Being able to move these human resources across functions relating to threats creates resiliency and redundancy in skills. This cross-functionality is something that security and intelligence planners in the public and private sectors should make better use of; they would benefit from it.

Not everyone adapts easily. Understanding a team's strengths and weaknesses is essential to all aspects of incident response. This allows for a team to leverage strengths and work smarter to be compliant and prepared without unnecessarily burdening a particular member of the team. Knowing what the leadership and team styles are helps determine what role each member should be assigned in emergency planning. Are there diversity strengths? Has the team worked together before or is it just getting acquainted? Being introduced for the first time in a crisis puts a team at a disadvantage, but getting through the crisis is possible if the right people come together—those comfortable with change, high stress, the unknown, unpredictable danger, and chaos. Those are the people who should be preselected to handle evacuations, serve as floor wardens, help first responders, and help with recovery efforts.

I have studied the behavior of humans for quite some time and now have taken an informal interest in animal behavior. Instinctively and often subconsciously, I find myself comparing the intelligence and instinct of humans to those of animals. It is unsettling to discover that some animals have far more superior intelligence and instinct, in an observable situation than some human beings. Their quick thinking and instincts determine if they will live or die, whether in the wilds of Africa or on the city streets of America. They do not have a lot of time to calculate risks, but their innate sense of danger is keen. That sense just kicks in, and they act accordingly. They do not hesitate. They do not waste a lot of time analyzing the situation. They move with a purpose, which indicates that they are wired to act this way, and evolution and technology simply have not tampered with their wiring. Even monkeys that communicate with humans through the use of computer technology have not been affected.

Some animals, elephants in particular, are like duplicates of humans in nearly every respect, with the same capacity for mental and emotional intelligence. Only, I have noticed that not all humans have that capacity— some lack mental and emotional intelligence. What is interesting about elephant behavior is that the herds maintain order and follow a certain social hierarchy. There are various role players, and there are babies, adolescents, and matriarchs. If one of the teenagers or one of the babies shows any signs of rebellion or resistance to group norms or attempts to deviate from socially acceptable behavior, the herd will not allow it. In a study that I performed 10 years ago on prisoner behavior, there was an emerging theme that reflected that of elephant behavior. Memorably, in the prison study, the prisoners' pre-prison behaviors were responsible for their prison sentences; society did not tolerate their behavior. The prisoners were imprisoned because they could not conform to socially acceptable behavior. Once in prison, there were also social norms. Even within the prison, some prisoners could not adapt to "prison-acceptable behavior." The prisoners had a way of policing their own and found ways to control unacceptable behavior. If animals and prisoners do not tolerate unacceptable behavior, should we as a society accept terrorism as a social norm in our country?

DYSFUNCTIONAL GROUP DYNAMICS

There are countless work behaviors that hinder an employee's ability to operate efficiently in the workplace and, if not recognized, these instances of dysfunctional work practices will also hinder efforts to assess threats and secure assets against them. The following two examples demonstrate how people often enable one another down the path of dysfunction without appearing to be aware of it.

Example 1: "The Road to Abilene | Groupthink" is a story by Jerry Harvey, as told by the Reverend John H. Nichols.* In this story, a family is sitting around on their porch in Coleman, Texas. The temperature in Coleman is 104 degrees, and it is very muggy, but the porch is shaded, and everyone is comfortable. Then, Jerry Harvey's father-in-law says, "Let's get in the car and go to Abilene and have dinner at the cafeteria." In the back of Jerry's mind, a little voice said, "This is nuts. I don't want to travel 53 miles in the heat of summer in a 1958 Buick to have dinner in a lousy cafeteria." But Jerry's wife said, "It sounds like a great idea." And Jerry heard himself saying, "Sounds good to me. I hope your mother wants to go." And Jerry's mother-in-law said, "Of course I want to go." Four hours and 106 miles later, they returned. The heat had been brutal. Perspiration and dust stuck to their clothing and bodies. The food, as Jerry guessed, had been awful. Later that evening Jerry said, quite dishonestly, "It was a great trip, wasn't it?" Nobody spoke. Finally, his mother-in-law said, "To tell the truth, I really didn't enjoy it much. I would rather have stayed home, and I wouldn't have gone at all if you hadn't pressured me into it." To which Jerry responded, "I didn't pressure you. I was happy here. I only went to make the rest of you happy." His wife said, "You and Dad and Mamma were the ones who wanted to go. I just wanted to make you happy." And his father-in-law said, "I never wanted to go to Abilene. I just thought you might be bored sitting at home with the rest of us." So, they all made a 106-mile round trip in the God-forsaken desert under furnace-like conditions to eat unpalatable food in a dingy cafeteria, a trip nobody had been looking forward to and nobody wanted to take.

Example 2: *"Challenger* | Groupthink" tells the story of the *Challenger* Space Shuttle. Seventy-three seconds into its mission, the *Challenger* Shuttle Mission STS-5 exploded, killing the entire crew. This disaster has been studied extensively to determine what went wrong and what were the immediate and the underlying causes of the disaster. The finding was that the fixture was sawed off and an attaching bolt was drilled out before closeout was completed. During this delay, the crosswinds exceeded limits at the Kennedy Space Center's Shuttle Landing Facility in Florida. There was a final delay of 2 hours when a hardware interface module

---

* Jerry Harvey, "The Road to Abilene | Groupthink," PDF, http://www.boisestate.edu/bsuaop/The%20road%20to%20abilene.pdf.

in the launch-processing system, which monitors the fire detection system, failed during liquid hydrogen tanking procedures. The *Challenger* finally lifted off at 11:38:00 A.M. EST. The decision-making process on the day of the incident was cited as an example or fault of *groupthink*, where the groups had convinced each other to think the same way with no one emerging to challenge even things that stood out as going counter to the group's decision. Although groupthink was clearly at play, it was not what caused the accident. The accident was caused by poor leadership.

According to the Rogers Presidential Commission's *Report on the Space Shuttle Challenger Accident,*[*] the direct cause of the accident was the failure of the O-rings. "They didn't fail because of groupthink; they failed because of the piss-poor engineering specs they were designed to, the lack of concern for mission failure under which the specs were created, and the launch decision being made despite all this. That's poor leadership, *not* groupthink."

Groupthink only comes into play as a contributing cause of failure on the day of the launch, in the meeting of managers of one of the contractors. Their decision to ignore their engineer's recommendations is talked about in the report, but they also talk about why there should have been other systems at work to question that decision, to ensure it was correct, and to ensure it was safe. The absence of that checks and balances process has nothing to do with groupthink, either.

> The unrelenting pressure to meet the demands of an accelerating flight schedule might have been adequately handled by NASA if it had insisted upon the exactingly thorough procedures that were its hallmark during the Apollo program. An extensive and redundant safety program comprising interdependent safety, reliability and quality assurance functions existed during and after the lunar program to discover any potential safety problems. Between that period and 1986, however, the program became ineffective. This loss of effectiveness seriously degraded the checks and balances essential for maintaining flight safety.[†]

What these findings seem to suggest is that teams that could end up making disastrous decisions should perhaps have a second team or member behind them whose sole purpose is making sure the team does not fall into groupthink.

---

[*] Presidential Commission, *Report on the Space Shuttle Challenger Accident*, 1986, http://history.nasa.gov/rogersrep/genindex.htm.
[†] Ibid.

DISCUSSION VERSUS DIALOGUE

It is important to understand dialogue—not stage acting but in the context of task accomplishment. Meetings are usually held to arrive at decisions. The outcome that most people would want from a meeting is that the *best* decision is made, not that just any decision is made or that another sub-committee is formed, but that a decision that delivers results is made. The group can then move forward. People busily hustle from meeting to meeting, and often achieve nothing in the way of measurable results, except to end up with yet another subcommittee all because they have lost the art of dialogue. So the question is, "What is the difference between dialogue and discussion?"

Discussion is the vehicle through which most people communicate. During discussion, we present our ideas and everyone analyzes and dissects them from their points of view. The underlying purpose of discussion, though, is to persuade, to make sure our own point of view is the one that is accepted. During the discussion, we will support our ideas and give our points more strongly until, eventually, others agree with us. We want to prove that we are right and the most knowledgeable, as does everyone else in the discussion. Great! With everyone trying to win the argument, no decision is ever made, and we eventually need to form a subcommittee to decide. Or the CEO or team leader uses his or her divine autocratic right and decides for the team.

Dialogue, on the other hand, is an exploration of ideas. It is not a new form of communication, but is the way the ancient Greeks and many so-called primitive societies are seen to explore ideas. During dialogue, everyone works together, contributing toward the idea. Remember that the team is greater than the sum of its parts; therefore, more is achieved from the dialogue as each person's ideas are added to the list of ideas. In a dialogue, no one is trying to win. Everyone is trying to learn and create, suspending individual assumptions in order to explore ideas and issues. It is a free flow of ideas where participants continue to think, watch, and teach each other. The great physicists Werner Heisenberg, Wolfgang Pauli, Albert Einstein, and Niels Bohr had many discussions among themselves on their individual theories and findings. As we know from history, however, it was their conversations (dialogue) that changed traditional physics because what they could achieve as a group exceeded what each could do as individuals.

HOW TO GET YOUR TEAM TO DIALOGUE

One of the leading experts on management communications is Graeme Nichol of Arcturus Advisors, who has successfully provided management consulting across industries and who shares the following observations:*

1. *Everyone suspended their assumptions.* Dialogue came to a halt when someone demanded, "It will be done my way." They needed to suspend their assumptions to really see the reality at hand. Suspending one's assumptions is not easy, as often they are so deep-seated that we do not even know that they are assumptions! Instead, we take them for being the truth.
2. *Team members were thought of as colleagues and equals.* If people see each other as colleagues, they will interact as colleagues. Team members will feel less vulnerable and less likely to either want to dominate the discussion or not say anything at all. Thinking of everyone as colleagues can be difficult in a hierarchical workplace environment. If individuals who are in authority come down from their lofty positions and talk to everyone else as equals, it facilitates dialogue; but if they like being in their elevated position and pontificate wildly, no dialogue will be possible while they are in charge.
3. *There was often a facilitator.* Note that a facilitator can help ensure that *all* assumptions are suspended. This means questioning statements and beliefs as they are mentioned. Facilitators are also important in keeping the dialogue moving. As a team gets better at dialogue, the need for a facilitator is reduced.

People are closer to achieving dialogue when team meetings are filled with questions. Questions indicate an attempt at understanding. Next time you attend a meeting, see how often a question is asked. No questions signal no dialogue. Teams can effectively use dialogue if everyone knows what is expected of them in advance, and if everyone has bought into it and truly wants the results created through dialogue. Dialogue is a more effective way of communicating, and everyone must be willing to practice using it. Learning to use dialogue can allow for better two-way communication.

---

* Graeme Nichol, "Dialogue vs. Discussion," *Ezine Articles*, June 2005, http://ezinearticles. com/?Dialogue-vs.-Discussion&id=43241.

LEADERSHIP VERSUS MANAGEMENT

Management consultant David Straker of Syque and author of the Changingminds.org Web site offers much academic and practitioner advice on leadership and management principles for positive influence and persuasion of individuals.*

What is the difference between management and leadership? It is a question that has been asked more than once and answered in so many ways. The biggest difference between managers and leaders is the way they motivate the people who work for them or follow them, and this sets the tone for most other aspects of what they do. Many people, by the way, try to be a little of both but are not very successful because the ability to be both is very difficult to acquire, let alone master. You are usually either a leader, or a manager with a birds-eye view, or in the trenches. Some people are great managers but ineffective as leaders, and vice versa.

By definition, managers have subordinates, unless their title is honorary and given as a mark of seniority. The manager and leader style differences can be described as follows:

> *Authoritarian, transactional style*—Managers have a position of authority vested in them by the company, and their subordinates work for them and largely do as they are told. Management style is transactional, in that the manager tells the subordinate what to do, and the subordinate does this not because he or she is a blind robot or a puppet, but in essence, because he or she has been promised a reward (at minimum, a salary) for doing so.
>
> *Work focus*—Managers are paid to get things done (they are subordinates too), often within tight constraints of time and money. Thus they naturally pass their pressures downward to their subordinates.
>
> *Seek comfort*—An interesting research finding about managers is that they tend to come from stable home backgrounds and lead relatively normal and comfortable lives. This causes them to be relatively risk-averse, and they will seek to avoid conflict where possible. In terms of people, they generally like to run a "happy ship."
>
> *Leaders have followers*—Leaders do not have subordinates, at least not when they are leading. Many organizational leaders do have subordinates, but only because they are also managers. But when they want to lead, they have to give up formal authoritarian control,

---

* David Straker, "Leadership vs. Management," Changingminds.org, March 2008, http://changingminds.org/disciplines/leadership/articles/manager_leader.htm.

because to lead is to have followers, and following is always a voluntary activity.

Charismatic, transformational style—Telling people what to do does not inspire people to follow. One has to appeal to them and show them how following will be beneficial. They must want to follow enough to stop what they are doing and perhaps walk into danger and situations that they would not normally consider. Leaders with a strong charisma find it easier to attract people to their cause. As part of their persuasion, they typically promise transformational benefits, such that their followers will not just receive extrinsic rewards but also somehow become better people.

People focus—Although many leaders have a charismatic style, to some extent, this does not require a loud personality. They are always good with people. Their style gives credit to others and accepts responsibility. They are very effective at creating the loyalty that great leaders instill. Although leaders are good with people, this does not mean they are friendly with them. In order to keep the mystique of leadership, they often retain a degree of separation and aloofness. This does not mean that leaders do not pay attention to tasks; in fact, they are often very achievement-oriented. What they realize, however, is the importance of motivating others to work toward a vision.

Seek risk—In the same study that showed managers as risk-averse, leaders appeared as risk-seeking, although they are not blind thrill seekers. When pursuing their vision, they consider it natural to encounter problems and hurdles that must be overcome along the way. They are comfortable with risk, will see routes that others avoid as potential opportunities for advantage, and will happily break rules in order to get things done. A surprising number of these leaders had some form of handicap in their lives that they had to overcome, such as traumatic childhoods, or dyslexia. This perhaps taught them the independence of mind that is needed to go out on a limb and not worry about what others are thinking about you.

The difference between leaders and managers is best captured in Table 7.1. This is, of course, an illustrative characterization, and there is a whole spectrum between either end of the scale along which each role can range. Some people (very few) can lead and manage at the same time, so they would display a combination of behaviors.

Table 7.1   Leaders versus Managers

Subject	Leader	Manager
Essence	Change	Stability
Focus	Leading people	Managing work
Have	Followers	Subordinates
Horizon	Long-term	Short-term
Seeks	Vision	Objectives
Approach	Sets direction	Plans detail
Decision	Facilitates	Makes
Power	Personal charisma	Formal authority
Appeal to	Heart	Head
Energy	Passion	Control
Dynamic	Proactive	Reactive
Persuasion	Sell	Tell
Style	Transformational	Transactional
Exchange	Excitement for work	Money for work
Likes	Striving	Action
Wants	Achievement	Results
Risk	Takes	Minimizes
Rules	Breaks	Makes
Conflict	Uses	Avoids
Direction	New roads	Existing roads
Truth	Seeks	Establishes
Concern	What is right	Being right
Credit	Gives	Takes
Blame	Takes	Blames

ROADBLOCKS TO EFFECTIVE TEAMWORK

As reported in a study "Communication in the Workplace,"* by Kate McLeod, Project Management Professional (PMP), of Algonquin College, there are barriers that impede effective communication in any operating environment. By breaking down and categorizing the issues, we find that there are three major roadblocks. These resonate with problems that DHS and industry face today as well as other organizations not linked to home-

---

* Kate McLeod, "Communication in the Workplace," http://www.allpm.com/modules.php ?op=modload&name=News&file=article&sid=986&mode=thread&order=0&thold=0.

land security. The problems in understanding each other impact the ability to share information or communicate information effectively.

One of the most annoying examples of easily misunderstood communication comes from the various numerical formats used to represent dates. For example:

02/04/03 could mean any one of the following:

April 3, 2002
April 2, 2003
February 4, 2003
March 4, 2002

It all depends on your perspective (i.e., where you have worked, where you are from, the context of the date, etc.) as to how the information will be interpreted at the receiving end. It is impertive to set up some ground rules or common language that the end users can rely on.

Roadblock 1: Lack of Proper Foundation

The first roadblock to assembling and maintaining a high-performing team is the failure to establish a firm foundation. Diverse teams need a foundation upon which a working relationship can be built. Ideally, a team establishes this foundation from the beginning, and continues to periodically discuss and modify elements of the team foundation throughout the duration of its efforts. A team's foundation consists of several components: mission clarity, stated values, empowerment limitations, and defined processes. Some experts in the field of team dynamics point to an unclear team mission as the single largest reason for a team's failure to perform at optimal levels. A team's mission may seem obvious, but it is vital that each member understands the team's purpose, vision, and goals in the same way. To achieve this common understanding, the team's project manager (PM) or leader must provide a shared purpose; short-term, long-term, and endgame goals; measures for goal achievement; and a timeline for goal achievement.

Next, team members must generate and believe in a shared value system of team interaction. Clear ground rules must be formulated by the team and accepted by each team member. These ground rules form the rules of engagement, and a framework for team conduct when interacting with one another and externally beyond the team. A code of behavior would be included under the rules of engagement and would address that which is important to team members, such as conduct for meetings,

171

integrity (keeping promises), timely communication of information, mutual respect, conduct for customer interaction, and speaking with a unified voice on settled issues. The rules of engagement should be established and then periodically reviewed. They should be modified at any time the team believes it is necessary, and the rules can be used as a compass to help find common ground when team conflict arises.

The term *empowerment* seems to be overused and misunderstood in segments of today's workforce. Empowerment is not a ticket for management to exclude themselves from the working level and then point a finger of accountability should things go awry. Nor does it provide the working level with unlimited authority. Instead, when managed appropriately, empowerment is documented with well-defined limits that are understood by team leaders, individual team members, and functional area managers outside the program. For instance, to help clarify roles and ease any issues between the program office and functional managers, drafting a memorandum of understanding defining limits of the team has been very effective. This is particularly important to ensure that members have authority to make most decisions regarding their functional area without having to constantly check with superiors. In addition, by assigning team and individual responsibilities, problems can be avoided that might otherwise arise when authority is perceived or unduly assumed. The delegation of authority must be visible to the entire team and can be shown via letters of authority or introductions at staff meetings. Team empowerment, when appropriately applied, provides a sense of mutual accountability, and is vital to the long-term health of the team. Equally important is the manager or PM's support of decisions that are delegated.

Roadblock 2: Linguistic Differences

Men and women often use different methods of interruption during group interactions. A typical male behavior is to jump in and interrupt the speaker, while on the other hand females frequently wait for a pause in the discussion. These differences can lead men to mistakenly believe a woman is not participating. Women can misinterpret the situation as well, believing that men are bulldozing them and stifling their input.

Men and women also have different linguistic styles. Linguistic differences can lead men to not always recognize women's ideas or to fail to give women credit for ideas generated in a team discussion. For example, women often include the use of an add-on question in their speech. The comment, "Normalizing the data shows a trend, doesn't it?" can make men think a woman is unsure of her conclusion when in reality the add-on question is simply a speech mannerism. Another example of linguistic differences is that men will often use the pronoun *I*, while women will often use the term *we*. This, too, can lead men to misinterpret a woman's statements and vice versa.

A final example of linguistic differences that can lead to miscommunication is the common use of qualifiers in women's speech. Men are not as prone to tag qualifiers such as *probably* onto the end of sentences, and this stylistic difference can add to confusion and misinterpretation. One method of turning team conflict into synergy is to teach team members to recognize conflict and then reinforce self-resolution. Team members need to be trained in conflict resolution methods to enable problem solving without finger pointing. The lack of training can result in a failure to understand differences and may increase the conflict level. Once trained, team members in conflict must agree that there is a problem, agree on just exactly what the problem is, search for a solution, agree on what each must do to mitigate the issue, and then follow up. Individuals learn to resolve differences by acting early to acknowledge conflict, directly engaging the other party with whom the conflict exists, responding rationally and without emotion, and dealing with each other honestly.

At times, management needs to recognize when self-resolution approaches are not effective and intervene in the situation. In such cases, the manager or PM should resolve the conflict with all parties present. The first step is to hold a meeting for the sole purpose of resolving the conflict. The PM needs to get those in conflict to recognize a problem exists and allow them to define the problem. Technology should not be used to avoid uncomfortable issues; face-to-face meetings work best. Initially the PM should strive to mediate, not judge. This is best achieved by being open-minded and actively listening. Active listening fosters feelings of acceptance and appreciation, saves time, keeps team members responsible for the issue, and builds relationships. The goal is to create an environment of healthy discussion of viewpoints and to foster candor. As such, the person at the top should withhold judgment until the situation is fully understood.

Roadblock 3: Conflicts

The third roadblock to effective teaming is the inability to resolve conflicts. Conflict in any team is inevitable, and many successful managers agree that team conflict is healthy—even vital. However, conflict becomes unhealthy if not managed appropriately. Typical reasons for conflict include role ambiguity and disagreements over methods, goals, procedures, responsibilities, values, or facts. Team facilitators and project managers can ensure the most prevalent sources of conflict are avoided by addressing the roadblocks identified. Yet, even those who carefully plan to avoid the principal roadblocks must still actively manage conflict. It is best to manage conflict by providing team members the tools to resolve conflicts themselves and by quickly addressing issues when self-resolution approaches are not successful.

Another challenge in making teams function efficiently is when they are composed of civilians and military members or industry-mixed people. While this situation is often not a significant issue, it sometimes can hinder team capability. Issues can stem from perceptions; biases of the other group; differences in organizational backgrounds and cultural backgrounds; and power interests.

For instance, due to typically brief job assignments, military personnel tend to hold a shorter-term focus while civilians often have a longer-term focus. This can result in differing priorities and conflict. When conflict exists, civilians tend to think military personnel treat civilians as second-class citizens; however, the military team members are often unaware of the perception. Military members also sometimes perceive that civilians are less motivated and are driven more by money than by doing the right thing for the effort, organization, or team. Furthermore, civilians are sometimes perceived as clock watchers (implying a lack of commitment to a cause), so it is a good idea to set guidelines for schedule adherence.

In general, military participants are considered better leaders because they are good at caring and coaching, but they often apply these skills only to military subordinates and often overlook the need to coach civilians. Should this type of conflict creep its way into a planning environment, a leader would be well advised to take time to train each group about the other's culture. "Dictate and take-charge types" will be most effective when they recognize and alter their leadership style from the field to the corporate setting. Each group type needs to recognize the benefit of both functional expertise and operational experience.

CHAPTER EXERCISE

Diversity in a team is great, and often people learn from the differences of other members, but it is important to keep one factor in mind: the differences should be distinct so as to lend helpful ideas to the group effort, but not so far apart that group members cannot relate to, understand, or communicate with one another.

Here's an example: An owner has a dog and a cat; the dog and cat get along. They have lived together since they were a puppy and kitten. They tolerate each other, and sometimes the cat will even groom the dog, and occasionally they will be found sleeping beside each other. They are slightly different, but they seemingly relate to each other and get along. If we had tried to pair the dog with a small water turtle, however, the teaming effort might not have worked because they are too dissimilar. The dog might have tried to put the turtle in his mouth, thinking that the turtle was a toy. The turtle would probably have wanted to run away and not have anything to do with the dog.

A team needs to come together to solve a problem. The company is going to bring all the business unit managers together so that they can report on the progress of the DHS National Infrastructure Protection Plan (NIPP) and make decisions on what information is needed and how to submit the pertinent information to DHS that the company has braved to share.

The manager from human resources is present; others include the manager of finance and the manager of marketing. The manager of the IT department has sent a level 2 help desk support member in his place. The risk manager is being represented by a temp hired for the week. Is this a good diverse group? Was this proper delegation on the part of the IT manager and risk manager? The president has also showed up in place of the manager of operations. Will every member be able to provide the critical information and make the decisions required to achieve the objective? Why or why not? This is not an uncommon practice among companies in both the private and public sectors, and it is a problem that must not continue if we are to effectively plan for preparedness and develop solutions against terrorism.

8

Innovative Ideas for Change

Whatever your mind can conceive and can believe, it can achieve.

Napoleon Hill

OVERVIEW

Most businesses can often detect when an outsider (nonemployee) tries to access company data either physically or electronically. As soon as this awareness is recognized, the company can then mitigate the threat of the potential outsider theft. However, a thief is harder to detect when he or she is on the inside doing the dirty deeds from within. The most damage can be caused by the insider: the employee with legitimate access who can steal solely for personal gain, or who can spy or steal company information or products in order to benefit another organization or country. According to the FBI, theft of intellectual property is an increasing threat to organizations and can go unnoticed for months or even years. There are increased incidents of employees taking proprietary information when they believe they will be or are searching for a new job.

Appendix E at the end of the book provides an FBI brochure providing information on how to detect an insider threat and provides tips on how to safeguard a company's trade secrets. Congress continues to "expand and strengthen criminal laws for violations of intellectual property rights to protect innovation and ensure that egregious or persistent intellectual property violations do not merely become a standard cost of doing business."

A domestic or foreign business competitor or foreign government intent on illegally obtaining proprietary information and trade secrets may wish to resort to espionage and clandestine tactics in order to gain access to nonpublic information. Alternatively, they may try to recruit an existing employee to do the same thing.

Personal factors that cause insiders to steal include a variety of motives or personal situations that entice them or compel them to engage in espionage or theft against their employer, they include:

- *Greed or financial need*—A belief that money can fix anything. Excessive debt or overwhelming expenses.
- *Anger/revenge*—Disgruntlement to the point of wanting to retaliate against the organization.
- *Problems at work*—A lack of recognition, disagreements with coworkers or managers, dissatisfaction with the job, a pending layoff.
- *Ideology/identification*—A desire to help the underdog or a particular cause.
- *Divided loyalty*—Allegiance to another person or company, or to a country besides the United States.
- *Adventure/thrill*—Want to add excitement to their life, intrigued by clandestine activity, "James Bond wannabe."
- *Vulnerability to blackmail*—Extramarital affairs, gambling, fraud.
- *Ego/self-image*—An "above the rules" attitude or desire to repair wounds to their self-esteem. Vulnerability to flattery or the promise of a better job. Often coupled with anger/revenge or adventure/thrill.
- *Ingratiation*—A desire to please or win the approval of someone who could benefit from insider information with the expectation of returned favors.
- *Compulsive and destructive behavior*—Drug or alcohol abuse, or other addictive behaviors.
- *Family problems*—Marital conflicts or separation from loved ones.

Organizational factors that contribute to the insider's success include the availability and ease of acquiring proprietary, classified, or other protected materials; providing access privileges to those who do not need it; proprietary or classified information is not labeled as such or is incorrectly labeled; the ease that someone may exit the facility (or network system) with proprietary, classified, or other protected materials.

There are several measures one can take to protect from insider threat. Tighten up undefined policies regarding working from home on projects of a sensitive or proprietary nature. Do not create a perception that security is lax and the consequences for theft are minimal or nonexistent. Be careful not to place unnecessary time pressure that makes employees feel rushed. They may inadequately secure proprietary or protected materials, or not fully consider the consequences of their actions.

Employees are generally not trained on how to properly protect proprietary information. Take time to train and educate them. Be sure they understand the consequences of violating security procedures and policies. Never let any employee or consultant take proprietary or other material home via documents, thumb drives, computer disks, or e-mail without authorization particularly those of interest to foreign entities or business competitors.

The following is an abbreviated list of possible red flag indicators that someone is stealing information or taking it from your premises without authorization:

1. Unnecessarily copies material, especially if it is proprietary or classified.
2. Remotely accesses the computer network while on vacation, sick leave, or at other odd times.
3. Disregards company computer policies regarding installing personal software or hardware, accesses restricted Web sites, conducts unauthorized searches, or downloads confidential information.
4. Works odd hours without authorization; notable enthusiasm for overtime work, weekend work, or unusual schedules when clandestine activities could be more easily conducted.
5. Short trips to foreign countries for unexplained or strange reasons. Unexplained affluence; buys things that they cannot afford on their household income.
6. Engages in suspicious personal contacts, such as with competitors, business partners, or other unauthorized individuals.
7. Shows unusual interest in the personal lives of coworkers; asks inappropriate questions regarding finances or relationships.
8. Concern that they are being investigated; leaves "booby traps" to detect any searches of their work area or home; searches for listening devices or cameras.
9. Many people experience or exhibit some or all of the above to varying degrees; however, most people will not cross the line and commit a crime.

In order to minimize the risk of insider threat, organizations need to do their part to deter intellectual property theft, such as:

- Educate and regularly train employees on security protocols and policies.
- Ensure that proprietary information is adequately, if not robustly, protected.
- Use appropriate screening processes to select new employees.
- Provide nonthreatening, convenient ways for employees to report suspicious activities.
- Routinely monitor computer networks for suspicious activity.
- Ensure security (to include computer network security) personnel have the tools they need to do their job; make sure you have hired adequate people to perform security functions.

Getting Assistance from the Federal Bureau of Investigation

When it comes to insider threat, the FBI provides tools and resources to assist private businesses in securing their assets or assessing whether there is an insider threat crime in progress. If there is any suspicion that it is affiliated with a foreign government, report it immediately. Being aware of potential issues, exercising good judgment, and conducting discrete inquiries will help businesses ascertain if there is a spy inside their company.

If you believe one of your employees is a spy or is stealing company trade secrets, do not alert the person to the fact that he or she is under suspicion. Instead, seek assistance from trained counterintelligence experts such as the FBI or specialty consultants with experience in counterintelligence. The FBI has the tools and experience to identify and mitigate such threats. If asked to investigate, the FBI will minimize the disruption to businesses, and safeguard privacy and data. When necessary, the FBI seeks protective orders to preserve trade secrets and business confidentiality. The FBI also provides security and counterintelligence training, or awareness seminars, to the private sector upon request. The sections that follow address methods for assessing and building skills that are essential to change work cultures and improve security practices.

ORGANIZATIONAL LEADERSHIP

Organizational leadership (OL) is the study of efficiency and effectiveness in the workplace through input that maximizes output in an efficient and effective way. It includes the study of leadership and management dimensions, the effective and efficient use of teams, and successful team dynamics, among many other things. Both elements—efficiency and effectiveness—are important. We know that workforces can be efficient but not effective, and effective but not efficient. Here is the best example I can offer to demonstrate this concept: A dancer just completed rehearsing the steps to a Broadway show. The steps involved 60 minutes of 100 moves. The 100 moves were carried out smoothly, which was effective, but they took 75 minutes to perform, which was not efficient.

By understanding the many dimensions of people, it is possible to have a high-performing organization composed of people who understand their strengths and weaknesses, capitalizing on the collective strengths of the organization to achieve high-performance teams in the workplace, on the battlefield, at client sites, and in homeland security crises. Once we recognize that we have to implement change, how do we do that? We can change by doing the following:

- Watching others
- Repetition of a newly learned behavior or skills
- Using "mavericks" to influence groups
- From the top and bottom both simultaneously pushing the change to a meeting point

All organizations need a library. In your library, you should have security, intelligence, and terrorism knowledge materials; management tools to self-manage and project manage; as well as time management tools and resources. Tools can consist of anything that equips your organization with a better way of conducting business—from new methods, models, theories, books, videos, games, exercises, templates, and checklists to case studies. There is no particular ranking or listing of which tools to obtain first or which ones to apply first. This is a subjective process but one that can stimulate action and achieve the mutual goals of having preparedness plans in place for prevention, detection, and response to terrorism and other disasters at work and at home—and being a valued employee or team member to the organization.

The goal of this chapter is to provide solutions for increasing the knowledge and skills that are necessary to enable preparedness. It cannot present you with an all-encompassing set of solutions, but if you walk away with two or three ideas that help you or your organization to train, operate, and communicate more effectively and efficiently, that is a major achievement. Ultimately, people need to do what they can to build skills that contribute to the protection of critical infrastructures.

PROBLEM-SOLVING EXERCISES

These tools help you understand complicated, difficult situations. Without tools, problems might seem huge, overwhelming, and excessively complex, or quite simply people are working with "sensory overload" and simply need a checklist or quick reference guide to get through a problem.

The following techniques come from MindTools.com, a Web site offering many management tools for today's problems.* The following exercises help people conduct a rigorous analysis of the problems faced. They help people look at as many factors as possible in a structured and methodical way. They give you a starting point in business problem solving (and other problem-solving situations) where other people would just feel helpless and intimidated by the situation. In the area of homeland security, there are many problems that we need to solve to be effective.

Appreciation Exercises: Extracting Maximum Information from Facts

Appreciation is a very simple but powerful technique for extracting the maximum amount of information from a simple fact.[†]

How to Use the Tool
Starting with a fact, ask the question, "So what?" (that is, what are the implications of that fact?). Keep on asking that question until you have drawn all possible inferences.

Example
Appreciation is a technique used by military planners, so we will take a military example:

Fact: It rained heavily last night.
So what?
The ground will be wet.
So what?
It will turn into mud quickly.

---

[*] "Appreciation (Situational)," Mind Tools, http://www.mindtools.com/pages/article/newTMC_01.htm.
[†] Ibid.

So what?

*If many troops and vehicles pass over the same ground, movement will be pro-
gressively slower and more difficult as the ground gets muddier and
more difficult.*

So what?

*Where possible, stick to paved roads. Otherwise, expect movement to be much
slower than normal.*

While it would be possible to reach this conclusion without the use of a
formal technique, appreciation provides a framework within which you
can extract information quickly, effectively, and reliably.

Key Points

Repeatedly asking "so what?" helps you to extract all important information implied by a fact.

5 Whys: Quickly Getting to the Root of a Problem

Why Use the Tool?

The *5 Whys* is a simple problem-solving technique that can help you to get
to the root of a problem quickly. But that is all it is, and the more complex
things get, the more likely it is to lead you down a false trail.

Made popular in the 1970s by the Toyota Production System, the *5
Whys* strategy involves looking at any problem and asking, "Why?" and
"What caused this problem?"

Very often, the answer to the first why will prompt another why, and
the answer to the second why will prompt another, and so on, hence the
name "5 *Whys* strategy."

It helps to quickly determine the root cause of a problem. It is easy to
learn and apply.

How to Use the Tool

When looking to solve a problem, start at the end result and work
backward (toward the root cause), continually asking why. This will
need to be repeated over and over until the root cause of the problem
becomes apparent.

183

Example

The following is an example of the 5 *Whys* analysis as an effective problem-solving technique:

> Why is our client, Hinson Corp., unhappy? Because we did not deliver our services when we said we would.
>
> Why were we unable to meet the agreed-upon timeline or schedule for delivery? The job took much longer than we thought it would.
>
> Why did it take so much longer? Because we underestimated the complexity of the job.
>
> Why did we underestimate the complexity of the job? Because we made a quick estimate of the time needed to complete it and did not list the individual stages needed to complete the project.
>
> Why didn't we do this? Because we were running behind on other projects. We clearly need to review our time estimation and specification procedures.

Key Points

The 5 *Whys* strategy is an easy and often effective tool for uncovering the root of a problem. Because it is so elementary in nature, it can be adapted quickly and applied to almost any problem. Bear in mind, however, that if it does not prompt an intuitive answer, other problem-solving techniques may need to be applied.[*]

WHY WORKFORCE BREAKDOWN IS CRITICAL (BY PERSONALITY TYPE, LEADERSHIP STYLE, AND TEAM ROLE)

It is imperative that organizations understand their workforce in terms of their personality type, leadership style, and team role. By understanding its workforce, an organization will be able to predict decision making, reactions, values, motivations, and skills of their employees and put these factors to their highest and best use for the organization's success. Organizations will also be able to understand and appreciate the differences between all of their employees and realize that each one has something different to contribute. In understanding their leadership type, an organization will be able to create a team of individuals who operate as a whole.

---

[*] "5 Whys," Mind Tools, http://www.mindtools.com/pages/article/newTMC_5W.htm.

Another reason why it is important to understand your workforce breakdown is because your workforce will determine whether your organization will survive an attack. By realizing that all employees do not react in the same way to a crisis situation or to chaos, employers will be better prepared to deal with the reactions and educate their employees so that they can survive an attack. In general, people will react in one of four ways to stress or crises: (1) the employee will be calm, take a leadership role, and direct others in a manner that will lead to survival; (2) the employee will follow a leader, do what he or she is told, and contribute to the survival; (3) the employee will be catatonic, he or she will not be able to function at any level, and someone else will have to physically move him or her in order for the latter to survive; and (4) the employee will be out of control and possibly create more stress and chaos. Clearly, if an organization understands this and provides education for its workforce so that they understand this too, everyone will benefit and the chances for survival of an attack increase.

Theory X and Theory Y

Employees come in many varieties but can be generally divided into two groups: employees who take charge of their job, take responsibility for their actions, and operate with little or no supervision; and employees who are unmotivated by their job, lack focus, and are thought to operate only when tightly supervised and told what to do, when to do it, and how to do it. This all boils down to motivation.

Social psychologist Douglas McGregor of Massachusetts Institute of Technology (MIT) expounded two contrasting theories on human motivation and management in the 1960s.* Douglas McGregor's Theory X and Theory Y models make assumptions about how motivation affects different employees. In Theory X, employees are assumed to dislike working, are unmotivated, and therefore need constant pushing, tight supervision, and direction to complete their job tasks. Theory Y employees are assumed to like working, are motivated, and therefore do not need the push, tight supervision, or constant directions; they complete their job tasks on their own. While these are just theories, it is easy to understand how, in some circumstances where an exact product or outcome is expected, Theory X supervision with harsh controls and constant direction would be expected so that the product or outcome can be predicted. However,

---

* "Douglas McGregor," http://www.mindtools.com/pages/article/newLDR_74.htm.

under Theory Y, supervision understands that most employees want to feel in control of their job, and they want to contribute to the organization. They want to be treated as responsible and valued employees, and when treated as such, they feel like a part of the organization and want to do an even better job.

As employees are the greatest asset an organization has, it is critical that management understands that most employees should filter under Theory Y if they want to have an organization that operates as a unit and comes together during times of chaos or crises. Employees, when properly motivated through education, pay increases, or other perks, can provide imagination, creativity, and ingenuity that can help organizations achieve their potential, solve work issues, and improve retention and recruitment. Management should never underestimate employees' potential and should learn how to motivate all employees to each reach their potential, be a part of the organizational team, and share in the successes of the organization that they helped to create by their efforts. Conversely, if a manager feels that an employee falls under Theory X, it would be wise to determine what role such a person could be counted on in a crisis, where there is little room for tight supervision.

Myers-Briggs Type Indicator

The Myers-Briggs Type Indicator (MBTI) is a personality questionnaire designed to identify certain psychological differences according to the typological theories of Carl Gustav Jung, as published in his 1921 book *Psychological Types* (English ed., 1923).[*] The original developers of the indicator were Katharine Cook Briggs and her daughter, Isabel Briggs Myers, who initially created the indicator during World War II, believing that a knowledge of personality preferences would help women who were entering the industrial workforce for the first time identify the sort of wartime jobs where they would be "most comfortable and effective."[†] The test indicates a certain predisposition to being extroverted, introverted, sensing, feeling, judging, perceiving, and feeling or thinking. While there is much controversy about tests like this, there is value to be appreciated in a setting where one has to determine how responders are going to react

---

[*] Carl Jung, *Psychological Types*, trans. H. Godwyn Baynes (New York: Harcourt Brace, 1923).
[†] Wikipedia, "Myers-Briggs Type Indicator," http://en.wikipedia.org/wiki/Myers-Briggs_Type_Indicator.

in a crisis. I am not convinced that this test is appropriate as a hiring tool, but military officers have been tested using this tool. The test indicates that there are 16 personality types and there are sufficient people in the workforce who have taken the test and know what they scored. The purpose of knowing the composition of one's team is to understand who has a mind for detail and who is not suited for it. For more information on the Myers-Briggs Type Indicator, go to the Myers-Briggs Foundation Web site, http://www.myersbriggs.org. There are 16 personality types:

ISTJ—Introverted Sensing with Thinking	ESTP—Extroverted Sensing with Thinking
ISFJ— Introverted Sensing with Feeling	ESFP—Extroverted Sensing with Feeling
INFJ—Introverted iNtuition with Feeling	ENFP—Extroverted iNtuition with Feeling
INTJ—Introverted iNtuition with Thinking	ENTP—Extroverted iNtuition with Thinking
ISTP—Introverted Thinking with Sensing	ESTJ—Extroverted Thinking with Sensing
ISFP—Introverted Feeling with Sensing	ESFJ—Extroverted Feeling with Sensing
INFP—Introverted Feeling with iNtuition	ENFJ—Extroverted Feeling with iNtuition
INTP—Introverted Thinking with iNtuition	ENTJ— Extroverted Thinking with iNtuition

Keirsey Temperament Sorter

Another similar test to the Myers-Briggs is the Keirsey Sorter. It has taken what Myers and Briggs developed and modernized it with other dimensions.* All 16 personality types are narrowly focused on four types of temperaments.

Idealistic NFs, being *abstract* in communicating and *cooperative* in implementing goals, can become highly skilled in *diplomatic integration*. Thus, their most practiced and developed intelligent operations are usually teaching and counseling (NFJ mentoring), or conferring and tutoring (NFP advocating). The Idealist temperament has an instinct for

---

* http://www.keirsey.com.

interpersonal integration, learns ethics with ever-increasing zeal, sometimes becomes diplomatic leaders, and often speaks interpretively and metaphorically of the abstract world of his or her imagination.

Rational NTs, being *abstract* in communicating and *utilitarian* in implementing goals, can become highly skilled in *strategic analysis*. Thus, their most practiced and developed intelligent operations tend to be marshaling and planning (NTJ organizing), or inventing and configuring (NTP engineering). And they would if they could be wizards in one of these forms of rational operation. They are proud of themselves in the degree to which they are competent in action, respect themselves in the degree to which they are autonomous, and feel confident of themselves in the degree to which they are strong willed. Ever in search of knowledge, this is the "Knowledge-Seeking Personality"—trusting in reason and hungering for achievement. They are usually pragmatic about the present, skeptical about the future, and solipsistic about the past, and their preferred time and place are the interval and the intersection. Educationally they go for the sciences, avocationally for technology, and vocationally for systems work. Rationals tend to be individualizing as parents, mindmates as spouses, and learning oriented as children. Rationals are very infrequent, comprising as few as 5 percent and no more than 7 percent of the population.

Artisan SPs, being *concrete* in communicating and *utilitarian* in implementing goals, can become highly skilled in *tactical variation*. Thus, their most practiced and developed intelligent operations are usually promoting and operating (SPT expediting), or displaying and composing (SPF improvising). And they would if they could be virtuosos of one of these forms of artistic operation. Artisans are proud of themselves in the degree to which they are graceful in action, respect themselves in the degree to which they are daring, and feel confident of themselves in the degree to which they are adaptable. This is the "Sensation-Seeking Personality"—trusting in spontaneity and hungering for impact on others. They are usually hedonic about the present, optimistic about the future, and cynical about the past, and their preferred time and place are the here and now. Educationally, they go for arts and crafts, avocationally for techniques, and vocationally for operations work. They tend to be permissive as parents, playmates as spouses, and play oriented as children. There are many Artisans to be found in many places where the action is, and they are at least 35 percent and as many as 40 percent of the population.

Guardian SJs, being *concrete* in communicating and *cooperative* in implementing goals, can become highly skilled in *logistics*. Thus, their most practiced and developed intelligent operations are often supervising and inspecting (SJT administering), or supplying and protecting (SJF conserving). And they would if they could be magistrates watching over these forms of social facilitation. They are proud of themselves in the degree to which they are reliable in action, respect themselves in the degree to which they do good deeds, and feel confident of themselves in the degree to which they are respectable. They are in search of security as they are the "Security-Seeking Personality"—trusting in legitimacy and hungering for membership. They are usually stoical about the present, pessimistic about the future, and fatalistic about the past, and their preferred time and place are the past and the gateway. Educationally they go for commerce, avocationally for regulations, and vocationally for material handling work. They tend to be enculturating as parents, helpmates as spouses, and conformity oriented as children. There are even more Guardians than Artisans around, at least 40 percent and as many as 45 percent of the population.

If you have any coworkers who you feel are strange, it could be that they slipped into a work environment where they may not be a good fit. People tend to gravitate toward like-minded people, and tests often show that they have similar personalities.

GROUP ROLES AND TEAM ROLES

Glenn Parker is an author and consultant on high-performing teams, and has developed tools to build and sustain such teams.[*] The Parker Team Player Survey (PTPS) is an easy-to-use self-assessment exercise that helps individuals identify their primary team player style: contributor, collaborator, communicator, or challenger. They discover how to most effectively use their style for improved team performance and how to adjust the role they play on the team to meet the team's needs.[†]

Keep in mind that these categories are not fixed in any way. Any given person may show different behaviors in different groups or different

---

[*] Glenn Parker, *Team Players and Teamwork* (San Francisco, CA: Jossey-Bass, 2008), http://www.glennparker.com/products/book-team-players-and-teamwork.html.
[†] http://www.cpp.com/products/parker/index.asp, Parker Survey.

behaviors in the same group at different points in time. However, most people tend to favor one of the four styles.

Knowing what styles exist in a group helps with appropriate assignments when teams meet to solve problems, design plans, or respond to threats or homeland security alerts, crises, disasters, or attacks. These are the four styles. Which one do you think you are?

1. *Contributor*—The Contributor is described as a *task-oriented* team member who is willing and able to share knowledge and information. Contributors like to provide technical and clinical information to team members. The Contributor may frequently take on the role of trainer or mentor to new members. They are described as dependable, responsible, and helpful.

2. *Collaborator*—The Collaborator is described as a *goal-directed* team member who helps others remain focused on the overall purpose, mission, and goal of the team. Collaborators are "willing to extend themselves beyond their traditional boundaries or comfort areas"; they will "do whatever is necessary to get the job done." Collaborators do not mind working behind the scenes. They are willing to take on a variety of jobs and duties in order to meet a goal. They are hardworking, flexible, open-minded, and enthusiastic team members.

3. *Communicator*—The Communicator is described as a *process-oriented* team member. Communicators care more about the team *process* than the end product. Communicators monitor the interpersonal climate of the team and take measures to improve relationships among team members. Communicators take an active role in facilitating consensus building and conflict resolution. They show concern for integrating new members and maintaining positive interactions among existing members. They take steps to ensure a supportive team environment.

4. *Challenger*—Challengers are described as questioning and critical. They express their opinions honestly and directly. They are very concerned with maintaining high ethical standards and high standards of quality. They are not afraid to express a dissenting opinion if they perceive a "higher good" in doing so. Challengers are willing to question authority "and will not accept decisions simply because 'that's the way it's always been done.'" Challengers force the team to think in new ways. Principled and candid, they have been described as the "conscience" of the team.

LOW-CONTEXT AND HIGH-CONTEXT COMMUNICATIONS

My experience of operating as a team member or leader of hundreds of teams in the United States and abroad in public and private sector critical infrastructure operations demonstrates that certain aspects of language are critical but not understood. Some cultures create people who are high-context communicators, while others create low-context communicators. These traits, while more prevalent in regions abroad, and carry over into the culture of first-, second-, third-, or fourth-generation Americans. This varied method of communication can affect operational efficiency during normal operations and in a crisis if we do not understand this.

When workers from high-context and low-context cultures have to work together, problems often occur with the exchange of information. These problems can be categorized as differences in *direction, quantity,* and *quality.* Regarding differences in direction, employees from high-context cultures like China and France adapt to their good friends, families, and close colleagues (in-group members). They communicate with them intensively (quantity difference) and exchange specific or detailed information about many different topics. The result is that every in-group member is constantly up-to-date with the facts around the business.*

In comparison to high-context cultures, low-context cultures like the United States and Germany orientate on many people in their daily life because they do not differentiate as much as high-context cultures between in- and out-groups. So their direction of communication is orientated on personal characters and refers to situations (direction difference). They mostly communicate within their out-groups in a broad and diffuse way (quantity difference). Within communication, they exchange information just to the necessary extent so that work can be done, and they do not discuss or exchange information constantly in their work environment and among colleagues (quality difference).

In China, communication tends to be very efficient because of their information flow at work and in privacy. The Chinese discuss everything in advance and consider meetings as an official "ceremony" where the already commonly agreed upon decision will be announced. This is important in the way of "giving and keeping face." The Americans and Germans, in contrast, inform the participating attendants in a meeting

---

* William B. Gudykunst and Young Yun Kim, "Communication with Strangers"; Lisa Hoecklin, "Managing Cultural Differences: Strategies for Competitive Advantage"; "High Context versus Low Context Paper," http://www.via-web.de/273.html (accessed March 2008).

about the hard and necessary facts. The decision-making process takes place within the meeting. In France, it is similar to their Asian counterparts. They are also well informed before they meet each other. Many explicit and detailed discussions would probably be seen as an insult because everything is already clear.

REACTIVE VERSUS PROACTIVE LANGUAGE

Being proactive may be the single most important habit change that a person could ever achieve. By being proactive, a person takes control and chooses what life is about. Life is not "happening" to them anymore. Stephen Covey explains that when he was attending university, he found the following quote in one of his marketing books:[*]

There are 5 types of companies:

Those who make things happen
Those who think they make things happen
Those who watch things happen
Those who wonder what the heck happened
Those that didn't know anything had happened

He thought this was true for people as well. Being proactive is about making things happen. But in this case, it can help organizations adopt proactive approaches that instill confidence in their operations or homeland security roles, thus building a strong foundation for any program. Table 8.1 is an example of how Covey feels reactive language can be reframed to make it proactive.

Table 8.1   Reactive versus Proactive Learning

Reactive Language	Proactive Language
There's nothing I can do about it.	Let's look at our alternatives.
That's just the way I am.	I can choose a different approach.
They won't allow that.	I can control my feelings.
I have to do that.	I can create an effective presentation.
I can't.	I choose.
I must.	I prefer.
If only …	I will.

---

[*] Stephen Covey, *The 7 Habits of Highly Effective People* (New York: Simon and Schuster, 1989).

Active Listening

What to Avoid

When we encounter people with a problem, our usual response is to try to change their way of looking at things, to get them to see their situation the way we see it or would like them to see it. We plead, reason, scold, encourage, insult, prod—anything to bring about a change in the desired direction, that is, in the direction we want them to travel. What we seldom realize, however, is that, under these circumstances, we are usually responding to our own needs to see the world in certain ways. It is always difficult for us to tolerate and understand actions that are different from the ways in which we believe we should act. If, however, we can free ourselves from the need to influence and direct others in our own paths, we enable ourselves to listen with understanding and thereby employ the most potent agent of change available.

What We Achieve by Listening

Active listening is an important way to bring about changes in people. Despite the popular notion that listening is a passive approach, clinical and research evidence clearly shows that sensitive listening is a most effective agent for individual personality change and group development. Listening brings about changes in the attitudes of people toward themselves and others. It also brings about changes in their basic values and personal philosophy. People who have been listened to in this new and special way become more emotionally mature, more open to their experiences, less defensive, more democratic, and less authoritarian.

How to Listen

Active listening aims to bring about changes in people. To achieve this end, it relies upon definite techniques—things to do and things to avoid doing. Before discussing these techniques, however, we should first understand why they are effective. To do so, we must understand how the individual personality develops.

What to Do

Just what does active listening entail, then? Basically, it requires that we get inside the speaker, that we grasp, from his point of view, just what it is he is communicating to us. More than that, we must convey to the speaker that we are seeing things from his point of view. To listen actively, then, means that there are several things we must do. First, we must listen for total meaning. Any message a person tries to get across usually has two components: the content of the message, and the feeling or attitude underlying this content. Both are important; both give the message meaning. We try to understand the total meaning of the message. For example, a machinist comes to his foreman and says, "I've finished that lathe setup." This message has obvious content and perhaps calls upon the foreman for another work assignment. Suppose, on the other hand, that he says, "Well, I'm finally finished with that damned lathe setup." The content is the same, but the total meaning of the message has changed—and changed in an important way for both the foreman and the worker. Here, sensitive listening can facilitate the relationship. Suppose the foreman were to respond by simply giving another work assignment. Would the employee feel that he had gotten his total message across? Would he feel free to talk to his foreman? Will he feel better about his job and more anxious to do good work on the next assignment? Now, on the other hand, suppose the foreman were to respond with "Glad to have it over with, huh?" or "Had a pretty rough time of it?" or "I guess you don't feel like doing anything like that again," or anything else that tells the worker that he heard and understands. It does not necessarily mean that the next work assignment needs to be changed or that he must spend an hour listening to the worker complain about the setup problems he encountered. He may do a number of things differently in the light of the new information he has from the worker, but not necessarily. It is that extra sensitivity on the part of the foreman that can transform an average working climate into a good one.

THE FORMING, STORMING, NORMING, PERFORMING MODEL

The "Forming, Storming, Norming, Performing" four-stage model, introduced by Bruce Tuckman in 1965, explains that when teams or groups come together for the first time, they inevitably go through a predictable development process before they are able to work together efficiently and effectively. The four stages are depicted in Table 8.2.

The model evolved out of Tuckman's observations of group behavior in a variety of settings. After completing his doctorate, Tuckman worked with the industrial psychology lab at Princeton University and then undertook research on small-groups and organizational behavior as a research psychologist at the Naval Medical Research Institute in Bethesda, Maryland. He postulated that groups were likely to go

Table 8.2 Forming, Storming, Norming, Performing Model

Stage	Activity
Forming	High dependence on the leader for guidance and direction. Little agreement on team aims other than those received from leader. Individual roles and responsibilities are unclear. Leader must be prepared to answer lots of questions about the team's purpose, objectives, and external relationships. Processes are often ignored. Members test tolerance of system and leader. Leader directs (similar to Situational Leadership® "Telling" mode).
Storming	Decisions do not come easily within group. Team members vie for position as they attempt to establish themselves in relation to other team members and the leader, who might receive challenges from team members. Clarity of purpose increases, but plenty of uncertainties persist. Cliques and factions form, and there may be power struggles. The team needs to be focused on its goals to avoid becoming distracted by relationships and emotional issues. Compromises may be required to enable progress. Leader coaches (similar to Situational Leadership "Selling" mode).
Norming	Agreement and consensus largely form among team, who respond well to facilitation by leader. Roles and responsibilities are clear and accepted. Big decisions are made by group agreement. Smaller decisions may be delegated to individuals or small teams within group. Commitment and unity are strong. The team may engage in fun and social activities. The team discusses and develops its processes and working style. There is general respect for the leader, and some of leadership is more shared by the team. Leader facilitates and enables (similar to the Situational Leadership "Participating" mode).
Performing	The team is more strategically aware; the team knows clearly why it is doing what it is doing. The team has a shared vision and is able to stand on its own feet with no interference or participation from the leader. There is a focus on overachieving goals, and the team makes most of the decisions against criteria agreed with the leader. The team has a high degree of autonomy. Disagreements occur, but now they are resolved within the team positively, and the team makes necessary changes to processes and structure. The team is able to work toward achieving the goal, and also to attend to relationship, style, and process issues along the way. Team members look after each other. The team requires delegated tasks and projects from the leader. The team does not need to be instructed or assisted. Team members might ask for assistance from the leader with personal and interpersonal development. Leader delegates and oversees (similar to the Situational Leadership "Delegating" mode).

through four distinct stages as they come together and begin to function.* These characteristics of human behavior in each stage might be recognized by participants, but there may only be a limited consciousness of the changes and their implications. The obvious implication was that if people could develop a better appreciation of the processes surrounding group development, then it would be possible to enhance group effectiveness and functioning.

All models and theories have elements of information that can be critiqued or valued. The model is not included here because we are not conducting psychological analysis or testing, or endorsing or attacking reliability or validity. What is clearly logical is that we need not be too concerned with why it has been critiqued. What we should do is take the value of this model for its simplicity. Instead of struggling with the idea that people on the team do not see eye to eye on all group ideas, embrace the fact that this is normal and acceptable. But hurry up and experience the attributes of the early stage so that the team can get to the *Performing* stage. You can almost see how all the pieces come together— moving in synchronicity because every team member knows his or her role and simply performs it. Figure 8.1 shows some of the most common work groups who would benefit from this model.

As you can see from the characteristics of each stage in the Tuckman model, it is typical for private and public sector team members, task forces, working groups, working committees, "red teams, tiger teams" (if they still exist), joint military forces, and coalition forces to exhibit the behavior dynamics associated with each stage.

It is important to understand that team-member behaviors and emotions are likely to get in the way of collaboration when they first come together. This is normal and to be expected. But once each stage has been normalized, so to speak, the group can move to the next stage and be more effective. Each time it progresses to the next stage, the group learns valuable lessons about its members' abilities and strengths, and about ways to capitalize on these strengths to achieve the group's objectives. Nearly all work in the future can be expected to be performed by groups. All groups will experience conflict and chaos. Now, instead of allowing conflict to escalate and impede group progress, the group can demonstrate an opportunity to proactively address how to move forward.

---

* M. K. Smith, "Bruce W. Tuckman: Forming, Storming, Norming and Performing in Groups," *Encyclopaedia of Informal Education*, 2005, http://www.infed.org/thinkers/tuckman.htm.

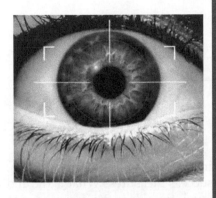

- DHS and the Private Sector

- Public to Public Sector Workgroup

- Corporate Incident Response Team

- Homeland Security Preparedness Plan Committee

- Business Continuity Plan (BCP) and Disaster Recovery Planning Team

- Emergency Planning Team

- Government Contractor Support Team

Figure 8.1 Teams and groups.

Change is not permanent. If a group learns to apply Tuckman's model to be more effective in meeting its corporate or homeland security goals, the change will need constant reinforcement and nurturing. Often corporations will be proud that they brought a change agent consultant or a facilitator to help implement change. A few months later, managers complain that they wasted thousands of dollars because everything went back to the way it was before. They are very disappointed, and you can see it in their faces: the cost, the time spent, and the glory of the moment—all seemed very promising but went nowhere.

The reason that this change did not take effect is because the behaviors need constant reinforcement. They need to be repeated regularly. Someone needs to measure the change and log the moments of deviation. Intervening forces need to be launched when groups start deviating back to their old, normal behaviors.

CHAPTER EXERCISE

Utilizing Figure 8.2, apply the model to one of your group activities. How is your group performing? What stage of development would you say your group is in? Check the space that best illustrates what stage your group is in at this time. How many days, months, or years does this group have before the intended project should be completed? Does everyone

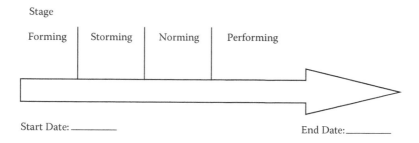

Figure 8.2 Current team stage.

in the group have a clear understanding of the group's vision, mission, objectives, milestones, deadlines, and success measures? What is the end goal? Given the group deadline, how much time does the group have to progress through the following stages? What can the group do to effectively achieve the desired goal in time?

9

Training and Exercises
Touch It, Feel It, Live It, Breathe It!

The free world is now consumed with a global and fateful struggle against terrorism! If terrorism is defeated under the leadership of the United States, a foundation for positive interaction will be built among diverse societies and a new plateau of human progress may be achieved. But if terrorism prevails—the potential exists for the regression of humanity into an age of darkness.

Lebanon General Michel Naim Aoun

OVERVIEW

Training needs to be a constant in the workplace—to broaden an individual's perspective, obtain task-specific knowledge and skills, obtain state-of-the-art knowledge and skills, and prepare people to perform a job, a new function, or a new procedure. Of all the things that can be done for prevention, preparedness, and response to a terrorist attack, the most important "proactive activities" are conducting effective training and continuous education of people.

Millions of dollars are spent daily in the public sector on security prevention, detection, and response technologies. It is not understood why very little effort and time are set aside for employee training, education, and plan exercising. Manufacturers of security technology and managers of organizations that purchase technology seem to forget that no matter how sophisticated the technology, the weakest link is the human factor, either as the operator of the technology or as the employee circumventing it and using his or her own shortcuts because it is too hard to get used to or created extra work.

Employees are our greatest assets in protecting our organizations. They should be considered the "organization's neighborhood watch." The real value of their potential capabilities is rarely recognized. Properly trained employees can provide early warning and create an atmosphere of a hard target just by being aware and reporting suspicious activities (e.g., strangers showing undue interest or asking out-of-the-blue questions that usually cause people to scratch their heads afterward). In this context, strangers who show this type of interest are probably conducting reconnaissance and surveillance as part of the terrorist operations cycle to assess vulnerabilities, and gathering intelligence to determine if the facility or organization makes a good target. Proper training can educate employees on threats, specifically terrorists' capabilities and methods of gathering intelligence about the target (their facility), as discussed in Chapter 5. The information gathered may not be secret or confidential, but it can be useful in the wrong hands. However, knowing what to do and how to do it requires training and education.

When the terrorist plotters of the Fort Dix attack were captured, it was discovered that they had considered a list of targets—one of them was McGuire Air Force Base (AFB), the next-door neighbor to Fort Dix. McGuire AFB was not selected because it was too hard of a target. The whole aim of this book will be missed if people do not "deduce, conclude, and put two and two together" to deny terrorists the ability to attack. We need education so we can figure out what needs to be done to protect ourselves from attacks like 9/11. We need tools and new ways to frame the problems we face today and will continue to face in the coming years, and we can always consider how the terrorists think (or the hackers or any other threats).

BENEFITS OF TRAINING

Effective training programs produce many benefits. They can decrease the time it takes to perform a task, increase effectiveness and efficiency for maximum productivity and positive bottom-line impact, improve the quality of products or services, reduce accidents and lower insurance premiums, implement new systems or procedures, and even reduce employee illness and stress through health-oriented work approaches. Effective training can also help deter terrorist attacks. The Israelis rely extensively on humans and less on technology. They use technology but only to complement what humans do. The Israeli population has an advantage on its side: everyone has to serve a short tour of duty in the military. A former Israeli officer once told me that someone's grandmother was responsible for providing as early a warning as possible in the face of an imminent attack: A suicide bomber was getting ready to get on a bus, and the grandmother was sitting opposite the entry with a full view of people entering the bus. "His rank was upside-down on his uniform. I thought something was off about his uniform, and that caused me to alert the bus driver," she would later report. The bus driver could only react by jumping out of his seat and pushing the guy out of the bus with his body. The suicide bomber and the driver died, but the rest of the passengers lived. Can we expect our citizens to be that alert and educated? We can strive and aim for it. Maybe our society is not there yet, but we can start today.

ADULT LEARNING

Training and exercises are essential in transferring knowledge that is critical to discovering human weaknesses that are sure to exist, and to do it right requires understanding adult learning: how adults sense information, how they receive it, how they process it, and how they recall it.

One interesting point is that if the training fails—and conditions are extremely dire—the body will unleash the brain's potential to enable survival. For example, adrenaline gets released, and the body slows down nonessential functions (cell renewal, hunger, etc.) to enable all bodily systems to concentrate on the required task: survival by means of running to safe ground or getting to where help is available. The body will even tell itself to start eating its own flesh if the person is in a situation where he or she is stranded at sea for days or trapped in a cave while cave diving and starving to death.* I am not sure that the hidden brain comes out when we are in normal everyday situations or in situations of less than dire need. We therefore still need to learn and receive education.

Research has consistently shown that there are considerable differences between adult and child-adolescent learning styles. Additionally,

---

* Discovery Channel: "The Human Body: Pushing the Limits" aired March 9, 2008, http:// dsc.discovery.com/tv/human-body/more-about-human-body/more-about-human-body. html.

since adults do not learn in the same manner as children, one cannot teach adults using techniques that were originally developed for use with children. Teaching adults requires the utilization of the process model rather than the content model.* Remarkably, people can learn from the moment of birth. Learning can and should be a lifelong process. We constantly make sense of our experiences and consistently search for meaning. In essence, we continue to learn. We can learn from everything the mind perceives (at any age). Our brains build and strengthen neural pathways no matter where we are, and no matter what the subject or the context.

In today's business environment, we must find better ways to learn—learning propels organizations forward. Strong minds fuel strong organizations. We must capitalize on our natural learning styles and then build systems to satisfy needs. Only through an individual learning process can we recreate our environments and ourselves to be a more highly evolved society.

Adults vary tremendously in how they acquire knowledge and there is also a difference in the way adults and children learn. Table 9.1 shows this comparison. Anyone who is still using techniques that are appropriate for children will not have success.

TRAINING METHODS

Adults learn by various methods: through the senses (listening, seeing, feeling, touching); through experience (social interaction, music-based activities, numbers-based activities, interactive activities [we should design more antiterror games like *PDR* for the average American]; and by using technical details, creative colorful images, and computers. Sometimes the learning styles are so dominant—people do not know this—that it will show in the training evaluation results.†

Instructor-led training (Figure 9.1) is most effective when interaction is required and educational material is being introduced or provided.

Table 9.2 provides a list of options to consider when you develop your training. Whatever you do, systematize it. If a threat causes damage, you may be asked to bring your training records to court.

---

* http://www.utoledo.edu/colleges/education/par/Adults.html; S. Stroot, V. Keil, P. Stedman, L. Lohr, R. Faust, L. Schincariol-Randall, A. Sullivan, G. Czerniak, J. Kuchcinski, N. Orel, and M. Richter, *Peer Assistance and Review Guidebook* (Columbus: Ohio Department of Education, 1998).

† From Malcolm Knowles, *The Adult Learner: A Neglected Species* (1984).

Table 9.1 Children versus Adult Learning

Assumptions	Children	Adults
Learner's concept	Dependent	Independent, self-directed
Learner's experience	Inconsequential	Rich in resource learning
Learner's readiness	Based on physical, mental, and social development	Based on need
Relevancy	Later application	Immediate application
Curriculum environment	Subject centered, authority oriented, formal, and competitive	Problem centered, collaborative, informal, and respective
Planning	By teacher	Mutual
Determination of needs	By teacher	Mutual and self-diagnosis
Lesson design	Sequenced in terms of subject matter, content focused	Sequenced in terms of need, problem focused
Activities techniques	Transmittal of information	Experiential
Evaluation	By teacher	Mutual

Figure 9.1 Instructor-led training.

203

Table 9.2 Training Methods

Training Methods	Advantages	Disadvantages
A		
Class instruction	Revised easily	Scheduling is difficult
	Developed quickly	Travel costs
	Face-to-face contact	Differences from class to class
Online group training	No travel costs	Requires computer equipment
	Developed quickly	No face-to-face contact
Videoconferencing and video/online	Supports large groups and multiple sites	High equipment costs
	No travel costs	Logistically challenging
On-the-job coaching	Effective knowledge transfer	Differences from instructor to instructor, session to session
	Related to trainee's job	Costly in terms of instructor-to-trainee ratio
	Face-to-face contact	
Online self-directed training	Consistent training content	High development costs
	Convenient access to training	Lengthy development time
Printed material	Portable	Less interesting
	Trainee sets own pace	Requires computer equipment
	Reuse does not require trainer participation	
Web-based training	Easy to modify	Limited bandwidth causes slow download times
CD-ROM/DVD	Supports complex multimedia	Difficult to modify
	Trainee sets own pace	
	Developed quickly	

Table 9.2 (continued)   Training Methods

Training Methods	Advantages	Disadvantages
B		
Video DVD or audio CD	Consistent training content	Requires playback equipment
	Can share copies	Can be costly to develop
	Trainee sets own pace	Difficult to modify
Just-in-time training	Available when needed at trainee's convenience	Costly to develop
	Related to trainee's job	Requires computer equipment
Continuous improvement	Promotes employee involvement	Requires training resources that are readily available on a continuous basis
	Promotes creative solutions	Differences from instructor to instructor
Computer-mediated	Accessible at the trainee's convenience	Requires computer equipment
Asynchronous collaboration	Promotes creative solutions	Can require computer software
	Promotes employee involvement	

CRAWL–WALK–RUN METHODOLOGY

Well-developed training supports the crawl–walk–run methodology for effective learning. This methodology has been used successfully for many years by the military. Table 9.3 details the three steps in this methodology, what they mean, and how they work. In every step, learning is verified before moving to the next step. Table 9.4 details the type of scenarios and conditions that are used in each phase. This methodology is easy to apply and is used extensively in business and military environments. Many people train this way without ever realizing it. This methodology makes sense, like a child developing and growing up: they crawl first and learn it before they walk, and they have to know how to walk before they can run.

To make training successful, it must be integrated into the corporate culture. Training must be a recurring event that is funded, planned,

Table 9.3 Crawl–Walk–Run

Phase	Meaning	Description
Crawl	Explain and demonstrate	Describe the task step by step, indicating what must be done to successfully complete the task
Walk	Practice what was learned with some assistance if required	Provide a scenario or task, use knowledge learned to complete the task step by step
Run	Perform the task to standard without assistance	Provide a realistic scenario or task, use knowledge learned to complete the task to standard or be able to meet the objective

Table 9.4 Crawl–Walk–Run Description

Phase	Description of Exercise to Support the Phase
Crawl	Situational training exercises that require coaching by the trainer or consultant
Walk	Situational training exercises using few tasks and favorable environmental conditions (e.g., day)
Run	Situational training exercises using multiple complex tasks, developing situations, and unfavorable conditions (e.g., environmental, lack of communications, or key personnel missing)

and supported by management with full commitment and buy-in by all involved.

One thing we can learn from Al Qaeda is that if they apply money, time, and resources to train their people to attack, shouldn't we spend just as much money, time, and resources to train our people to defend? Their effective use of training methods is evidenced by their standardized methods no matter where the terrorists are trained (e.g., Malaysia, Syria, the Philippines, Yemen, the United States) and regardless of what language in which the training is taught. They use curricula that are "modular": self-contained and focused on the basics. If you learn the basics of anything you want to learn, and learn them well, they will be second nature when needed.

Over the years, Al Qaeda has expanded the use of the Internet from a means of spreading propaganda to communicating with operatives to educational purposes. The use of roving Web sites, biweekly electronic journals, blog sites, and Web-based training also provides for the sharing of lessons learned immediately after they are learned and makes an ideal training medium for personnel located all over the world. Non-Al Qaeda Web sites also play a major role in providing security, intelligence, military, and emergency response training to interested Muslims and U.S. militant groups. If the Internet is beneficial to them, obviously it can be used to effectively train employees to benefit us in the fight against terrorism. But don't forget that they follow training with practical exercise.

VIDEO EXAMPLE FOR TRAINING

Videos are one of the best methods for training (seeing). Depending on the topic, there are many good videos that can teach the desired security and other skills needed to be productive and security conscious employees.

The movie *Catch Me If You Can* is a great display of effective training material for "social engineering" in action. Social engineering is the ability of a human being to be able to trick others into unwittingly giving up something, generally information. In the movie, the main character—based on a real person—tricks those around him into believing that he is whatever he wants to be. One day he is a pilot; the next day he is a doctor. With confidence, the main character does his due diligence to learn what he must know in order to carry off the ruse. He becomes comfortable in the skin of the person he is going to be, and then he prepares himself to be that person. The people around him never question him because he never gives them a chance to question any of his actions. He is able to stay in character, and therefore be completely believable. Social engineering is a powerful tool in the terrorist's arsenal—we are all vulnerable to a nice-looking face, a confident demeanor, and a lovable character. Why should we question those qualities when they are qualities we admire?

Another Show Solving a Problem

Attention to detail and awareness of your surroundings are critical to solving problems. A kidnap victim on the former CBS series *Numbers* is rescued because the investigators paid attention to the details and the victim made herself aware of her surroundings. The victim is a journalist reporting on a shady real estate developer who is about to close escrow on a very large deal with the city. The journalist has found information about the developer that showed he had suppressed the price of certain parcels of land so that he could buy them at a reduced rate and have the land to proceed with his large deal. The developer has the journalist kidnapped to keep her out of the way so that his escrow can close. The investigators paid attention to the details of the recent reporting that the journalist had done; they investigated the stories that she had been working on; they talked to colleagues about her stories; and they found the link between her stories and the developer. By using math, the investigators were able to correlate recent land purchases the developer made with a list of numbers that was found at the journalist's house. The list of numbers turned out to be the parcel numbers of the land that had been purchased. There were two parcel numbers for land that the developer had purchased that did not appear on the journalist's list. By researching these two parcels, the investigators discovered that one of the parcels was a piece of vacant land, and the other parcel was located a distance from the other parcels and had a building on it. They deduced that this could be where the journalist was being held. It turned out that she was there. She heard the investigators and began making noises so they would find her. She was rescued.

You can probably come up with your own films for training tools. They draw interest and appeal to both visual and audio learners. This is just an example of how films can speed up the learning process—it is almost like being there. The learning needs to involve touching, feeling, and breathing it, as if the person being trained is there experiencing the event.

EXERCISES

People go into exercises thinking they already know everything and how everything works; you get to throw them for a loop. Exercises work because people get to breathe it and live it as if it were the real thing. For example, in a red team exercise that was conducted at a critical infrastructure, the security guys were overwhelmed, alarms did not work, they did not know what to do next, their faces turned white, and soon they just stopped functioning because everything was going wrong. It is okay to make a mistake here because it is safe, but you can have a heart attack too! And you can get arrested and use up valuable police time if your exercise is not properly coordinated. One person actually did have a mild heart attack, and they had to deal with that emergency immediately. This left no reserves to deal with any other emergency had there been one. The exercise showed that people could not seem to make basic or commonsense decisions. In situations like this, the environment is primed for groupthink.

Many have an idea of what DHS expects in the way of training and exercises for terrorism preparedness. DHS provides extensive funding and support. Those exercises have standards and guidelines that need to be met, and many participants, from government agencies to private companies, participate. One can get an idea of what these exercises might entail by watching the movie *Dirty War,** a film about how many components need to come together quickly, efficiently, and effectively, or people could cause the ordeal to worsen. The movie begins:

> In a post-9/11 world, how do you prepare for the unthinkable? Is it possible to stop a coordinated radioactive-weapons attack by determined terrorists in an international city? And what, if anything, should the public be told about such a threat? This HBO Films thriller shows how a "dirty bomb" attack might be planned and executed in London, despite the best efforts of police and intelligence forces—as well as how devastating the consequences of such an attack could be.†

Exercises complement training and education, and validate the training as effective. It is the one method of training that invariably opens the eyes of the organization to the fact that it may not be as prepared as it thought to detect and respond to a serious event. Terrorist organizations such as Al Qaeda spend just as much money, effort, and time on training, rehearsing, and practicing (henceforth referred to as *exercising*) their plans as they do on developing them. They understand the importance of training and exercising, and if personnel are not trained properly and the plan is not exercised, the risk of failure increases exponentially. So why don't we seem to have the same approach?

Too often, the word *test* is used to validate plans and preparedness. From our early childhood school days, we have been programmed to fear this word. The mere sound of *test* leads one to believe that it means pass or fail. No wonder it is avoided. To promote a learning environment, the word *exercise* should be used to evaluate and validate training, security, and response plans.

Although many executives and managers may think they have good plans, they are not prepared unless they exercise their plan. We do not mean exercising just the bits and pieces of the plan, such as performing a tabletop drill, or doing the exercise when all the cell phones are working and all the key players show up and the skies are blue. Organizations should exercise enough to reach the point where they can honestly say

---

* HBO Films, *Dirty War*, http://www.hbo.com/films/dirtywar/.
† Ibid.

that their exercise was an intense experience and things went wrong, the way they would in real life, and leaders had to make tough decisions. Exercises should not be conducted just to say they were done, to check a block or meet an audit requirement. Why? Because practice makes perfect.

In truth, everyone wants to be prepared for the worst-case terrorist scenario, so why is it so difficult to get organizations to complete preparation plans and follow through with training? Sometimes there is a bias that serves as a barrier to conducting an effective exercise. Why? Because management does not understand the true purpose of an exercise and does not want to look bad after a lot of money and effort have been put into a plan or a program or department. Departments have to compete for a slice of the budget. What if someone strong and influential—a secret favorite department—gets funding and purchases many fancy gadgets that did not serve their purpose, and now there is no budget? Or what if the training budget was used to buy equipment, pagers, or golf carts that security personnel thought they needed to do their job, and now there is no money for training? The human factor enters the picture, and suddenly people realize that the funds were misspent, so the training component gets undercut and the company or organization just has to get by. This is the result of poor leadership and poor management. Management is supposed to be able to manage, control, track, and report. Leaders are supposed to inspire others to achieve a vision through many of the "manager" processes. Often decision-making skills and "people-managing" abilities are lacking in the workplace. How many of the 200 million or so adults in our population do you think have been trained or mentored by good leaders and managers? If you want to know what will happen to societies that do not continue to learn, rent or download a must-watch film called *Idiocracy*. Even if it's not your style of humor, you should watch this film. It portrays what would happen if people stopped learning.

Essentially, today's managers develop scenarios for success instead of realism. Results and identified gaps in a plan are toned down, and excuses are developed that include, "If this had been a real incident, we would have done …"

It is interesting evaluating exercises and watching people go into them thinking they are ready; and then, as the exercise scenario develops and evolves, they find out how complex the scenario is, the cascading effects of decisions that are made, and how much coordination with other agencies and organizations is required. They walk away with new insight and the realization that it is easy to make mistakes. There is no better place to make a mistake than under a controlled environment where it is safe rather than during a real incident where lives are at stake. Exercises are a learning vehicle. Knowledge is gained and skills are developed. People learn to communicate and coordinate the necessary support and logistics needed. They develop the ability to make complex, high-risk decisions in a changing environment filled with ambiguities.

A senior consultant for top *Forbes* companies in security and emergency preparedness who has conducted evaluations of organizations' preparedness across the nation, both in the private sector (technology, transportation, water, and finance) and in government (the Department of the Army and the Department of Homeland Security), had several observations on the topic of exercises:

> Across the industries I evaluated, there were similar responses when senior management and executives were asked why their plans had not been exercised:
>
> Funding
> Lack of time
> High turnover of key management personnel (KMP)
>
> Companies that conducted training and exercises fell into two distinct categories:
>
> Tabletop exercises only
> Exercises with unrealistic scenarios

He said the mere idea that they attempted exercises deserved applause. At least they had conducted some sort of exercise. It was more than what some of their competitors and counterparts did to evaluate the effectiveness of their plans, but despite the attempt, they failed in the execution.

Over the years, DHS has administered $22.7 billion in federal grants to states, territories, urban areas, and transportation authorities to strengthen prevention, protection, response, and recovery capabilities at all levels of government and throughout our critical infrastructure. In fiscal year 2014, DHS will award $1,043,346,000. "Grantees are encouraged to utilize grant funding to maintain and sustain current critical core capabilities through investments in training and exercises, updates to current planning and procedures, and lifecycle replacement of equipment."* So, how much do you think will be used for training versus technology improvements, and will the money used for training and exercising be used effectively?

---

* Department of Homeland Security, "DHS Announces Grant Guidance for Fiscal Year (FY) 2014 Preparedness Grants," March 18, 2014, http://www.dhs.gov/news/2014/03/18/dhs-announces-grant-guidance-fiscal-year-fy-2014-preparedness-grants.

For too many organizations, developing a security or response plan ends when the plan is developed and written, and then is placed on the shelf for auditor reviews. To effectively have the capability for prevention, detection, and response plans, participants must be trained in their roles and rehearsed in the procedures they are expected to perform. Effective security against terrorism is a multiphase process that must include internal and external feedback loops, management sponsorship, and activity relationships with all levels of an organization, that is, effective training and exercising.

One of the most effective methods of evaluating security plans is conducting "red team" exercises. These exercises were originally developed by the military as a game theory exercise to evaluate plans; increase understanding of the enemy's abilities, equipment, and tactics; and develop strategies to defeat them. Today, they are also used as a method of evaluating security plans, policies, and procedures. Experienced role-players are used to simulate the threat—they are competent, completely understand the methodologies used by the threat, and use them to challenge the customer's security.

The purpose is to validate perceived vulnerabilities or weaknesses in the overall security of a facility; to test security operations and procedures, tactics, and equipment; and evaluate employee training by testing their security awareness. DHS and several other federal departments and agencies have long used red team exercises to test security. The Department of Energy uses red teams to evaluate security and test response plans. The Federal Aviation Administration uses red team exercises to evaluate security and its ability to detect attempts at smuggling contraband onto aircraft. These exercises evaluate not only the human factor but also the technology used to detect threats. The "National Strategy for the Physical Protection of Critical Infrastructure and Key Assets," published by the White House in February 2003, calls on DHS to use red teams to "evaluate preparedness" based on an "accurate assessment of national-level critical assets, systems, and functions."

One of the weaknesses of red team exercises is that their results are often skewed by senior management and government officials suppressing findings; they reject the red team's conclusions or do not follow through with recommendations. Someone, usually in management, forewarns those being evaluated so that after the exercise the results do not look bad. Another problem area is not using qualified role players. This usually happens when exercises are conducted internally to save money. An effective red team exercise requires specially qualified and experienced people. They should thoroughly know the methodologies used by the threat; have training and experience in gathering information, surveillance, and elicitation; be able to think like the threat; be able to think on their feet when the situation changes; and be able to live the lies they develop to play out their roles in the exercise. Another problem is unrealistic scenarios, or developing scenarios that are too restrictive or are not based on threat assessments. These problems are not exclusive to any single industry. They really stand out when you have had a chance to serve as an exercise controller or role player.

Red teams have been used for years in the corporate world to evaluate information technology security, plans, policies, and procedures. They are often referred to as ethical hacking. Kevin Mitnik is well known for his knowledge and experience in using social engineering. He has written several books on the subject of organizational weaknesses and how vulnerable information security systems and people are in the corporate world, thus making it easy for "threats" to exploit vulnerabilities—threats being terrorists, spies, hackers, or others who wish to inflict harm or loss. There are many critical infrastructure sectors that would benefit from red team exercises, for example, water treatment facilities, chemical plants, and transportation systems.

BUILDING AN EXERCISE

An exercise plan should include, at a minimum, the development of a scope and objectives, exercise duration, management buy-in, and budget approval to meet the exercise plan's scope and objectives.

Other Key Factors

- Having the right participants—internal and external.
- Having adequate supplies and equipment.
- Building the scenario. Probably the most time-consuming scenarios are those based on threat and vulnerability assessments that have already been conducted.
- Incorporating postexercise reviews to identify gaps, identify follow-up actions, assign responsibility with deadlines, update plans, and plan for the next exercise.

213

When planning and conducting an exercise to validate a security or response plan, organizations should ensure that the following steps (at a minimum) are performed:

1. Obtain management sponsorship (funding and forecasting).
2. Initiate project.
3. Collect data: vulnerability and threat assessments.
4. Select a project development team.
5. Develop realistic and measurable objectives (no more than three to five).
6. Develop a safety plan.
7. Identify exercise participants.
8. Develop the scenario.
9. Select an exercise controller, evaluator, and observer group who are nonplayers and unbiased—external and internal.
10. Identify logistics and external support required.
11. Implement the exercise.
12. Document the results.
13. Conduct a "hot wash," a postexercise brief that includes both participants and observers.
14. Identify good points and gaps in the exercise, plans, training, and logistics.
15. Document findings.
16. Develop a realistic and measurable plan to improve procedures and plans.
17. Plan for follow-on training and the next exercise.

How Often Should You Exercise?

There are many variables that affect how often exercises should be conducted, including the regulatory requirements of each industry, if the organization is a critical infrastructure, and, of course, budget. But at a minimum, based on experience and best practices, a plan should be fully exercised annually. This does not include the tabletop or walk-through exercises that should be performed leading up to the full exercise.

Exercises should provide challenges to the participants that require innovative problem solving in a time-effective manner. Exercises provide participants with a skill that would be impossible to obtain in any other way without risking injury in a real event.

TRAINING EVALUATION

Adults learn though various methods. Whether there is a formal training program, a corporate university, or a "train-as-needed" program, one important element is to get feedback. Training evaluations need to be performed in order to accomplish the following:

- Ensure that the material that was supposed to be learned was learned.
- Ensure that knowledge transfer occurred.
- See if the information learned was retained so it can be recalled and applied.
- See if there is a return on investment (ROI).

Often, this is accomplished by asking the participants to fill out a critique form, but other methods include administering a test, conducting random spot-checks, and testing knowledge.

In much of my experience, random knowledge testing was often included as part of a red team exercise or as the information-gathering component of vulnerability assessments. We would determine that a certain percentage of the organization would be randomly quizzed. The persons selected would be scheduled for "employee survey interviews." We would not tell them we were evaluating their knowledge; we would tell them that we were conducting a survey on different aspects of their organization and wanted to gather some information—and we were always introduced by their managers. We would use a questionnaire similar to the following, tally the results, and report them to top management, as well as include them in final reports.

1. What is your job in this organization?
2. Tell me a little bit about what that entails.
3. What would you consider to be an obstacle in this job?
4. Can you tell me what the corporate policy is on talking to the media?
5. Can you tell me how your company conducts training on security topics?
6. What is the regulation on (fill in the blank; e.g., list a policy, guideline, or directive) that you would refer to if the threat level suddenly changed from Bravo to Charlie (or from Yellow to Orange, or to Code Red)?
7. What is "Code Red?"

8. How are you informed that the threat level has changed?
9. In an emergency evacuation, where do you go to assemble?
10. Would you know where the emergency kits are located if you had to retrieve one right now?
11. Do you have a copy of the evacuation plan (or bomb threat checklist)? May I see it?

Sometimes, if the scores were really low, we had to share the information with other stakeholders besides the senior executives of the organization. In our environment, the results of training evaluations or feedback could feasibly be required to be presented in court if a catastrophe occurred (i.e., a terrorist attack). This is especially true in public sector organizations. In the aftermath of a disaster, it is often labeled "fact finding," but it is really meant to be "Who's at fault for this?" and "Can they be held liable for this disaster?" In such a case, the feedback results may and often do end up on the Internet because if court records are not sealed, they become public information. These days it is not uncommon to find court records posted to the Internet.

There are more comprehensive methods for evaluation that can be better addressed by a company's training department. It can be performed as a large group or one-on-one, as in Figure 9.2. The random testing method provided earlier could easily be adapted and customized

Figure 9.2   Training evaluation feedback.

when there is no method in place to test knowledge learned or knowledge that one received through training in their recent past. People need periods of knowledge reinforcement where the knowledge is allowed to settle and then the recall ability can be assessed. Evaluation does not have to be done in one session immediately following the training. But it is critical to perform it, more than most people realize. Otherwise, the training could end up being wasted money that did not serve the purpose, and in the worst-case scenario, the training would be questioned in a court of law in the aftermath of an attack or other catastrophe.

"Give me your worst scorers and your best scorers" is one method that some organizations prefer for training evaluation. Using this method, they ask the ones who scored high and retained information why they thought they did so well. Often it was because the method in which the training was delivered was engaging, but sometimes it was that they already had some knowledge and this training served as a refresher. The ones who scored low often said, "It did not hold my interest" or "It was not explained very well." This type of response reinforces that adult learners learn by doing or by methods other than what teachers use in schools, where mostly it is a one-way delivery method of instruction with little time to deviate.

EDUCATIONAL PROGRAMS

In 2012, I was invited to serve on the Advisory Board of the UCLA Extension Homeland Security and Emergency Management Certificate Program and I also teach a course based on this book, which inspired the creation of this program. This program provides core knowledge and skills essential to leaders in today's world of emergency planning, security, protection, and emergency response. The certificate is offered on campus and online. It is designed to prepare candidates for management and supervisory positions in the growing industry of homeland security and prepares professionals to lead security, protection and recovery identification and planning; resource management; predisaster risk mitigation; postdisaster recovery; and best practices for protecting people, especially employees, and assets. The curriculum is for

- Government agency employees (federal, state, local)
- Private business managers in such areas as human resources, finance, project management, communications, and facilities management

- Real estate and private property managers
- Military personnel transitioning into civilian careers
- Current college students or recent college graduates looking for socially satisfying careers

Curriculum like this and that of other similar programs creates a foundation based on DHS standards and emergency management protocols for new students and transitioning career professionals. For example, in this program there are partnerships and collaboration between the program managers and InfraGard Los Angeles. InfraGard is a national education and information sharing program created by and between the Federal Bureau of Investigation (FBI) and the private/public sector. There are InfraGard groups in cities around the country. Their individual and combined objectives include the mitigating of local, state, and national vulnerabilities, which terrorists might attempt to exploit.

According to Roger Torneden,* "Future programs must relate more to private sector risks, liabilities, resiliency vs. bankruptcy, recovery plans/ expenses and, most importantly, employee and asset protection. Many governmental bodies and public agencies are actively involved in collaboration, coordination, skill development and hiring in this area but companies, large and small, remain 'out of the loop.'" Curriculum breadth needs to expand to include business case studies, effective best practices in identifying high severity loss exposures (natural, man-made, and marketplace), loss mitigation strategies, and contingency plans. Many companies may be too small to have a full-time emergency preparedness manager (or equivalent) but would strongly benefit from one or more of their existing managers (i.e., facilities, human resources, insurance, risk manager, etc.) having emergency planning, preparedness, and event management expertise.

> Present and future employers should be encouraged to take a step back from their hectic day-to-day operations and look at their "systemic" or strategic risks. Having access to a number of real case studies and

---

* Roger Torneden, interview by Elsa Lee, April 2014. Torneden is the Director of Business, Management and Legal Programs, UCLA Extension. He earned his Ph.D. in International Business from New York University with his dissertation resulting in a book published by Praeger Publishers. He earned his CFP(R) while consulting with a large private U.S. bank. Torneden's international career includes senor vice president of Worldwide Marketing for AIU and director of International Development for JCPenney as well as CEO of a large privately owned financial services company. He has taught part time for more than five years with UCLA Extension as well as part time with MBA/Ph.D. programs as adjunct professor with Webster University and adjunct assistant professor with Baruch College in New York City.

references would be most valuable. For example, how many know that the community of Avila Beach, California, had to have its entire downtown rebuilt by Union Oil because of an underground oil pipeline leak? How many of the hundreds of thousands of businesses counting on merchandise from the Port of Los Angeles have resiliency plans in the event of a port shutdown for several days or several weeks? How many have recovery plans for a "Black Swan" economic event (e.g., a long bank closing "holiday"). Yesterday's unthinkable is thinkable in today's environment; mitigation and recovery is key to business survival.

The biggest challenge in UCLA Extension's mission to working professionals in homeland security and emergency management is getting the involvement of private sector businesses as well as the coordination between the public and private sectors. We are presently working to establish more awareness and value-added in the following ways:

- Working with the insurance industry to get insurance premium reductions for companies having excellent emergency preparedness and management programs and company exercises.
- Designing tailor-made programs for quasigovernmental entities (e.g., airports) that bring together public and private protection and resiliency priorities.
- Offering programs that respond to increasing regulations that are aimed at protecting employees and "guarantees of best practice compliance" (e.g., Sarbanes-Oxley).
- Highlighting business cases that illustrate real business risks and recovery costs.

Our challenges are not uniquely ours as FEMA and the DHS, in general, have similar challenges in integrating public and private emergency response. Given the challenges, UCLA Extension is well positioned in one of the world's largest metroplexes to succeed and, hopefully, generate models for best practices for other cities and countries, especially with our world-wide on-line course capabilities.[*]

TRAINING CASE STUDY

Shortly before 8 A.M. on September 16, 2013, Aaron Alexis drove to the front gate of the Washington Navy Yard and displayed his access card. He was admitted by security, parked his car, and walked to Building 197.

---

[*] Roger Torneden, e-mail to, and interview by Elsa Lee, April 2014.

Upon entering that building, Alexis encountered two additional security layers: an automated turnstile, which required a valid access card, and an armed security guard posted near an entrance. Eight minutes after Aaron Alexis cleared security, he began shooting coworkers using a Remington 870 shotgun he had successfully concealed and a Beretta handgun he obtained during the attack. He managed to kill 12 people and wound 4 others before he was shot and killed by law enforcement officers.

Alexis held a U.S. government secret security clearance, allowing him to obtain a position at the Navy Yard with a company called The Experts and an access card to gain entrance to the facility in which he worked. So how did this Navy contractor employee, who reportedly suffered from delusions, had an arrest record, and who also had a history of violent behavior and indebtedness—all discoverable with minimal investigative effort—obtain and maintain a secret security clearance?

Although, as the internal review report on the Navy Yard shooting makes abundantly clear, the series of errors that allowed Alexis to be granted access to sensitive information was largely a result of U.S. government system failings, the private sector should also be reviewing the aftermath of incidents like this to determine ways it can mitigate the risk of an active shooter event. No organization is invulnerable. The Navy Yard internal review report, like many postincident analyses, is publicly available online.

The truth is that even if Alexis had been denied a security clearance and therefore would not have worked at the Navy Yard, he would have sought employment elsewhere, probably in the private sector. Unless a company takes steps to protect itself, it runs the risk of inadvertently inviting an active shooter or other insider threat into its workplace—even one with possible access to sensitive company information. It is imperative that companies examine its internal practice for hiring and its facility security procedures. Consider the following:

- Corporate policy on background investigations conducted prior to hiring employees
- Facility entrance procedures
- Insider threat training
- Workplace violence training

TRAINING FAILURES

Critical infrastructure components and other regulated industries are under the scrutiny of evaluators and investigators reviewing their training frequency and methods. Most of the time, it is a paperwork drill, that is, until something happens or they test the effectiveness of security using role players to attempt to defeat security during a red team exercise. Over the years, airport security and training has come into the limelight. One of the most common comments by investigators has been that poor employee training and weak compliance to security procedures has led to the defeat of security measures.

Other training failures include the executive or employee who frequently travels overseas and either avoids required foreign travel training that could protect him or her abroad or perhaps attends but does not pay attention to the training provided. Why? Is it complacency, or is it that the employee felt it was not important, did not have the time, and has traveled overseas for many years and never experienced an incident? Not taking this type of training seriously could result in death or facing other hazards.

In evaluating security training for over 20 years, I have found it amazing how many people are motivated during training because what they learned was an eye-opener, yet within a few days or weeks they forgot everything they had learned. Most of the time, it is because the training was ineffective and was not reinforced once it was over.

Many organizations make attempts to comply with regularly scheduled training. But less than half are successful because they are not skilled in this arena.

INTERVIEW OF REAR ADMIRAL TIM SULLIVAN

In my interview with Rear Admiral Tim Sullivan, I asked what he sees as a common element in the mishandling of a disaster, crisis, or terror attack.[*] He stated,

---

[*] Rear Admiral Tim Sullivan, interview by Elsa Lee, April 2014. Sullivan recently completed a 36-year career with the U.S. Coast Guard (USCG) with tremendous afloat and ashore operational experience, and since then has been a maritime safety and security consultant assisting both public and private ventures. He served as a key advisor and Principal Federal Official as designated by the Secretary of the Department of Homeland Security. Sullivan has tremendous knowledge of maritime transportation issues ranging from strategic planning to domestic and international port security. He supports international maritime capacity building projects and operational assessments as well as actively participating on several boards. Admiral Sullivan is a senior instructor/subject matter expert and mentor for the U.S. Departments of State and Defense as well as private industry delivering Maritime Port Security Management, as well as major emergency management training courses/assessments internationally and domestically. He also instructs at the UCLA Extension Homeland Security and Emergency Management program.

The common element in mishandling of a crisis is a combination of not being able to demonstrate professionalism under pressure as well as not understanding both one's own internal and external communications plans. Are people properly trained, calmly/safely led, and equipped to respond? Communications both inside the responding organization have to be quick and efficient. Likewise, getting information truthfully as well as quickly to the affected public and media needs to happen concurrently. When a disaster hits it is likely that a secretary or a gate guard will be the first interface with the media. How will they handle it? What are they allowed to speak on and who will back them up. What is their training and policy? Both of these can happen as a result of both poor planning as well as policy. Are the right people properly trained to do the job at hand? Do you have the right people that can communicate truthfully about what is happening especially to the affected public?[*]

I also asked him what he felt was the one thing that most organizations, private or public, can do to be prepared for most disasters or crises, be it terrorism or a man-made disaster?

In a word … exercise! This needs to be a combination of hands on exercises (really launching boats, planes, response equipment, and people) as well exercising tough, real-world scenarios as tabletops with both leaders and the media present.[†]

When asked to briefly discuss one case where the response either worked well or failed horribly, and reasons it worked or did not work, Sullivan said,

A great example of things done right was the U.S. Coast Guard response to Hurricane Katrina. Operationally, all units evacuated people and equipment at the last minute and then quickly came back when the winds were still howling to save thousands of people from rooftops and flooded homes. Helicopters and boats were staged from all over the country ready to come in. Their personnel and equipment were interchangeable due to training and policy. In the first few crucial days, the professionalism of these crews as well as professionally trained public information and affairs personnel told a great

---

[*] Rear Admiral Tim Sullivan, interview with Elsa Lee, April 2014.
[†] Ibid.

and heroic story. In all the negative things that happened during this major disaster one of the few positive organizations who was held up as a role model was the U.S. Coast Guard.[*]

A SUBJECTIVE METHOD FOR CALCULATING RETURN ON INVESTMENT (ROI)

Return on investment is important, and very few companies take the time to evaluate and analyze costs and benefits. It is only prudent to see what you got for your money. So if the training is being conducted to protect business, people, critical functions, and assets, and it costs $5,000, $10,000, or $20,000, what do you have to show for it? How many terrorists did you stop? How many hackers were identified on your network? How many disgruntled employees or potential workplace violence events did you identify and preempt? Was there a decrease in security violations? Do you know how many you had in the first place?

Hypothetically speaking, let us posit that in the last year, your company spent $20,000 on training, $50,000 on physical security technology, $500,000 in security labor, and $10,000 on risk insurance premiums. The cost of your security can be summed up as $580,000. What was the cost of incidents responded to in the previous year? In a typical year, it would be conceivable for a company to experience the incidents listed next. For the sake of this high-level subjective exercise, let's calculate at the high end what the losses might have been if the resources cost $120,000 (per employee compensation) and they work an average of 1,920 hours per year. The purpose of this exercise is not to be precise but to suggest one quick method of estimating the cost to benefit ratio. The first nine events are the security issues followed in the next section by the estimated cost of each line item:

1. Damage from one successful network intrusion from an outsider (3 days of labor for 12 resources to investigate and remediate).
2. Theft of five laptops with critical information (without data, $6,000; with privacy information, $25 to $300 per identity for 200 identities; trade secrets loss or loss of market share, a $35,000 to $1,000,000 loss of market share).

---

[*] Rear Admiral Tim Sullivan, interview with Elsa Lee, April 2014.

3. Labor to investigate and remediate 25 incidents of potential workplace violence (25 days of labor for one resource; compensation rate divided by 1,920 annual labor hours).
4. Labor to reinstall firewalls and other equipment (three resources for two weekend days and downtime; only calculating the labor cost of two resources).
5. Labor to respond to a virus attack (3 days of labor for 20 resources).
6. Labor to file police reports and appear in court as a witness to an incident on your property (2 days of labor for one resource).
7. Brand damage from negative publicity (loss of market share or business, $100,000).
8. Turnover of security personnel five times in the year (average cost of turnover is $100,000 per person in loss of productivity from the labor gap and time to get new employees trained).
9. The insurance premium increased by $5,000 due to thefts.

Hypothetically, let's say the cost of these events was as follows:

1. $18,000
2. $1,012,000
3. $12,500
4. $8,000
5. $30,000
6. $1,000
7. $100,000
8. $500,000
9. $5,000

The estimated cost of security issues was $1,686,500.

These numbers are one method of attempting to determine the cost of security. To perform it more comprehensively would require input from several sources and your "numbers" people. The point of this exercise is to ask: Does technology provide a good return on investment over training? Simply stated, training employees is an absolute necessity that is often not given the importance it warrants in order for an organization to be profitable, productive, efficient, effective, compliant, and to also be good corporate Samaritans who prepare and equip employees to succeed in the workplace. The benefits are often not quantifiable.

10

You Can Deter,
But You Can't Interdict
Don't Cross the Line!

I, Elsa Lee, do solemnly swear that I will support and defend the Constitution of the United States against all enemies, foreign and domestic; that I will bear true faith and allegiance to the same; and that I will obey the orders of the President of the United States and the orders of the officers appointed over me, according to regulations and the Uniform Code of Military Justice. So help me God.

Elsa Lee

KNOW THY LIMITS

We have arrived at a point, hopefully, where everyone knows much more about the topics of threat prevention, detection, and response, and the many activities that go into the processes of achieving preparedness. The greatest place to be is here—with newly acquired knowledge to actually contribute in measurable ways to homeland security. It is also the most dangerous place to be, having just received a dose of privileged information that at one time was reserved for elite units and senior government leaders. Today, we are all on a need-to-know basis because of the world in which we now live. Of course, on that note, everything shared with you is publicly available information. Nevertheless, you are either trying to help

225

protect this country or you have ulterior motives, in which case I hope you now see the light. Perhaps you can join the rest of us who are trying to preserve humanity and its precious resources.

There is a fine line between security awareness, proactive preparedness measures, and crossing the line and breaking the law or acting in a manner that is unethical. If that line is crossed, there are serious consequences—the least of which is personal safety. Nothing is worth breaking the law.

DISTINCTIONS BETWEEN COLLECTING INFORMATION AND COLLECTING INTELLIGENCE

I mentioned in earlier chapters that we do not all speak the same language. Please understand that this can create problems, and we should all work to establish a few basic rules. The proper way to refer to the process of collecting information in the private sector should be "collecting information." The intelligence community will refer to it as "intelligence collection," and they have to undergo many levels of approval in order to collect that intelligence. So for you to say, "I was doing my own intelligence collection last week and found ...," well, you may get a funny look in security or intelligence circles due to "intel types'" discomfort with this language. It is very specific to intelligence activities. In the intelligence community, if people are found to be engaging in such a task (intelligence collection) and then "blabbing" about it, people feel inclined to report them for possible compromise of security protocols.

In the private sector, we engage in activities for prevention, detection, and response, and we may uncover suspicious activity. We are allowed to conduct an inquiry and conduct internal investigations, but our authority to perform those tasks ends inside the company premises. If the inquiry or investigative activities involve following people, it could turn into surveillance, and now the person's privacy is being violated. If a person must be followed, it should be for something reasonable, such as the person is in danger or the police have been called and you are only following—at normal speeds—until you can "do a handoff." I have only encountered a situation one time where it was necessary to engage in this activity, and it was because the person feared for his safety and needed a third party to witness a financial transaction. In that case, he had to be followed to a bank.

Private sector employees do not conduct surveillance. "They monitor their perimeter or facilities." They maintain situational awareness.

They follow someone safely, if possible and if necessary just to obtain a license number; otherwise, they do not follow anyone. Terrorists and criminals conduct surveillance against their targets to collect intelligence (not to be confused with intelligence collection). Terrorists perform reconnaissance—they recon an area. Companies can recon too, but companies do not conduct surveillance. Law enforcement and intelligence agencies conduct surveillance. Terrorists are not supposed to conduct surveillance either, but they do.

Private sector employees do not interdict; they monitor, and if something suspicious is noted or discovered, it gets reported to law enforcement. Employees do not conduct interrogations. They do not talk to subjects. They do not secretly tape-record conversations. They do not engage in search and seizure unless it involves property they own (for example, computers) and it is on their premises.

Some of the worst things that will happen if your company breaks the law or is perceived to have broken the law, include the following:

- Suffer brand damage
- Face possible prison time (it will not be considered a minor violation, and you will get more than a slap on the wrist)
- Botch up a possible lawful ongoing investigation or operation
- Let the bad guys get away
- Get hurt or killed
- Get sued
- Pay a fine

HOW TO AVOID BOTCHING AN INVESTIGATION

The investigative process is very thorough and sensitive in nature, requiring discretionary actions. A great deal of complexity is a constant because of resources that have to be pulled together, coordination that has to take place by multiple agencies, measures that must be taken to avoid a compromise, and legal obligations to be considered to ensure that a case does not fall apart because of a technicality.

All lawful investigations require an extraordinary amount of diligence and planning. Law enforcement agencies spend endless hours in liaison meetings coordinating the various aspects of their operations, areas of responsibilities, and dedication of investigative assets and equipment to ensure the desired end result. Prosecutors and private sector experts also engage in a similar collaborative process, such as when acts that can cause loss of life, the unauthorized disclosure of defense information, or when corporate crimes are being committed. Imagine how a security manager working for a corporation can complicate an investigation when he or she, or the corporation, takes matters into their own hands as if they had the same authority or power.

There are many former military intelligence personnel, ex-law enforcement officers, and private security officers who may have experience, former training, and a certain skills set to conduct an investigation; but what they lack that officials have are technical resources, investigative teams, legal permission, authority, and the proper training to conduct specific investigations. As a former counterintelligence agent, and having been trained in intelligence matters, it would be out of my scope and training to conduct a criminal investigation. Similarly, ex-investigators who have been trained in certain disciplines would not be equipped to investigate matters outside of a theft or a violation of a company's Internet policy.

Law enforcement agencies also face similar concerns in their own investigation to ensure they do not interfere with a covert operation by another agency. This type of scenario is not uncommon when local (county or municipal) agencies are investigating crimes within their jurisdiction while a federal agency is running an undercover investigation or operation.

Where corporations, private security companies, and investigative consultants run a risk is when they go beyond the steps of preliminary fact-finding activities to detect a problem, if indeed a crime has been committed. The reason the aforementioned entities run a risk is because they may unwittingly prevent a required set of circumstances that investigators need to conduct a thorough and effective investigation and tamper with evidence or obstruct justice.

An example of how a company may be outside of its scope of investigation is a department store where there is an unexplained shrinkage in inventory and perhaps other crimes are also being committed, but the security manager investigates further and inadvertently alerts the perpetrators that the company is aware of their activities. In a situation like this, it is—and imperative—to immediately bring in law enforcement officials so that the perpetrators can be arrested and so that the level of the threat can be fully identified.

Companies that hire ex-law enforcement, counterintelligence personnel, or special operations forces should provide special training to their hires and review the position's scope of duties with them to clarify any ambiguities or assumptions. These resources bring exceptional skills, but sometimes they may cross certain lines because they are not familiar with the way things work in the private sector and they have been used to having authority in a previous career.

STUMBLING ACROSS EVIDENCE OF A CRIME: HOW TO PRESERVE IT AND RELINQUISH IT TO LAW ENFORCEMENT AGENCIES

The advent of the Internet has helped us in many ways to make our globe smaller—and, at the same time, has made it easier to commit crimes. Many companies have strict guidelines and policies on the usage of the Internet for business purposes. Unfortunately, some people will also use the Internet at work to surf pornographic sites or conduct illegal or unethical activities. When employees access child pornography sites, they are putting their company at risk in many ways (disrupting business when all computers are seized or servers are shut down for an investigation by law enforcement) and also committing a federal crime. 18 USC 2252 makes it a federal offense to knowingly receive child pornography. Companies may be more apt not to report this because of the fallout that may occur as a result, such as loss of customers or business, a loss of consumer confidence in procedures, and ethical questions on how a business is operating. People with information about a crime like this may also be more reluctant to report it for fear of losing their jobs. A perfect case study happened in California, where a librarian reported a man for accessing child pornography to police authorities and was consequently fired for reporting it.

Obtaining digital evidence of suspicious activities over the Internet or crimes being committed over the Internet is crucial for investigators to determine the level of damage and harm that has been done. Such evidence helps prosecutors to arrest and bring to justice perpetrators or criminal elements who are committing fraud, violent acts, or white-collar crimes, such as stealing proprietary information and then selling it. Other illegal activities taking place in the workplace may include the following:

- Sexual harassment by employees
- Theft of company resources
- Sabotage of company property (intellectual)
- Securities & Exchange Commission (SEC) or Sarbanes-Oxley Act of 2002 (SOX) violations
- Unethical or questionable activities

We are living in a world with an uncertain future, but we can determine the outcome. It does not have to be every man for himself. Through unified efforts and communities of teams we can all be gainfully employed, productive, prosperous, and contributing to our nation's homeland security.

Going forward, these should be common goals:

- Understanding the fundamentals and more about terrorism
- Hardening all facilities
- Building the pillars of preparedness
- Using simple models to relearn skills and reframe problems
- Relying more on the human factor before it becomes a lost art

We should consider the use of tools and models to help us better organize, solve problems more efficiently, and leverage the natural abilities and skills of team members to help in the overall effort to protect our country from terrorist attacks and other threats. We all have strengths, but that is not enough to perform all the tasks that go into preparedness. Imagine how far we can go when people with diverse skills and abilities take one idea and continuously build up to the succeeding step(s). Khalid Sheikh Mohammed (or KSM), the mastermind behind 9/11, considered himself an entrepreneur, and he applied the "one idea leads to another" concept until he developed the 9/11 plot.

Now we know what needs to be done to protect our businesses, our critical infrastructure, and our nation. If you don't know how to begin or cannot accomplish it all on your own, hire someone to help you.

The last point in this book is to keep all operations and activities aboveboard.

APPENDIX A: SAMPLE SECURITY PLAN

The following sample security plan was put together by Elsa Lee for a fictitious company named AlphaBravoCharlie. Because of the increasing focus on small business security, I am reviewing security practices to put together a security plan.

SECTION 1: ABOUT AlphaBravoCharlie

I am a one-person business providing consulting services as a single-person company. Although I have zero staff, from time to time, I contract to other vendors. For example, Printshop Delta provides all of my marketing material.

Objectives

This security plan takes a broad view of the security risks that my business faces to produce a snapshot for next actions so I can reduce risk exposure to myself, my business brand, and the homeland. Recent featured stories about active shooters going on killing rampages really scare me and I want to be protected from such threats. By conducting a self-review, I hope to properly plan for and protect against threats that I know about as well as those that I don't know about.

I can't operate like Fort Knox or the CIA but I can take steps to have adequate security measures and plans in place at a reasonable cost and have some assurance that I am being proactive about risks.

Doing nothing is not an option and that in itself is risky business.

My Security Plan Is Proprietary

This document contains important security information and is therefore confidential; to be kept under lock and key when not in use and not openly shared unless there is a "real need to share it." As my business grows, I will determine who can have access to it.

SECTION 2: ASSESSMENT RESULTS

My assessment produced the following results. I work from home, from my car, and from client sites.

- I do not know the security measures or posture of my clients.
- I do not know what threats they face, but while I am in their space, I, too, am at risk from their threats.
- My personal safety is at risk when I am at client sites more so than when I work from my own office or my car.
- My computer files are not locked and there are times when I have visitors or family members who might accidentally see or delete these files.
- My computer is running very slowly; there is a chance it may be infected with viruses.
- I do not know if any viruses or key logger programs are running on my computer, or if any passwords to personal or business files are compromised.
- My kids use my work computer sometimes and I do not have guest accounts created for their use.
- The vendors who provide services for my business are not located in the United States, and I have no way of knowing if they protect my data or follow U.S. guidelines for cybersecurity.
- Someone broke into my office within this year and I have not changed the locks.
- I do not know what, if anything, is required of me by Homeland Security offices in my city.

Security

I have taken a physical walk around my workspace's interior and exterior perimeter.

- *Virus protection*—Not present on six computers; not up-to-date on four computers; generally, most users are aware of viruses but are a bit unsure about what they can do to prevent them.
- *Spam-filtering software*—Many users have begun to complain about spam, but no protection is in place.
- *Firewall*—We thought the ISP's router included a firewall, but it doesn't; so, we don't have one.

- *Updates*—All the Windows XP Professional systems are up-to-date because they are automatically checked and updates are downloaded, accordingly. However, several installations of Microsoft Office need updating, and the Windows 98 computers are not updated at all.
- *Passwords*—A random sampling found that most people aren't using passwords at all or had them written on Post-it notes. In particular, none of the laptop computers are password protected.
- *Physical security*—We had the insurance people in last year, so the window locks, doors, and alarms are pretty good. However, none of the computers has a serial number etched on its case, and we do not have a log of the serial numbers. We also noticed that everyone is using the same printer including the VP and two directors, which means that there is a risk of confidential documents being left on the printer by accident.
- *Laptop computers*—All the laptop computers have shiny bags with big manufacturer logos. No security locks.
- *Wireless networking*—We are wide open here. It turns out that we just set the thing up and it worked, so nobody touched any of the settings. The wireless network is open to people who have wireless access capability to snoop on the network or freeload on the Internet connection.
- *Web browsing*—Everyone thinks that having fast Internet access is a great perk, but they are using it all the time and without much thought to the risks. Through a content-filtering audit (free with Secure Computing), we found that 20 percent of our Web browsing was unrelated to work. We don't have a policy on acceptable use, and no one is taking any security measures.
- *Backups*—We back up data on the server to a Digital Audio Tape (DAT) drive on a weekly basis, but we haven't tested restoring the data; unless people remember to copy local files to the server, those files are not backed up, which is unsatisfactory. The server contains our primary customer database, so well-tested backups are essential, as is reaining a copy of backups off-site.

Assets

In addition to the physical property, our main assets are:

- Our product designs and marketing collateral
- Records of our contracts with vendors

- Our e-mail database and archive of past e-mail messages
- Sales orders and the customer database
- Financial information
- Line-of-Business (LOB) software for online booking and reservations
- Paper legal records stored in various filing cabinets

All these assets are considered secret and should be accessible only on a need-to-know basis. In addition, they need to be protected and backed up as safely as we can manage.

Risks

We believe the risks break down into four main categories:

1. *Intruders* (viruses, worms, hijacking of our computer resources or Internet connection, and random malicious use). These are the risks faced by anyone using computers connected to the Internet. High risk, high priority.
2. *External threats* (rivals, disgruntled ex-employees, bad guys after money, and thieves). They are likely to use the same tools as hackers, but in deliberately targeting us they may also try to induce staff members to supply confidential information or even use stolen material to blackmail or damage us. We need to protect our assets with physical and electronic security. High risk, high priority.
3. *Internal threats*. Whether accidental or deliberate, a staff member may misuse his or her privileges to disclose confidential information. Low risk, low priority.
4. *Accidents and disasters*. Fires, floods, accidental deletions, hardware failures, and computer crashes. Low risk, medium priority.

Priorities

1. Intruder Deterrence
   - Firewall
   - Virus protection
   - Strengthening the wireless network
   - Replacing the four computers running Windows 98 with computers running Windows XP Professional with SP2
   - Ensuring that all computers are configured to be updated automatically
   - Ongoing user education and policies

2. Theft Prevention
   - Laptop computer security
   - Security marking and asset inventory
   - Moving the server into a secure, lockable room
   - Security locks for desktop and laptop computers
3. Disaster Prevention
   - More frequent backups with off-site storage
   - Ensure backup of users' local data
   - Off-site backup of critical paper documents
   - Regularly testing the backups by performing a restore
4. Internal Security and Confidentiality
   - Strong password policy and user education
   - Secure printers for accounts, HR, and directors
   - Review security for filing cabinets and confidential documents

SECTION 3: SECURITY PLAN

After performing our assessment, we have devised the following security plan.

Action Items

- Select, purchase, and install a hardware firewall (or ask our ISP or technology consultant to provide one).
- Enable Windows Firewall on the server and on all desktop computers.
- Make sure that antivirus software is installed on all computers and that it is set to automatically update virus definitions.
- Configure computers running Office Outlook 2003 to use junk e-mail filtering. Select, purchase, and install spam-filtering software on the mail server, if necessary.
- On the wireless network, disable service set identifier (SSID) broadcasting, choose and configure a sensible SSID, enable WPA encryption, enable MAC filtering, and configure the access point to only allow traffic from the desktop and laptop computers in the office.
- Replace the four computers running Windows 98 with computers running Windows XP Professional with SP2.
- Review all machines to make sure they are fully updated, and set them to automatically refresh those updates.
- Buy new, nondescript laptop computer bags and locks.

- Security mark all desktop computers, laptop computers, and their components.
- Log all serial numbers.
- Buy and install desk security locks for desktop computers.
- Find a suitable, lockable room for the server and move it there.
- Review backup and restore procedures. Ensure that user data is either stored on the server or copied across regularly prior to backups. Implement daily backups. Ensure that a full backup goes offsite once a week. Ensure that the backup is password protected and encrypted. Review paper documents and make photocopies for secure off-site storage of critical documents.
- Configure Small Business Server 2003 and individual machines to enforce reasonably strong passwords. Discuss with users what would be an acceptable balance of convenience and security. (We do not want anyone writing down new passwords.)
- Configure workstations to log users out and require a password to log on again if the workstation is idle for more than 5 minutes.
- Buy cheap printers for accounts, HR, and the two directors so that they can have private documents printed securely.

Policy Changes

Kim will update the staff handbook to include new policies on:

- Acceptable use of e-mail and the Internet
- Use of passwords
- Who can take company property away from the office

After she has completed a first draft, it will be reviewed by the directors and the company's attorneys before being rolled out.

User Education

We expect to plan up to two hours of user training in small groups as a result of these changes. Training will cover:

- The importance of security
- Passwords
- Laptop computer security
- Virus prevention
- Safe Internet browsing
- Updating software and operating systems from a server

- Introducing the new staff policies
- Making sure employees understand the consequences for not complying with policies
- Assessing employees' understanding of the new policies
- Periodically reviewing the practice of the new policies

Project Time Line and Responsibilities

The top three priorities—firewall, virus protection, and strengthening the wireless network—will receive urgent attention from our security consultant, Jeremy. The remaining tasks will be done by our own staff in order of priority.

We expect the top three priorities to be completed within a week and the remaining tasks within 30 days. Steve will be responsible for purchasing and implementing the technical changes. Kim will be responsible for all the policy and training requirements. Denise will oversee the project and be responsible for any other tasks that arise.

Response Planning

In the event of a security breach, we will contact Jeremy. His company has a one-hour response policy during office hours and a four-hour response policy at all other times to deal with serious incidents, such as virus infections. In addition, Steve will monitor the server and firewall regularly to make sure that no breaches have occurred.

Ongoing Maintenance and Compliance

Steve will be responsible for security on a day-to-day basis, with Denise taking overall responsibility. Steve will continue his own self-education on the topic, subscribe to security bulletins from Microsoft and our antivirus software supplier, and liaise with Jeremy on a regular basis to monitor compliance with the new policies.

On a monthly basis, Steve will make sure that Windows and our antivirus software are updated, and that the backup and restore procedures are working properly. He will also be responsible for ensuring that new computer equipment is properly configured and up-to-date.

Kim will be responsible for ensuring that new staff joining the company are fully trained in the company's security policies and procedures.

There will be a full, formal review of this plan in six months.

APPENDIX B: BOMB THREAT CHECKLIST

Keep the caller on the line as long as possible!

Exact time and date of call:

Exact words of caller:

Voice
- ☐ Loud
- ☐ High-Pitched
- ☐ Raspy
- ☐ Intoxicated
- ☐ Soft
- ☐ Deep
- ☐ Pleasant
- ☐ Other

Language
- ☐ Excellent
- ☐ Fair
- ☐ Foul
- ☐ Good
- ☐ Poor
- ☐ Other

Accent
- ☐ Local
- ☐ Foreign
- ☐ Race
- ☐ Not Local
- ☐ Region

Speech
- ☐ Fast
- ☐ Distinct
- ☐ Stutter
- ☐ Slurred
- ☐ Slow
- ☐ Distorted
- ☐ Nasal
- ☐ Lisp
- ☐ Other

Manner
- ☐ Calm
- ☐ Rational
- ☐ Coherent
- ☐ Deliberate
- ☐ Righteous
- ☐ Angry
- ☐ Irrational
- ☐ Incoherent
- ☐ Emotional
- ☐ Laughing

Familiarity with Threatened Facility
- ☐ Much
- ☐ Some
- ☐ None

Background Noise
- ☐ Factory Machines
- ☐ Bedlam
- ☐ Music
- ☐ Office Machines
- ☐ Mixed
- ☐ Street Traffic
- ☐ Trains
- ☐ Animals
- ☐ Quiet
- ☐ Voices
- ☐ Airplanes
- ☐ Party Atmosphere

Questions to Ask the Caller
When is the bomb going to explode?

Where is the bomb right now?

What does it look like?

What kind of bomb is it?

What will cause it to explode?

Did you place the bomb?

Why did you place the bomb?

Where are you calling from?

What is your address?

What is your name?

* * *

If the voice is familiar, who did it sound like?

Were there any background noises? PA system, street noises, machinery, booth, music, motors?

Telephone number call received at:

Person receiving call:

Any additional remarks:

Dial 911 immediately, report threat, and contact security for evacuation procedures.

APPENDIX C: BEST PRACTICES FOR MAIL CENTER SECURITY

There are millions of businesses that use the mail. The vast majority of these have only "one to a few" person(s) responsible for mail center–type operations. Of these millions of businesses, there are thousands of large, complex corporate mail center operations. The best practices listed next are a summary of well-developed mail center security procedures that can be used by any mail center. Procedures applicable primarily to large mail centers are identified as such.

These recommendations come from businesses that use the mail and have been shared with the U.S. Postal Service (USPS) for distribution to its customers. Since needs and resources are often different, every suggestion may not apply to all businesses. Security managers should determine which are appropriate for their company and conduct periodic security reviews of their operation to identify needed improvements. The following list contains general security concepts and a few specific examples of how to accomplish them.

GENERAL MAIL OPERATION PREVENTIVE RECOMMENDATION

- Appoint a Mail Security Coordinator (*and an alternate if a large mail center*).
- Organize a Mail Security Response Team, as practical, depending on the size of the mail center staff.
- Create, update, and/or review standard operating procedures (SOPs), security procedures, disaster plans, and operating plans. Keep a backup copy of plan(s) off-site.
- Train personnel in policies and procedures relative to mail security, i.e., biological or chemical warfare, weapons, or natural disasters.
- Include from the staff, when possible, certified firefighters; biohazard handlers; and/or corporate safety, environmental, and health personnel; or train personnel in these duties.

- Members of the team should be equipped with cell phones or pagers and should be available up to 24 hours a day, 7 days a week, as is appropriate for the situation.
- Information and updates about the personnel and response procedures should be published and distributed company-wide.
- Publish an after-action report or incident report after every incident.
- Have senior management buy-in and sign-off on the company's mail security procedures.

EMPLOYEE SECURITY PROCEDURES

- Maintain good hiring practices.
- Provide in-depth screening and background checks when hiring new employees.
- Make arrangements with one or two temporary employment agencies to ensure that a restricted, pre-screened group of individuals is available when needed to supplement the workforce.
- Enforce and institute a probationary period for the evaluation of employees.
- Establish a strict employee identification and personnel security program.
- Require employees to wear photo ID badges at all times.
- Instruct employees to challenge any unknown person in a facility.
- Where provided to employees, utilize uniforms with names and logos stitched on them for employees to wear at work.
- Provide a separate and secure area for personal items (e.g., coats and purses). Prohibit employees from taking personal items into the main workspace.
- Establish incoming–outgoing personal mail procedures.
- Hire or designate security personnel for the mail center area (*primarily for large mail centers*).
- Establish health safety procedures.
- Have on-site medical personnel (*large mail centers*) or arrange for an off-site facility and personnel.
- Encourage employees to wash hands regularly, especially prior to eating.
- Encourage employees to see a doctor if suspicious symptoms occur.

- Encourage employee attendance for health seminars, talks, and informational updates.
- As practical, establish or take advantage of company health programs (e.g., shots and checkups).
- Provide approved personal protection equipment according to Centers for Disease Control and Prevention (CDC) guidelines.

GENERAL SAFETY AND SECURITY PROCEDURES FOR INCOMING–OUTGOING MAIL AREAS

- Notify internal and external customers, as appropriate, of steps taken to ensure safety of mail.
- Control or limit access of employees, known visitors, and escorted visitors to the mail center with sign-in sheets, badges, and/or card readers. (*For large mail operations, include plant, workroom floor, etc.*)
- Subject to emergency exit safety requirements, lock all outside doors and/or prohibit doors from being propped open.
- Require deliveries to be made in a restricted, defined area.
- Restrict drivers to areas (rest areas) that are separate from the production and mail center facilities.
- Use video cameras inside and outside the facility and docks, as feasible.
- Keep the area for processing incoming and outgoing mail separate from all other operations, as feasible.
- If a separate processing area is used, it should not be part of the central ventilation system.
- Shutoff points of the processing area's ventilation system should be mapped and should be part of an emergency procedures handout.
- A separate processing area should include appropriate personnel protection equipment and disposal instructions for such equipment, as approved by the CDC.
- Designate, publish, and post evacuation routes for emergency situations.
- Conduct training, emergency preparedness drills, and informational update meetings, as necessary.
- X-ray all incoming mail (*large mail centers*).

- Maintain a Suspicious Package Profile.
- Ensure appropriate emergency access numbers are posted by or on every phone. Such numbers should include 911; the CDC at 770-488-7100; the local postal inspector; and the local police and/or fire department.
- Maintain updated employee lists (name, address, phone, and cell phone), and keep a backup copy off-site.
- Provide only vacuum systems for cleaning equipment, not forced-air systems.
- If not already done, alter receiving procedures to require a manifest with all shipments, and practice the acceptance of "complete" shipments only.
- Discarded envelopes, packages, and boxes should be placed in a covered container and transported to the loading dock for removal. (Ensure local arrangements are in place for the disposal of such material.)

ACCESS TO INFORMATION: EDUCATION AND COMMUNICATIONS

- Maintain a library of publications, videos, and brochures from appropriate information sources, and facilitate employee access to them as needed. Sources should include the USPS, CDC, and Occupational Safety and Health Administration (OSHA).
- Maintain and publish a list of useful Web sites from appropriate authoritative sources. Bookmark appropriate Web sites for easy access, that is, those of the CDC, OSHA, the USPS, and the General Services Administration (GSA). Monitoring twice a day is a minimum recommendation, as situations warrant.
- Maintain and publish a list of phone numbers to call in an emergency: postal inspectors, the local fire department, the CDC, OSHA, the local police, etc.
- Present updated best practices from the CDC, OSHA, the GSA, the USPS, and the local fire department.
- Company-wide communications concerning mail center security procedures should be implemented.
- Require and encourage applicable employees to attend all local meetings pertaining to mail security issues.

GUIDELINES FOR MAIL CENTER THEFT PREVENTION

Mail is sometimes lost or stolen from company mail centers, or while en route to or from the post office. Much of this mail is quite valuable, containing cash, jewelry, and other high-value items. Needless to say, such losses are costly to the company and its investors. The following are some suggestions for improving theft prevention in your mail center operation:

- *Know your employees.* Don't put your new hires in your mail center without a criminal record check.
- *Secure your mail center.* Prevent access by unauthorized persons. Keep it locked whenever possible, especially when no one is on duty. Maintain a sign-in sheet for persons entering and leaving the mail center, including times of arrival and departure.
- *Keep Registered Mail™ separate from other mail.* Document transfer of Registered Mail by requiring the receiver to sign for custody.
- *Protect company funds.* If company funds are handled as part of the mail center operations, establish adequate controls to fix individual responsibility for any losses that may occur.
- *Keep postage meters secure.* Postage meters should be secured when not in use. Check mail periodically to determine if employees are using company postage meters for their personal mail.
- *Vary times and lines of travel between the post office and plant.* If currency or other valuable mail is sent or received, check periodically to see if mail messengers are making unauthorized stops or leaving mail unattended in unlocked vehicles.
- *Employees caught stealing should be prosecuted.* There is no greater deterrent to a potential thief than the fear that he or she may go to jail. The Postal Inspection Service will extend its full cooperation.

APPENDIX D: FACT SHEET ON DIRTY BOMBS

BACKGROUND

A "dirty bomb" is one type of a radiological dispersal device (RDD) that combines a conventional explosive, such as dynamite, with radioactive material. The terms "dirty bomb" and "RDD" are often used interchangeably in the media. Most RDDs would not release enough radiation to kill people or cause severe illness—the conventional explosive itself would be more harmful to individuals than the radioactive material. However, depending on the scenario, an RDD explosion could create fear and panic, contaminate property, and require potentially costly cleanup. Making prompt, accurate information available to the public could prevent the panic sought by terrorists. A dirty bomb is in no way similar to a nuclear weapon or nuclear bomb. A nuclear bomb creates an explosion that is millions of times more powerful than that of a dirty bomb. The cloud of radiation from a nuclear bomb could spread to hundreds of square miles, whereas a dirty bomb's radiation could be dispersed within a few blocks or miles of the explosion. A dirty bomb is not a "weapon of mass destruction" but a "weapon of mass disruption," where contamination and anxiety are the terrorists' major objectives.

IMPACT OF A DIRTY BOMB

The extent of local contamination would depend on a number of factors, including the size of the explosive, the amount and type of radioactive material used, the means of dispersal, and weather conditions. Those closest to the RDD would be the most likely to sustain injuries due to the explosion. As radioactive material spreads, it becomes less concentrated and less harmful. Prompt detection of the type of radioactive material used will greatly assist local authorities in advising the community on protective measures, such as sheltering in place or quickly leaving the immediate area. Radiation can be readily detected with equipment already carried by many emergency responders. Subsequent decontamination of the affected area may involve considerable time and expense.

Immediate health effects from exposure to the low radiation levels expected from an RDD would likely be minimal. The effects of radiation exposure would be determined by the following:

- The amount of radiation absorbed by the body
- The type of radiation (gamma, beta, or alpha)
- The distance from the radiation to an individual
- The means of exposure—external or internal (absorbed by the skin, inhaled, or ingested)
- The length of time exposed

The health effects of radiation tend to be directly proportional to the radiation dose. In other words, the higher the radiation dose, the higher the risk of injury.

PROTECTIVE ACTIONS

In general, protection from radiation is afforded by the following:

- Minimizing the time exposed to radioactive materials
- Maximizing the distance from the source of radiation
- Shielding from external exposure and from inhaling radioactive material

More detailed guidance can be found at the sources (see "Other Contact Information") provided at the end of this appendix.

SOURCES OF RADIOACTIVE MATERIAL

Radioactive materials are routinely used at hospitals, research facilities, and industrial and construction sites. These radioactive materials are used for such purposes as diagnosing and treating illnesses, sterilizing equipment, and inspecting welding seams. The Nuclear Regulatory Commission (NRC), together with 33 "agreement states" that also regulate radioactive material, administers over 21,000 licenses of such materials. The vast majority of these materials are not useful for an RDD.

CONTROL OF RADIOACTIVE MATERIAL

NRC and state regulations require owners licensed to use or store radioactive material to secure it from theft and unauthorized access. These measures have been greatly strengthened since the attacks of September 11, 2001. Licensees must promptly report lost or stolen high-risk radioactive material. Local authorities also assist in making a determined effort to find and retrieve such sources. Most reports of lost or stolen material involve small or short-lived radioactive sources not useful for an RDD.

Past experience suggests there has not been a pattern of collecting such sources for the purpose of assembling an RDD. It is important to note that NRC states that the radioactivity of the combined total of all unrecovered sources in the United States over the past five years (when corrected for radioactive decay) would not reach the threshold for one high-risk radioactive source. Unfortunately, the same cannot be said worldwide. The U.S. government is working to strengthen controls on high-risk radioactive sources both at home and abroad.

RISK OF CANCER

Just because a person is near a radioactive source for a short time or gets a small amount of radioactive dust on him- or herself does not mean he or she will get cancer. Any additional risk will likely be extremely small. Doctors specializing in radiation health effects will be able to assess the risks and suggest mitigating medical treatment once the radioactive source and exposure levels have been determined.

There are some medical treatments available that help cleanse the body of certain radioactive materials. Prussian blue has been proven effective for ingestion of cesium-137 (a radioactive isotope). In addition, potassium iodide (KI) can be used to protect against thyroid cancer caused by iodine-131 (radioactive iodine). However, KI, which is available as an over-the-counter pill, offers no protection to other parts of the body or against other radioactive isotopes. Medical professionals are best qualified to determine how to best treat symptoms.

OTHER CONTACT INFORMATION

A number of federal agencies have responsibilities for dealing with RDDs. Their public affairs offices can answer questions on the subject or provide access to experts in and out of government. Their Web sites and phone numbers are as follows:

Department of Energy: www.energy.gov; 202-586-4940
Department of Health and Human Services: www.hhs.gov; 202-690-6343
Department of Homeland Security: www.dhs.gov; 202-282-8010
Department of Justice: www.usdoj.gov; 202-514-2007
Environmental Protection Agency: www.epa.gov; 202-564-9828
Federal Bureau of Investigation: www.fbi.gov; 202-324-3691
Federal Emergency Management Agency: www.fema.gov; 202-646-4600
National Nuclear Security Administration: www.nnsa.doe.gov; 202-586-7371
Nuclear Regulatory Commission: www.nrc.gov; 301-415-8200
Transportation Security Administration: www.tsa.gov/public/; 571-227-2829

APPENDIX E: THE INSIDER THREAT

U.S. Department of Justice
Federal Bureau of Investigation

A company can often detect or control when an outsider (non-employee) tries to access company data either physically or electronically, and can mitigate the threat of an outsider stealing company property. However, the thief who is harder to detect and who could cause the most damage is the insider—the employee with legitimate access. That insider may steal solely for personal gain, or that insider may be a "spy"—someone who is stealing company information or products in order to benefit another organization or country.

THE INSIDER THREAT

An introduction to detecting and deterring an insider spy

> Disgruntled
>
> Working odd hours
>
> Unexplained affluence
>
> Unreported foreign travel

This brochure serves as an introduction for managers and security personnel on how to detect an insider threat and provides tips on how to safeguard your company's trade secrets.

251

PROTECT YOUR INTELLECTUAL PROPERTY

Theft of intellectual property is an increasing threat to organizations, and can go unnoticed for months or even years.

There are increased incidents of employees taking proprietary information when they believe they will be, or are, searching for a new job.

Congress has continually expanded and strengthened criminal laws for violations of intellectual property rights to protect innovation and ensure that egregious or persistent intellectual property violations do not merely become a standard cost of doing business.

A domestic or foreign business competitor or foreign government intent on illegally acquiring a company's proprietary information and trade secrets may wish to place a spy into a company in order to gain access to non-public information. Alternatively, they may try to recruit an existing employee to do the same thing.

PERSONAL FACTORS

There are a variety of motives or personal situations that may increase the likelihood someone will spy against their employer:

Greed or Financial Need: A belief that money can fix anything. Excessive debt or overwhelming expenses.

Anger/Revenge: Disgruntlement to the point of wanting to retaliate against the organization.

Problems at work: A lack of recognition, disagreements with co-workers or managers, dissatisfaction with the job, a pending layoff.

Ideology/Identification: A desire to help the "underdog" or a particular cause.

Divided Loyalty: Allegiance to another person or company, or to a country besides the United States.

Adventure/Thrill: Want to add excitement to their life, intrigued by the clandestine activity, "James Bond Wannabe."

Vulnerability to blackmail: Extra-marital affairs, gambling, fraud.

Ego/Self-image: An "above the rules" attitude, or desire to repair wounds to their self-esteem. Vulnerability to flattery or the promise of a better job. Often coupled with Anger/Revenge or Adventure/Thrill.

Ingratiation: A desire to please or win the approval of someone who could benefit from insider information with the expectation of returned favors.

Compulsive and destructive behavior: Drug or alcohol abuse, or other addictive behaviors.

Family problems: Marital conflicts or separation from loved ones.

ORGANIZATIONAL FACTORS

Organizational situations may increase the ease for thievery:

The availability and ease of acquiring proprietary, classified, or other protected materials. Providing access privileges to those who do not need it.

Proprietary or classified information is not labeled as such, or is incorrectly labeled.

The ease that someone may exit the facility (or network system) with proprietary, classified or other protected materials.

Undefined policies regarding working from home on projects of a sensitive or proprietary nature.

The perception that security is lax and the consequences for theft are minimal or non-existent.

Time pressure: Employees who are rushed may inadequately secure proprietary or protected materials, or not fully consider the consequences of their actions.

Employees are not trained on how to properly protect proprietary information.

BEHAVIORAL INDICATORS

Some behaviors may be a clue that an employee is spying and/ or methodically stealing from the organization:

Without need or authorization, takes proprietary or other material home via documents, thumb drives, computer disks, or e-mail.

Inappropriately seeks or obtains proprietary or classified information on subjects not related to their work duties.

Interest in matters outside the scope of their duties, particularly those of interest to foreign entities or business competitors.

Unnecessarily copies material, especially if it is proprietary or classified.

Remotely accesses the computer network while on vacation, sick leave, or at other odd times.

Disregards company computer policies on installing personal software or hardware, accessing restricted websites, conducting unauthorized searches, or downloading confidential information.

Works odd hours without authorization; notable enthusiasm for overtime work, weekend work, or unusual schedules when clandestine activities could be more easily conducted.

Unreported foreign contacts (particularly with foreign government officials or intelligence officials) or unreported overseas travel.

Short trips to foreign countries for unexplained or strange reasons.

Unexplained affluence; buys things that they cannot afford on their household income.

Engages in suspicious personal contacts, such as with competitors, business partners or other unauthorized individuals.

Overwhelmed by life crises or career disappointments.

Shows unusual interest in the personal lives of co-workers; asks inappropriate questions regarding finances or relationships.

Concern that they are being investigated; leaves traps to detect searches of their work area or home; searches for listening devices or cameras.

Many people experience or exhibit some or all of the above to varying degrees; however, most people will not cross the line and commit a crime.

YOU CAN MAKE A DIFFERENCE

Organizations need to do their part to deter intellectual property theft:

- Educate and regularly train employees on security or other protocols.
- Ensure that proprietary information is adequately, if not robustly, protected.
- Use appropriate screening processes to select new employees.
- Provide non-threatening, convenient ways for employees to report suspicions.
- Routinely monitor computer networks for suspicious activity.
- Ensure security (to include computer network security) personnel have the tools they need.

Remind employees that reporting security concerns is vital to protecting your company's intellectual property, its reputation, its financial well-being, and its future. They are protecting their own jobs. Remind them that if they see something, to say something.

GET ASSISTANCE

Being aware of potential issues, exercising good judgment, and conducting discrete inquiries will help you ascertain if there is a spy in your midst. However, if you believe one of your employees is a spy or is stealing company trade secrets, do not alert the person to the fact that he/she is under suspicion, but seek assistance from trained counterintelligence experts–such as the FBI. The FBI has the tools and experience to identify and mitigate such threats. If asked to investigate, the FBI will minimize the disruption to your business, and safeguard your privacy and your data. Where necessary, the FBI will seek protective orders to preserve trade secrets and business confidentiality. The FBI is committed to maintaining the confidentiality and competitive position of US companies. The FBI will also provide security and counterintelligence training or awareness seminars for you and your employees upon request.

RECENT INSIDER THEFT CASES

en Chyu Liu, a retired research scientist, was sentenced in January 2012 to 60 months in prison, two years supervised release, a $25,000 fine and was ordered to forfeit $600,000. Liu was convicted in February 2011 of stealing trade secrets from his former employer and selling them to companies in China. Liu conspired with at least four current and former employees, traveled throughout China to market the stolen information, paid current and former employees for material and information, and bribed a then-employee with $50,000 in cash to provide a process manual and other information.

exue Huang was employed by two different US companies. He admitted that from 2007 to 2010 he delivered stolen trade secrets from both companies to individuals in Germany and China. The stolen materials were used to conduct unauthorized research to benefit Chinese universities. Huang also pursued steps to develop and produce the trade secrets in China. The aggregated loss from both companies was between $7 and $20 million. Huang pleaded guilty to charges of economic espionage and theft of trade secrets, and was sentenced in December 2011 to 87 months in prison and three years supervised release.

uan Li, a former research chemist with a global pharmaceutical company, pleaded guilty in January 2012 to stealing her employer's trade secrets and making them available for sale through Abby Pharmatech, Inc. Li was a 50% partner in Abby. Between October 2008 and June 2011 Li accessed her employer's internal databases, downloaded information to her personal home computer, and made them for sale through Abby. She was sentenced to 18 months in prison.

lliot Doxer sent an e-mail to the Israeli Consulate stating that he was willing to provide information from his employer that might help Israel. An undercover FBI agent posing as an Israeli intelligence officer spoke to Doxer and established a "dead drop" where the two could exchange information. For the next 18 months, Doxer visited the dead drop at least 62 times. Doxer provided customer and employee lists, contract information, and other trade secrets. He pleaded guilty to one count of foreign economic espionage and was sentenced in December 2011 to six months in prison, six months home confinement, and fined $25,000.

ergey Aleynikov worked as a computer programmer for a Wall Street company. During his last few days at that company, he transferred 32 megabytes of proprietary computer codes -- a theft that could have cost his employer millions of dollars. He attempted to hide his activities but the company discovered irregularities through its routine network monitoring systems. In December 2010, Aleynikov was found guilty of theft of trade secrets.

ichael Mitchell became disgruntled and was fired from his job due to poor performance. He kept numerous computer files with his employer's trade secrets; he entered into a consulting agreement with a rival Korean company and gave them the stolen trade secrets. In March 2010, he was sentenced to 18 months in prison and ordered to pay his former employer over $187,000.

halin Jhaveri gave trade secrets to a person he believed was an investor willing to finance a business venture in India, and confirmed that the information he had taken from his employer was everything he needed to start the business. In January 2011, he was sentenced to time served (one year and fifteen days), three years probation, a $5,000 fine, and a $100 Special Assessment.

anjuan Jin took a leave of absence from her US employer in 2006. While on leave, Jin worked for a similar company in China. A year later, Jin returned to the United States. Within a week of her return, she bought a one-way ticket back to China, and advised her US employer that she was ready to end her leave. Jin returned to work on February 26, 2007 and for the next two days downloaded hundreds of technical documents. On February 28, 2007, during a routine check at the airport, more than 1,000 electronic and paper documents proprietary to her US employer were found in Jin's luggage. In 2012, Jin was sentenced to four years in prison and fined $20,000.

reg Chung spied for China from 1979-2006. Chung stole trade secrets about the space shuttle, the Delta IV rocket and the C-17 military cargo jet for the benefit of the Chinese government. Chung's motive was to "contribute to the Motherland." He stole hundreds of thousands of documents from his employer. He traveled to China under the guise of giving lectures while secretly meeting with Chinese agents. He also used Mak (below) to transfer information back to China. In February 2010 he was sentenced to over 15 years in prison.

hi Mak admitted that he was sent to the United States in 1978 in order to obtain employment in the defense industry with the goal of stealing US defense secrets, which he did for over 20 years. He passed information on quiet electric propulsion systems for US submarines, details on the Aegis radar system, and information on stealth ships being developed by the US Navy. The Chinese government tasked Mak to acquire information on other technologies. Mak recruited family members to encrypt and covertly courier information back to China. In May 2007, Mak was convicted of conspiracy, failing to register as an agent of a foreign government, and other violations. He was sentenced to over 24 years in prison.

Report theft of trade secrets to your local FBI office or submit a tip online: tips.fbi.gov

254

INDEX